Inside a Pearl

Forgetting Elena
The Joy of Gay Sex (coauthored)
Nocturnes for the King of Naples
States of Desire: Travels in Gay America
A Boy's Own Story
The Beautiful Room Is Empty
Caracole
The Darker Proof: Stories from a Crisis
Genet: A Biography
The Burning Library: Essays
Our Paris: Sketches from Memory
Skinned Alive: Stories
The Farewell Symphony
Marcel Proust: A Life
The Married Man
The Flâneur: A Stroll Through the Paradoxes of Paris
Fanny: A Fiction
Arts and Letters: Essays
My Lives: A Memoir
Chaos: A Novella and Stories
Hotel de Dream
Rimbaud: The Double Life of a Rebel
City Boy: My Life in New York During the 1960s and '70s
Sacred Monsters: New Essays on Literature and Art
Jack Holmes and His Friend

Inside a Pearl

My Years in Paris

Edmund White

B L O O M S B U R Y

LONDON · NEW DELHI · NEW YORK · SYDNEY

First published in Great Britain 2014

Copyright © 2014 by Edmund White

The moral right of the author has been asserted

No part of this book may be used or reproduced in any manner
whatsoever without written permission from the publisher except in the
case of brief quotations embedded in critical articles or reviews

Bloomsbury Publishing Plc
50 Bedford Square
London
WC1B 3DP

www.bloomsbury.com

Bloomsbury Publishing, London, New Delhi, New York and Sydney

A CIP catalogue record for this book is available from the British Library

ISBN 978 1 4088 2045 2 (hardback edition)
ISBN 978 1 4088 3785 6 (trade paperback edition)

10 9 8 7 6 5 4 3 2 1

Typeset by Hewer Text UK Ltd, Edinburgh
Printed and bound in Great Britain by CPI Group (UK) Ltd, Croydon CR0 4YY

To Ann and Lincoln

. . . and the wit and the laughing awareness that is France made all of us alive.

—M. F. K. Fisher, *Long Ago in France*

Chapter 1

I discovered France through Marie-Claude de Brunhoff. I'd met her at a party in New York around 1975 and I'd been struck right away by how polished and elegant she was. Marie-Claude gleamed like the inside of a nautilus shell. She wasn't tall, but she held herself as if she were. She had a white ivory cigarette holder into which she screwed one cigarette after another. A small group of Americans had already begun to object to cigarette smoke in a closed room, but at a cocktail party it still seemed inevitable. I chain-smoked and thought nothing of it.

Marie-Claude was beautiful, with big, wide-awake eyes, a low voice, layers of pale clothes that billowed around her in floating panels, shoes that were immaculate and of a startling red. She seemed completely focused on the person she was talking to—me, in this case. But there was a slight lag in her responses, almost as if in spite of her excellent English she might first be translating everything into and out of French. Later, her English (or rather "American") became much more assured, pell-mell and rapid.

She seemed more interested in me than I merited, and I wondered if she'd mistaken me for someone more important. When I'd lived in Rome in 1970, I noticed that foreigners often promoted me a notch or two in their imaginations; I'd certainly benefited from this geographical social climbing. It wasn't that Marie-Claude treated me with deference. It was just that she bothered to ask me questions and flirt with me.

I was puzzled by the flirtation. Americans were, and are, the least seductive of people. After all, America and Britain are the countries where a politician can be pushed out of office or impeached if it's discovered he has a mistress—or even an overeager intern with no sense of discretion. In France, seduction is a form of politeness and means no more than any other courtesy. It is the necessary liquid in which all the denizens of the social fishbowl need to swim. A prime minister is mocked if he doesn't have a mistress.

I'd learn this only later, when I lived in France, but Marie-Claude was already using her warmth and femininity to flatter me. In France, *coquette* is a positive word, and even a little boy of five or six, say, who has tilted his new cap at a fetching angle, will be described approvingly as *coquet* (*"Comme il est coquet, le petit!"* his grandmother will say).

The next day on the phone, the hostess (who was also my agent) told me that that French woman was married to the man who did the children's books about Babar the Elephant. That hadn't been one of my books as a child; I think the American Babar readers were in a higher socioeconomic class, the sort of people who visited France, and maybe even spoke French, or wanted to. But even I knew *of* Babar, though the character struck me as very colonial, from the same era as pith helmets.

I dimly remembered a monkey, an old lady, and of course all those elephants in green clothes wearing crowns. There was a quaint, brightly colored charm about these images that I had a hard time imagining was still being generated in our day. My agent told me that Laurent de Brunhoff's father had started the Babar series in the 1930s, then died, before the war, of tuberculosis. He'd first invented the tales and drawings as bedtime stories for his three sons. In the 1950s, one of those sons, Laurent, began turning out new Babars. Of course, critics always compared Laurent's books unfavorably to his father's seven original Babars, but in fact Laurent created many beautiful books including a yoga-for-elephants book and a book of museum visits in which the Mona Lisa was an elephant, as was the nude woman eating lunch on the grass in the *Dejeuner sur l'herbe*.

I later learned that Marie-Claude was born in Paris on September 7, 1929, and that she'd been a literary critic for *L'Express*, *Le Monde*, and the *Quinzaine Littéraire*. She didn't look nearly so old when I met her, though years of tanning had taken their toll. She hated to have her picture taken, which is why so few exist.

I wondered if Marie-Claude had flirted with me because she wanted something. I was suspicious, like all New Yorkers. And hadn't she been told that I was the coauthor of *The Joy of Gay Sex* and impervious to her allure? But of course I was susceptible to it—and as my years in France later showed me, straight and gay women never shied away from taking a gay man's arm, serving him his favorite dish, remembering his pet peeves, deferring to his phobias, kissing him on both cheeks at the beginning of the evening and at the end (or three kisses in the South of France). In our years together, I knew that most of Marie-Claude's warmth came from a sense of friendship, but to that was always added a soupçon of seductiveness.

After the initial meeting, Marie-Claude wrote me from Paris several times in dark blue ink on her sky-blue stationery. The writing was very large, and ten or fifteen words could fill a whole page. As a result, each letter was short but looked long. She seemed to have no idea how to punctuate and her English spelling was at best impressionistic. Later, I learned she was no more orthodox in French orthography. She sent me a book, Michel Tournier's *The Erl-King*. She later wrote a fanciful portrait in English of Tournier. Everything about Paris seemed as glamorous as Gitane smoke to this States-confined guy.

I tried to read the Tournier, since it was an article of personal faith that I knew French. I'd studied it two years in high school and even won a county-wide *prix d'honneur*, but now, looking back, I wonder if our teacher could actually *speak* French. He was good at grammar and drilled us in it relentlessly, if patiently, as he knotted and unknotted his enormous pale hands. He'd somehow fought on the Gaullist side before we entered the war, and he had hung on the classroom wall a sort of diploma of gratitude from the Gaullist government that declared, *"Pour la gloire."* I'd read Rimbaud and Verlaine in *en face* translations obsessively, secretively—after lights-out in my boarding-school dorm, sitting on the toilet. I owned a volume of Madame de Sévigné's letters entirely in French, which I'd convinced myself I'd read, but all that had happened was that my eyes had passed, unregistering, over all the words. I was like someone who convinces himself he's dieting just by buying a few lo-cal foods.

For Time-Life Books, in the early 1970s, I'd co-written a book about *Homo erectus* called *The First Men* and had been invited by a staffer, a French woman named Simone, to a lunch with two French anthropologists. They were members of an important *Homo erectus* dig in the Dordogne and had been brought over to New York to advise us on our book. Simone agreed to translate. I amazed and pleased everyone by saying a few words in French at the beginning of the meal. But as I drank more and more white wine, I acquired a fatal confidence and soon was stringing together long chains of French words and tossing them like bouquets at the worried-looking experts. Finally, Simone said, unsmiling, "You know, you're not making any sense. No one can understand a word." When I think of that moment now, late at night, forty years later, I still cringe.

One night in New York I picked up a short, jolly French tourist (or was he a sailor from Marseilles?) who couldn't speak a word of English. We had great sex and convinced ourselves we were communicating effortlessly until he took me to see *Going Places,* one of Depardieu's early hits, during which if I glanced up even for a second from the English subtitles I was completely lost. The little Frenchman kept pushing my hand onto the enormous bulge in his trousers and whispering incomprehensible dirty words into my ear. His shamelessness alarmed me—and then I was chagrined that I was being so prudish and American. When the lights came up at the end the couple beside us were lesbians and smiled encouragingly.

I'd spent a few days in Paris in the mid-1960s with my officemate from New York. Then, in 1970, the poet Alfred Corn and I drove from Rome to Paris, where we stayed for a few nights in a hotel on the Île Saint-Louis. Al and I visited museums, surely, but what I remember were the Left Bank cafés, full of male students with suit jackets that they'd drape over their narrow shoulders without putting their arms through the sleeves. They were all murmuring this maddening, confident language, their mouths bitter with espresso, tiny glasses of cognac, unfiltered cigarettes, and words, words, words. The girls were all in black, their pale, cynical faces unpainted except for moon rings of mascara. Al and his then-wife, Ann, spoke French—that was the language they spoke to each other.

Paris still seemed like a set out of a nineteenth-century opera, with its broad avenues, narrow streets, skinny houses teetering up into the sky, and lines of four or five students linking arms, trotting out into the night, and laughing mirthlessly. A Hungarian friend of mine observed that the French resisted globalization, which meant Americanization, longer and more effectively than any other people. They had their own way of cooking, dressing, smelling, talking, which resembled no one else's. The cafés, which spilled out onto the sidewalks, glowed and pulsed in the misty night like pods about to spawn.

When I came back to live in Paris in the summer of 1983, I arrived armed with the success of a novel, *A Boy's Own Story,* and a Guggenheim fellowship for sixteen thousand dollars. Nicholas Wahl, a scholar who ran the Institute of French Studies at New York University, arranged for me to stay in an apartment he sometimes rented for a semester on the Île Saint-Louis. I think he intended for me to live there just a few months, but I ended up staying in that apartment for the next six years, depriving him of his favorite stopover. I stayed in France till 1998 but at two later addresses.

Oddly enough, people often asked me if as a writer I went to Paris for inspiration. That never occurred to me. I guess I didn't think writers were that influenced by their setting. And I didn't think of inspiration in that way. Was the idea that one would be moved by the residue of all the great writers of the past? Perhaps one was inspired by living writers one met and talked to—but to me they were more present in their work than in their presence, and presumably their work was available in Topeka as much as in Paris. The fact that Voltaire had once eaten at the Procope restaurant didn't affect me at all. And yet in some vaguer and more exciting way Paris was part of my fantasies about my future, which I usually dreamed about while flying home to New York. I'm the kind of guy who's always wanted to be elsewhere.

Chapter 2

I had a new lover, or rather companion, named John Purcell, who went with me somewhat grudgingly to Paris during the summer of 1983. Everyone says he or she wants to live in Paris, but the reality is somewhat daunting—a strange language spoken rapidly, a culture that rivals and a history that far surpasses America's, winters during which it rains every single day, an exorbitantly expensive town. No wonder so few Americans go there for long, just long enough for their fantasies to wear off and the cold, wet reality to dawn on them like a bad hangover.

I'd met John in a formal or at least old-fashioned way, long before I'd thought of moving to Paris. I'd been lonely in New York and Rudy Kikel, a Boston poet, introduced us. Rudy had said, "John is young and unbelievably sweet and cute and he'll cost you about ten thousand a year." John was in his mid-twenties and I was forty-three when we moved to France.

John had been studying design at Parsons in New York, and he transferred to Parsons Paris without much fuss. He wanted to be an interior designer, but only in a vague way since he had no immediate plans to work. What he liked was to build intricate models of houses and apartments that he would furnish in a glamorous way with tiny chaises longues and sofas. But what he liked even more was meeting preppy, muscular men, preferably black or Mediterranean, who'd court him in a traditionally romantic way and buy him lots of drinks. God should have made me aggressive in bed, since I was always attracted to passive boys but could never satisfy them. John was sexually a bit more versatile than I and for a while things worked out, but soon enough I'd fallen into my usual sexual indifference. For me, familiarity bred friendship, even love, but inevitably the incest taboo set in. If I went to London or Rome for work, John would often greet me on my return to Paris with passionate kisses, enacting scenes he imagined I expected. Or maybe he was trying to "save our marriage." He was entirely dependent on me financially and perhaps he feared I'd fall for someone else.

John and I had a lot of silly fun. We had a ratty-looking antique teddy bear named Peter, then Peters and eventually Petes. It was very important that Petes should see Europe; we were proud parents or maybe godparents introducing him to the Continent. We had lots of snapshots showing Petes looking out the windshield at Mont Blanc or the Duomo in Florence, back when private cars could still drive inside the city. We called each other Petes, too. Sometimes we put words in Petes's mouth: "Petes doesn't like it when you're grumpy. It scares him." When John was elated nothing was more exhilarating; a cartoonist depicting him would have had to plant rays of light in his eyes, his words dancing off his lips.

He always wanted me to tap my razor after I'd shaved to make sure the whiskers washed off the blade. He'd sing a little Disney sort of song, "Tap-tap-tap!" and I think of that even now every morning after I've shaved, although he's been dead for many years—just as when I pee for the first time in the morning I think of a friendly colleague at Time-Life Books who'd said he once passed out after urinating. Or whenever I go up a set of stairs I remember a character in a Scott Spencer novel who vows he won't hang on to the banister, in order to make his leg muscles work harder.

When I told John that I was worried about dying from AIDS, he said, "Don't worry, Petes, we'll take care of each other and have fun."

I'm not sure John wanted to save our marriage, but he did love soap operas. He'd gone to boarding school with a couple of rich girls who'd remained friends and, while we were still in New York, he'd get together with them to watch *As the World Turns* or *The Doctors*. His girlfriends lived on unsalted, unbuttered popcorn, which was filling but not fattening, and they'd sit around in Brooks Brothers shirts hugging their pretty, hairless legs and shake their curls and munch popcorn, their eyes huge, trained on the next adultery. Both girls were from famous families and bore the names of concert halls founded by their grandmothers or academic buildings where an ancestor had devised the "science" of sociology, although neither of them claimed to be a "brainiac" (their word). They talked about clothes and friends and boys, and they followed their soaps and little else. I can remember when Derek Granger, a British Granada Television producer, came to the States for the American launch of his miniseries *Brideshead Revisited*. I introduced him to the girls and John and they kept asking him what he did in life. Finally Derek sputtered, "I've been on every major American interview show and on the cover of half a dozen American magazines—but none of it seems to have gotten through to you!" Still, Derek invited us all to join him for an evening with the owners of the Leslie Lohman gay art gallery, in whose apartment everything including the ceramic ashtray and the corkscrew was either a penis or pair of buttocks. On one wall hung a big nude portrait of the same two men forty years earlier. The girls were intrigued but, I could tell, slightly revolted.

Once we were living in Paris, John was so frantic about missing out on plot twists of his favorite shows that he'd call the girls from a pay phone using a five-franc piece (less than a dollar); John called these quickies "five-frankers." For the allotted two minutes he would speak to them as fast as possible and one of the girls would respond with equal speed: "Helen has seduced Robbie and neglected her dying mother, who died, and her stepmother hates her and is trying to get the will annulled. Vanessa was hired to be a top model in New York and Ted has become an alcoholic and tried to beat her up and ruin her face so she won't leave him. Their baby turns out to be her *father's* child—yes! Vanessa slept with her own *father*!" Suddenly the line would go dead, leaving John with a look of bemused amazement. His eyes, which were appealingly asymmetrical and of two different colors, blue and brown, now looked even more dazed. "My God, Vanessa's son is her own brother!"

I tried to get excited about this amazing fact, but it spoke to me no more than my own books spoke to John. He'd been carrying *A Boy's Own Story* around for a month but never got beyond page 10. He said he was dyslexic, the vogue word of that decade for lack of literary curiosity, just as attention deficit disorder is the term now. I was with him when I received the first printed copy of the book, in a rented room in a crumbling house in Martha's Vineyard that belonged to some *nouveau pauvre* family John knew. It was the sort of house where a pine tree was growing up inside an abandoned Volkswagen on the lawn and where scions of old families inhaled oxygen from tanks every morning upon awakening to get over their hangovers. At the time, John had seemed genuinely excited about my book and all the other young inhabitants of the house passed it around from hand to hand as if it were a curious new fruit, possibly poisonous.

John didn't like Paris. He couldn't speak French and he thought of the language as an annoying habit contrived to irritate him. He'd lived in Florence for one year and was used to linguistic affectations, but that didn't mean he approved of them. He'd even made up an Italian word of his own, *traversiamo*, which meant "Let's cross the street." Television, his main source of amusement, was useless to him in French. He liked Venice but when I took him to Crete for a summer, he was so bored I had to send him to the gay resort island of Mykonos for a week of R&R. He came back with a camera full of snapshots of a hairy-chested Athenian he'd met on the beach and had a romance with. When we went to an island near Istanbul another summer, I sent him off to the southern coast of Turkey for a "vacation" from our vacation. I was a writer and went to quiet places to write, but what made them appealing to me maddened John.

For tax reasons I seldom went back to the United States during the many years I lived in France. If I stayed out of my native country and returned no more than thirty days a year, I owed no American taxes on the first seventy-five thousand dollars I earned—it was as if someone were handing me an extra twenty thousand dollars a year, especially as I paid no taxes in France. The small amounts I earned through my French publisher went through my agent in New York and counted as dollars. Susan Sontag, after we started feuding, used to say I could afford to live in Paris only because I worked for the KGB—how else could you explain my elaborate style of life? Somehow I qualified as a tourist in France by leaving the country at least once every ninety days, but only to go to London or Zurich or Venice, never far. I never had a *permis de séjour* and

I remember the American writer and poet Harry Mathews, who'd been in Paris since the fifties, telling me that neither did he. Although one year when he'd tried to go legit and apply for a visa, a government employee said it was all just too complicated and he might as well skip it.

John was at loose ends and would have liked to visit the States much more often. He walked around the city for hours every day. He said he was trying to memorize all the street names. His path would often take him to the Hotel Central, one of the few gay bars in Paris at that time. What he'd liked in New York were the early evening bars, especially Julius', where older businessmen, just getting off work, would buy him endless drinks late into the night. There were no such fun men in Paris. He took a course at the Cordon Bleu, which was what many Americans on extended stays did in Paris. The French couldn't understand the American mania to open restaurants; in France, a chef was the son of a chef. No one would willingly seek out a life of unending toil and perilous investment. At the Cordon Bleu the master chefs worked under ceiling mirrors and all the American ladies (as most of the pupils were) looked up and followed the procedures while a handsome young Canadian poet translated the chef's instructions. Eventually, everyone would work on her pie crust and the professors would walk among them, making their corrections. Every sort of teacher, it seemed, was called a *professeur* in France. At the gym, we were instructed by a *professeur du sport*. Our dog trainer was called, quite simply, *le professeur.* John came home from the Cordon Bleu after a month of classes with just two recipes under his belt. The one I recall fondly was for lobster bisque, which required hours of "reduction" and the employment of every last squirt of the lobster's coral or carapace. Of course the small European lobsters were so expensive that many middle-class French people ate them only once or twice in a lifetime, and then in a Norman restaurant beside the sea where the spiny versions were halved and broiled under a layer of buttery breadcrumbs, Lobster Thermidor. Later, when I was teaching for a brief time at Brown University, my first trick as host was always to take visiting French people to a lobster shack as soon as their plane from Paris had landed.

I worried that I was infantilizing John by not encouraging him to work, but a job would have been next to impossible for him to arrange in France. He took a course at the Alliance Française, as did I, and there he met a beautiful American lipstick lesbian. He went out with her to all the dyke bars, where he was often the only man, though several of the customers looked like men. He didn't have work papers. All the Americans we met working under the table were either fitness professors or personal assistants to rich American writers. Our friend Bill Corey lived on a houseboat, a *péniche*, tied up near the boulevard Saint-Michel. Bill typed manuscripts and took dictation from a Mr. Miller, and although Bill was mailing Mr. Miller's manuscripts off all the time to editors in the UK and the States, already there were a dozen unpublished novels in Mr. Miller's bottom drawer. Bill, who was a gee-whiz kind of guy, said loyally, "Mr. Miller's books are really, really good. He just needs a break. Mr. Miller is patient and confident—we just know he's going to get his big break someday soon and then he'll have a dozen novels to publish, one every month, as a follow-up to his first success. You laugh, but I really admire him. Of course, I don't know much about the publishing scene, but Mr. Miller says it's a tight, closed little world."

Whenever Mr. Miller was away in England visiting friends, or in Virginia inspecting his polo ponies, Bill would give cocktail parties on the deck of the *péniche*. It felt like the set of Puccini's *Il Tabarro*. The boat was permanently tied up in its prime location; the stairs descending from the quay (which was thronged with cars and pedestrians) led down into a quiet village of rotting ropes, uneven paving stones, the smell of gasoline, and the lapping of waves when a Bateau Mouche would slide by and rock the moored boat. We'd be down here on the water, five degrees cooler than the street, and looking up at historic buildings from an unusual angle, while that typically Parisian sound of someone playing a jazz saxophone under a bridge serenaded us. After many drinks, we'd all want to read Mr. Miller's novel manuscripts out loud, but Bill would forbid us to touch the beautifully typed pages. "That's private." Later, as a film student, Bill made a silent black-and-white short of me and my friends. For a dolly he rented a wheelchair and had someone pull it backward behind Notre Dame while with a handheld camera he shot me walking away from the cathedral. *A Day in the Life of Edmund White* was eventually shown at some of the earliest gay film festivals.

We were all afraid of AIDS—even straight people in those first years. Two foreign women I'd known in New York, famous for their orgies, had suddenly become monogamous. Even in Paris, the least hysterical and most fatalistic city in the world ("We all have to die sometime"), people, straight and gay, were suddenly circumspect. I had been one of the six founders of Gay Men's Health Crisis, in 1981, and its first president, and like everyone I'd seen the numbers swell. At that point no one knew what caused it—one exposure or multiple exposures. One just seemed too unfair and harsh; we voted for several, on the blame-the-victim theory that promiscuity was to blame. Cold comfort for me, since I had had literally thousands of partners.

Friends from America came to visit, including a huge, brainy bodybuilder named Norm who'd been my lover, who ordered two of everything in French restaurants. David Kalstone, my best friend from New York, came; I served him and others a giant tray of shellfish, a *plateau de fruits de mer*, on New Year's Eve, which made him wretch violently and which seemed to announce the onslaught of the AIDS that killed him. J. D. McClatchy wrote about the few feeble gatherings I could put together in those early days in an article in the *Yale Review* that made us all sound important and worldly.

My John was famous in our little world for his charm. The first truly out gay editor in New York, Michael Denneny, had been in love with John and was jealous when John moved in with me. Michael had met John in Boston, where John was living in a mansion at the foot of Beacon Hill with a Spanish prince, a Rockefeller, and two punk rock brothers. The house was full of valuable antiques and, as John described it, an eyebrow-raising amount of decadent behavior.

John was a pack rat. When he moved into my studio apartment in New York he arrived with twenty garment bags. And then he watched television all the time, which drove me crazy. I got him his own apartment in SoHo above an Ethiopian restaurant.

And then we moved to Paris. I bought him a tiny black-and-white TV, but our French was so bad we couldn't even follow the news. Then

I found out that I had to pay an annual *tax* for the boring, state-financed channels!

John exaggerated both the high points and the ordeals of his life to the degree of pure invention. He liked to picture his parents as monsters and his sisters as wicked, and he told horror stories about his abuse from a family member when he was twelve. It's true that there was something broken about John, something goofy and slightly off, as if a nurse had dropped him on his head. His social rhythm was sprung. He'd look around, blinking and uncomprehending. Then he'd lock into one of his horror stories about the tortures he'd suffered as a teen from his sisters, whom he portrayed as figures of pure malice, or from his stern, unforgiving parents. He'd start ranting, talking faster and faster, exhibiting what the psychologists call "forced speech." Moods of vacant inattentiveness would alternate with spells of obsessive talk. Exchanging these stories was almost a rite of passage in America, helping establish intimacy with a new friend. No American would openly question the veracity of a horror story about the hell of childhood. It was as if we were each granted credibility and attentiveness for one story only—our own. And if, like the story of saints' lives, it was a narrative of suffering and redemption, all the better.

John would have been deeply offended if someone had dared to question his martyrdom, but in Paris people merely drooped under the onslaught of so many shocking details. John's eyes would glitter like Savanarola's and his voice would take on all the solemnity of high conviction as he recounted the whole nightmare. Later, when I met his father, slender and handsome and half effaced, and his mother, ample and serene as Barbara Bush, it was hard to believe anything John had said against them. His mother was the first female selectman of Concord, Massachusetts, or so John claimed. His family owned the huge cosmetic firm Maybelline, or so he said. After a while he stopped mentioning that connection. His father was a doctor from the South. Or so he said. John didn't like to have his veracity doubted. The Taoists, or so I've been told, say that no one ever lies, that even an untruth can express a desire, an ideal, a longed-for reality. John certainly wanted to be seen as the sweet, wounded victim—and for him victimhood was more appealing when it befell a little aristocrat. If history had been at all real or interesting to him, he might have identified himself with Marie Antoinette. To be young, pretty, *and* beheaded would have struck him as a winning combination.

The French in general didn't seem to like such American tales of painful childhoods. "Everyone had a wretched childhood," they'd say airily. "We must just get on with it." Or they'd say, *"Pas de confessions!"* ("No confessions!"). I remember telling this to Jules Feiffer, and a French woman in a film he directed later is overheard telling another character, *"Pas de confessions!"* I knew, too, that anyone French my age would have lived through World War II from start to finish as well as the grim period afterward of material shortages and moral recriminations. How could any American spanking saga or Oedipal epic compare with the chilblains and lost limbs and bombings and concentration camps the Europeans had endured? There was a moment when I tried to serve Jerusalem artichokes to French friends. They threw their hands up in the air—"Oh no, Edmond! You can't expect us to eat *topinambours*. We choked on them all through the war." I could remember in my wartime childhood revolting meals of canned bony salmon mixed with breadcrumbs and formed into patties, but then we'd never gone hungry or cold.

Anyone younger who grew up in France before the events of May 1968 revolutionized everything could remember strict Catholic (or Communist) families, school uniforms, meals during which children were expected to be seen but not heard. When French friends read in translation *A Boy's Own Story*, bizarrely what struck them most was how little supervision I'd had as a teenager. I'd never thought about that. Both the British and the French praised me for my honesty and courage in relating my sexual "secrets" in that book. A fellow American would never have singled out those qualities, since we Americans all like to bray our secrets to complete strangers on a plane or at the next table.

To be sure, *A Boy's Own Story* was presented to the world as a novel rather than as a memoir, but not out of a sense of discretion or modesty. It was just that back then only people who were already famous wrote their memoirs. The victor of Iwo Jima had the right to sign a memoir, but not a battered housewife. The man who invented the rubber band could give us his success story, but not a child who'd been locked in the basement for a decade. All this would change by the end of the 1980s, when suddenly youngsters would ask me with a hint of superiority why I hadn't dared to call my book an autobiography. I remember in 1990 on a visit back to the States reading with astonishment an agency ad in the back of the *New York Review of Books*: "Were you incested as a child? Raped by your father? You might consider going on the lecture circuit and letting us represent you."

John was tall and slender and well mannered, with a sweet smile and a polite way of making small talk. His teeth were yellow from a sulfur drug he'd taken as a kid. People liked him, especially some women and older men who found him courtly and vulnerable. He had a very high voice, almost a young girl's voice, which sounded especially strange in a Latin country where most men spoke "from the balls" (with *"une voix des couilles"*). Everything about John was contradictory. He seemed docile and polite till he started relating his horror stories with all the half-mad zeal of a reforming saint. He "read" in a crowd as blond, but on closer inspection his hair was white, pure white. His hair color was polyvalent, if that means it had many shifting meanings. If he was looking boyish, people would laughingly deny his hair was white. "But it's blond," they'd insist. "Platinum blond." If he looked hungover and haggard, they'd take in his high voice, his youthful, preppy way of dressing in too-tight jeans, madras jackets, and pink, laceless sneakers and his way of tilting his head from side to side and observe that so many attempts to look young were repellent in a middle-aged man— when he was actually only twenty-five. He spoke seriously of interior decoration and his plans for the future, but it almost seemed he knew in advance he'd die young and would never work. French people were charmed to encounter a young man from the hometown of Emerson and Thoreau, but John knew more about how to do rubbings from Puritan gravestones and sell them to tourists than how to parse the essays of their nineteenth-century descendants.

Early on during our first year in Paris, he met a hairy-chested macho named Emmanuel who had a large apartment on a high floor overlooking the place de la Bastille. Not that there was much to see there except for the building site for the new Bastille Opera House. According to one story, all Paris was chuckling that President Mitterrand had been led into a room where five models for the opera house by five different architects were on display. He'd been coached to choose the one all the way to the right, by Richard Meier, but he became confused and chose the one all the way to the left by the unknown Carlos Ott, a Uruguayan working in Canada (he thought it was the one by Meier). And that's how Paris ended up with an opera house resembling a cow palace on the outside and on the inside a bathroom lined with black and white tiles.

I started to see Marie-Claude from time to time at her "state dinners," when she'd invite the newest celebrities of the moment, *les vrais génies du moment*. One of her prizes was Gae Aulenti, an Italian architect who between 1980 and 1985 undertook the immense job of turning the Gare d'Orsay into a museum. Gae was an intelligent, humorous, heavyset woman with short hair, cropped, unvarnished nails, and a frank, easy-going manner. She told us that the real problem of converting a vast turn-of-the-century train station into a museum was that the huge, empty vault above the tracks had to be crammed full of little squares, exhibition spaces, some five floors of them. It wasn't an easy or natural use of this space. Another problem was that the curator—who was often introduced as the granddaughter on one side of the painter Paul Signac and on the other of the founder of the French Communist Party—had decided the museum should reflect the taste of the people of the nineteenth century, not ours now, so the ground floor was full of big academic dud paintings whereas the masterpieces by Cézanne and Degas were relegated to the top floor—which many exhausted tourists never got to. When Gae needed to select the color of the entire interior she had to construct at great expense three identical models of the future museum each painted a different color, all so that Mitterrand could swan in, glance at the models and declare, "It shall be gray!" No other elected president in modern times has had such dictatorial powers over even the smallest details of his land. Of course, Mitterrand was the embodiment of grandiosity with a mania for building monuments to himself, *Les Grands Travaux*. He ended up bestowing on Paris the glass pyramid of I. M. Pei as the entrance to the new Louvre; the new Bibliotèque Nationale

(National Library) on the banks of the Seine; and the Grande Arche at the modern office center La Défense, a huge, rectangular arch lined up with the Napoleonic Arc du Carrousel at the Louvre and the Arc de Triomphe. The Bibliothèque Nationale, installed in four glass towers, was meant to resemble open books. After it was finally completed, one of the first things that had to be done to the building was to block out all that sunlight admitted by the glass, since light damages books—and in one stroke the whole concept of the transparent, sun-drenched towers was invalidated. Then the automated delivery system didn't work until many adjustments had been made. Worst of all was the location: the library was in a part of Paris few people visited.

Mitterrand also built the Bastille Opera House and the sprawling Finance Ministry spanning a highway (it collapsed soon after it was inaugurated but was quickly propped back up). Mitterrand gave Paris a new science museum in a former abattoir. Next to it he erected the Cité de la Musique. Of all his projects only the Louvre pyramid is a complete success, and that only for people on the political Left. In France I quickly learned that everything is political, even an opinion of a building. When the pyramid was unveiled I could tell who was a Socialist and who was a Gaullist according to their approval or dislike of the building; it was absolutely systematic. In America we wouldn't usually confuse aesthetics and politics, whereas in France everything is arranged according to extra-artistic allegiances. For instance, I learned that literary prizes such as the Médicis, the Femina, and the Goncourt, which determine sales figures in France, alternate among the three top publishing houses in a nearly unvarying way. One year a prize will go to Gallimard, the next to Seuil, and the third to Grasset, no matter the actual merits of the candidates (the collective noun is "Galligrasseuil"). A masterpiece published by some less prestigious house would never win, for instance, nor would a superior book from a publisher in the wrong sequence ("Oh, no. This year it's Gallimard's turn!").

Undoubtedly these remarks show what an anthropological approach I took toward "the French." Later I came to disapprove of this spirit of observation and speculation about the national character of what the Peace Corps calls "our host country nationals." I came to think that individuals should be judged on their merits and not used to build up a portrait of a whole nationality. I'd read somewhere that tracing national character was a puerile pursuit, not one to be encouraged, but one that Americans are especially prone to. Only about 30 percent of Americans have passports, and half of those have traveled only to Mexico or Canada. We are an insular, incurious nation—but there I go again.

In many ways Mitterrand was the best friend French capitalists ever had. Because he was supposedly a Socialist, the labor unions came to heel. For that, he'd mastered all the progressive rhetoric necessary. Although many bankers and investors initially fled Paris for New York, soon they came trickling back, especially when Mitterrand realized his more extreme policies (taxation of the rich) wouldn't work. I heard that Marie-Hélène de Rothschild said that New York was impossible because rich people there only socialized with other rich people of exactly the same level of wealth, and that our New York rich people worked long days and had to be in bed by ten, making social life impossible. No one had amusing artists or writers to dinner. And besides, everyone in America ate asparagus with knives and forks, instead of with their fingers as civilized people did.

I realized the rich had come home to Paris and were reassured the night I was asked to accompany the French editor of French *Vogue* to a masked ball given for a cause at the Palais Garnier, the old opera house. The two hosts were Madame Mitterrand and Madame Chirac (at that time wife of the mayor of Paris). For the first time every rich woman felt safe to bring out her jewels, no longer afraid they'd be confiscated. The evening started with the entirety of Verdi's *Un Ballo in Maschera* starring Pavarotti. Then in the lobbies there was a sit-down dinner for hundreds, followed by an actual masked ball. TV cameras were wheeling about lighting up one woman after another and televising her gown. It was the sort of stuffy evening I hate except to tell others about it. Years later, my partner Michael and I went to Elton John's fiftieth-birthday party, where hundreds were in costume. Elton was dressed like an eighteenth-century courtier with tiny cannon explosions going off in his white wig. He and his lover arrived in the back of a freight truck decorated inside like an eighteenth-century drawing room. Trumpeters lined the entranceway.

We were entertained by black singers from America singing spirituals and formally dressed couples from Wales demonstrating ballroom dancing onstage. Michael recognized every rock star attending, but I'd never heard of any of them. We were seated with Ismail Merchant, of the filmmaking duo Merchant and Ivory, and his date, a beauty who turned out to be Mr. Naples, who'd been flown in for the occasion. He turned and asked me in Italian who was the man he was accompanying. At another grand dinner, given by Diane von Furstenberg to launch a new perfume, I was seated next to France's then most famous model, Inès de la Fressange. I asked her what she did. The others at our table gasped. She thought it was funny and explained she'd just come back from India and was opening a dress shop of her own. In those days Diane von Furstenberg lived in Paris, not New York, and she was with André Elkan, the editor of *Panta,* an Italian magazine similar to *Granta.* He was doing a book-length interview of the very old Alberto Moravia, who was always seated in the corner.

And yet when I first moved to Paris I couldn't really socialize with French people because I couldn't speak the language. The best description of what it's like to speculate about what other people are saying in a language you're trying to learn comes from Ben Lerner's hilarious recent novel *Leaving the Atocha Station* (in which the narrator moved to Madrid): "Then she might have described swimming in the lake as a child, or said that lakes reminded her of being a child, or asked me if I'd enjoyed swimming as a child, or said that what she'd said about the moon was childish." Neophytes in a new language live from one hypothesis to another.

In the meantime, the expat I saw most often was Marilyn Schaefer, a friend from New York who came to Paris for a year in 1983. She'd been such a friend since I was fourteen that it was a real consolation to have her nearby (she's still a close friend). She understood French only very approximately. One night a waiter was saying something with such a tragic expression that Marilyn said, "Quel dommage." Her French-speaking date said the waiter had asked them if they wanted to be on their mailing list. I saw a lot of Sarah Plimpton, George Plimpton's sister (as serious as her brother was jokey), a slender woman who wrote poetry and painted and would eventually marry Robert Paxton, the great historian of the Vichy period. Sarah frowned skeptically at everything I said, as though she were hard of hearing or I were a liar. Over lunch I told her I was just planning to stay for a year. She said, "I thought the same thing. Just one year. Now it's nineteen years later. It's really the land of lotus eaters here."

She'd previously fallen for André du Bouchet, one of France's top poets, who, like Sarah, wrote in short, unpunctuated free verse lines, *la poésie blanche*. She sublet her Marais apartment to Marilyn, and the most remarkable thing about the apartment was the orgasmic yelping of a female neighbor each morning, her rhythmic cries filling the courtyard. When the woman descended the stairs and came into the courtyard, on her way out to do her shopping, applause would erupt from all around.

I asked myself why I was here. Sure, I'd won a Guggenheim and a small but regular contract with *Vogue* to write once a month on cultural life. Right now I was writing a piece about why Americans liked Proust so much. Back in America I'd worked around the clock heading the New York Institute for the Humanities and teaching writing at Columbia and New York University. I never seemed to have time for my own writing. When I was president of Gay Men's Health Crisis, the biggest and oldest AIDS organization in the world, I hadn't liked myself in the role of leader; I was power mad and tyrannical, much to my surprise, always ordering people to shut up and vote. And secretly I'd wanted the party to go on and thought that moving to Europe would give me a new lease on promiscuity. Paris was meant to be an AIDS holiday. After all, I was of the Stonewall generation, equating sexual freedom with freedom itself. But by 1984 many gay guys I knew were dying in Paris as well—there was no escaping the disease. Michel Foucault, for one, had welcomed me warmly during a brief visit in 1981, but he and Gilles Barbedette, a mutual friend and one of my first translators, had both laughed when I'd told them about this mysterious new disease that was killing gay men and blacks and addicts. "Oh no," they said, "you're so gullible. A disease that only kills gays and blacks and drug addicts? Why not child molesters, too? That's too perfect!"

They both died of AIDS, Foucault first, then Barbedette. I helped Foucault's surviving partner, Daniel Defert, start up the French AIDS organization AIDES. But I went to only a few meetings. Everything in France was different and beyond my competence. Whereas we in America could only think of having a disco benefit to raise money for research and treatment and prevention, in France AIDES had the cooperation of Mitterrand's minister of health, Édith Cresson. We brought our very sense of marginality and pessimism to the disease, whereas French gays made everyone recognize it was a national disaster. Whereas the public in America was hysterical, in France the government instructed journalists not to make too much of the at-risk groups lest there be a gay backlash. As a result gays weren't attacked, but they also weren't properly forewarned. Across the Channel, Mrs. Thatcher's scare tactics were much more effective in keeping the numbers of AIDS patients down. Or maybe, I thought, the English just tricked less. London was so spread out and the tube stopped running early.

I had moved to Rome from New York thirteen years earlier, when I turned thirty. I wanted to acquire some polish and international culture, but my mentor Richard Howard complained that in my letters I made Rome sound "like a kickier version of Scranton." According to Richard, I had failed to see that Rome was "one of the central cities of Western culture." I had re-created my New York life in Rome but in an inferior version. I drank too much sour white wine and, like a character in Chekhov, took too many naps.

I wanted to make my Parisian sojourn better than my time in either Rome or New York had been. Whereas Rome in those days had been a village and my New York was a gay ghetto, I wanted Paris to be a real grown-up, pansexual adventure. I had been a teacher for the last eight years—at Yale, Johns Hopkins, Columbia, New York University—and now I was a student again. Now that I was in my forties and had a successful novel to my name, I could either go on doing the same things until I retired—or begin anew. I stopped smoking and then, a year later, stopped drinking. David Rieff, Susan Sontag's son, said to me, "I guess you have to start all over again. You're too famous to live in New York, right?" Was that true—was I famous? I didn't feel famous, though Susan had told me, "You'll never be really poor again." She had already arranged for me to receive a cash award from the American Academy of Arts and Letters and to win a Guggenheim. *She* was famous; people nudged each other when she walked past. I suppose lesser lights like me always over-estimate or underestimate their celebrity ("But my novel wasn't listed by the *Times* as one of the best books of the year"). It seemed to me that only a few educated gay Americans my age had ever heard of me.

Here I was in Paris, where I knew only two people and couldn't speak the language. Rather than consolidating my position in New York and writing a sequel to *A Boy's Own Story*, I had disappeared into Paris and dived off a cliff and I was writing a novel that managed to satirize all the people who'd helped me, including Susan and Richard Howard as well as Richard Sennett, who'd given me my job at the New York Institute for the Humanities. It was called *Caracole* and was set in a weird amalgam of Venice and Paris and other centuries. I described it by saying it was as if you were taking a comparative literature course and fell asleep the night before the exam and had a bad dream. It was also sort of about the Austrian domination of Venice. Édouard Roditi, a new friend in his seventies whom I'd met when *Conjunctions* had asked us to interview each other, said, "*Caracole* is a very fine novel and you won't have a career if you write another one like it."

The only people who liked *Caracole* were Alan Jenkins at the *Times Literary Supplement* and the director Louis Malle. He and I met for lunch at a nearly empty restaurant on the Île de la Cité I'd suggested, and he said his father had brought him there as a child. He told me he wanted to option my book because it reminded him of his childhood in occupied France—since my book was about a superior people being tyrannized by conquering inferiors. He explained that he'd gone to a Catholic school during the war that had protected a Jewish boy from the Nazis—until the boy was betrayed and led off to a death camp.

I said, "Why bother with my novel? The story you just told—*there's* your next film."

Ultimately he agreed and went on to make *Au revoir les enfants*, one of his best movies.

Once again I'd shot myself in the foot.

Chapter 3

I attended French language classes at the Alliance Française, but there of course only the instructor could speak the language correctly and with a native accent. Our teacher seemed to sympathize with the Japanese students, who apparently shared not a single phoneme with the French. They were utterly incomprehensible, though they studied really hard and turned red with the effort to pronounce the tricky *r* and the nasal *on* and the flutey *ü*. The Arabs were all gifted linguists and lacked nothing but vocabulary. Many of them were enrolled just so they could have a student visa. They often added a harsh aspirated *h* where it didn't belong. One well-dressed Spanish woman was reproached for having a loud, metallic voice. The poor lady was told that her way of speaking, perhaps acceptable south of the Pyrenees, could only offend the soft-spoken French. An English girl was told that she had a misplaced confidence in her French, especially her faulty way of pronouncing *u* as *oo*.

Then one day we discovered our teacher was sort of crazy. She said she was sick of always asking the questions. Surely there were things we wanted to know about France. The Spanish woman, trying to moderate her tones, asked the teacher to inform us about Normandy. The teacher leapt into action. She drew a cow on the chalkboard and said, "Oh, Normandy is famous for its butter." Then she drew a fish: "And for its fishing industry." She drew a bed: "A fourth of all hospital beds are for the mentally ill." She wrote *1/4* on the blackboard and for emphasis repeated, "*La maladie mentale*. I myself have had electroshock treatments," then wrote, *Traitements par électrochocs*.

I was hanging out mostly with other Americans I met at the gym or at the Alliance Française or whom I'd first encountered in the States. It seemed all these Americans were always huddling together talking about *them*. The French, they complained, had no friends but only family members. They were incapable of making friends after child-hood. The French never went anywhere alone but always *en bande*. Or the French were never open and honest in love: everything *they* said was strategic. Frenchmen adored women and liked them as no American males did. Conversely, Frenchmen were bullies and pigs beneath all their hand kissing. The French thought we were naïvely kind and childish, *bons enfants*. If they *liked* an American, they'd say he or she was nice, "but not at all stupid" (*gentil mais pas de tout bête*), but *they* just as often accused us of being crudely materialistic, or *they* thought we were prudes and hypocrites—perverted in the boudoir and Tartuffes in the salon, rapists and puritans. The French alone had mastered *l'art de vivre*. The French had a fierce primitive respect for the peasant, though only 5 percent of the population lived on the land. The French thought Americans dined exclusively on hamburgers and the Italians on pizza. The French were snobs; *they*, after all, were the only truly democratic people—*they* had invented *égalité* and *fraternité*. *They* readily gave asylum to political refugees; conversely, *they* were the worst chauvinists and racists. The French were cheap (every busker and beggar said as much); conversely, the French owned more second homes than any other people. The French never invested in stocks, only in property—*pierres* ("stones"). *They* spoke of "evolved" attitudes all the time: *"Il est très évolué!"* I'm not sure we Americans could embrace the eugenicist biological principles underlying such a term. Was our multiculturalism compatible with the notion of an inevitable and uniform biological development?

It was all beginning to sound like Flaubert's dictionary of clichés, *Le Dictionnaire des idées reçues* ("Blondes are hotter. See brunettes." "Brunettes are hotter. See blondes"). If I had one generalization about the French, I formulated it thirty years ago and still believe it despite its eugenicist sound: they evolve faster than any other people, and what was true of them a decade ago is no longer true. The French are immersed in ideas and pride themselves on being rational. They can almost instantly discard a prejudice and embrace a new, better idea. Americans mostly cling to familiar ideas and repeat them year after year. Only the French change their minds.

Whereas Americans were spread across the continent, one in six French people lived in the greater Paris area. This concentration, of course, facilitated communication and social coherence. The French gathered to discuss ideas in "philosophical cafés." They favored book-chat shows on TV where serious issues were debated—and where sometimes quite outlandish ideas were advanced with daunting rhetorical energy and icy confidence. Just recently, while watching a rebroadcast of a French book-talk show on a New York cable channel, I heard an aging French male author, Patrick Grainville, argue that all experience could be reduced to the symbol of the octopus (*le pieuvre*)—which in his 2010 novel, *Le Baiser du pieuvre*, embraces a Japanese woman and brings her down to his watery realm. He spoke with such fervor about the sea creature that he seemed to have hypnotized himself into believing what he was saying. As one French critic asked, "Is the octopus a projection of the female sex or should we see in its tentacles a phallic allusion? Definitely, this animal spitting ink—wouldn't that be a fine metaphor for the writer?" No wonder the English think the French have no sense of humor—at least no feel for the ridiculous. I suppose the French can see when an enemy deserves to be laughed at, but they can't quite conceive when they themselves are courting ridicule. This imperviousness has permitted the French (unlike the English) to embrace Lacan and Derrida and to foster the avant-garde in literature, the theater, and the other arts. English humor—deflating, commonsensical, alert to the excesses of self-importance—is a prophylactic against all that is new or experimental. Humor, especially satire, is always conservative.

The French may make diagnostic pronouncements about their own culture, but they dislike it when foreigners do so. The English writer Theodore Zeldin won wide esteem in France when he published *France: 1848–1945* in five volumes, but he irritated the French reading public in 1982 when he brought out his book *The French,* about contemporary French society. Suddenly Zeldin went from being the unquestioned expert in French history to being one more unreliable British pundit. And as I write it, I'm wondering if this book of mine will ever be published in France.

Before moving to France I'd always assumed that the sort of educated people I would meet there would be progressive, even leftist, and always critical of their own government and even the whole nation. Back in New York, everyone I met socially was a Democrat, possibly a socialist, very occasionally a communist. They all loved making wry or stinging comments about the "military-industrial complex" ruling the United States. Our humorists were Mike Nichols and Elaine May, Mort Sahl, Jules Feiffer, Lenny Bruce—people who satirized themselves and their kind as slightly absurd, pretentious New York Jews and intellectuals, and who ridiculed America as an ignorant, destructive, war-mongering behemoth. I suppose I thought French writers and teachers and thinkers would be just as self-critical. I was shocked to discover they were patriotic. Maybe French leftists loved France because Mitterrand was a Socialist president, the first in half a century. The Left had elected him. The Left enjoyed some real influence, unlike radicals in the States who'd never governed and never would.

I quickly learned I could make a good impression by praising France to the French unqualifiedly as the center of world culture, the beacon of freedom, the epitome of fashion. My new friends loved their country—nor were they all leftists. I interviewed one aristocrat who'd known Genet and kept a photo of the far-right politician Jean-Marie Le Pen on his grand piano. People I knew in Normandy hung out a black flag on the anniversary of the day Louis XVI was beheaded, and our summer-rental landlady in Provence routinely called Marie Antoinette "Sa Majesté la Reine." Some were right, far right, even tending toward monarchism or fascism. I heard people murmuring anti-Semitic things—not so you could make an issue out of it: "But we're joking! You don't understand our humor." For the first time I was meeting charming, educated people who were frankly elitist, who believed in France for the French only and who assumed the French were superior to Arabs and black Africans and gypsies and Eastern Europeans. And Americans. Oh, there were good, i.e. Europeanized, Americans. But most of them were oafs who spoke loudly or put their feet up on the opposite seat of the train or chewed gum or didn't know how to wield their knives and forks or split the bill in a stingy way and were far from being generous hosts. Table manners seemed to enjoy a childish importance in France. How you held yourself at table (no slumping, naturally) and grasped your silverware (the fork always in the left hand, no switching back and forth to the right; soup spoon pointing away then turned 180 degrees to deliver the liquid to your mouth, and no sideways entry as required in America)—all proved or disproved your "upbringing": a word that in French was simply "*éduca-tion*." And never take twice from the cheese plate, though it is the one course you may refuse altogether. Marie-Laure de Noailles's mother, the comtesse de Chévigné, told her that only plebeians ate cheese, anyway. The more snobbish the family, the more their cheese plate was only six kinds of goat cheese, the least stinky of all varieties.

Although Americans were far more religious than people in France, no one faith back home had the universal prestige of French Catholicism. I remember a French lover of mine telling me about his aunt and grandmother in Nantes standing for half an hour in the front hall every Sunday morning before going out to mass. They were both dressed in navy blue suits and they were both picking tiny, nearly invisible bits of lint off of each other. That image of their anxious weekly preparation for their ritual crept into my imagination. It became an emblem of the French bourgeoisie—not chic, certainly not glamorous, but *correct*. That was the word they used for everything they approved of. A restaurant was "correct." A hotel was "correct." An office party was "correct." Nor was the word ever accompanied by an ironic smile. It was a grim badge of acceptance, not enthusiastic approval. Just a weary way of saying nothing had been disturbing or disorderly or shocking. A negative form of tolerance, the ground zero of disapproval.

Some American friends of mine owned a farm two hours south of Paris and an hour north of Tours. They were seldom in France and gave me the keys for four months at a time. I bought an old Renault Cinq and drove down there and stayed sometimes to do a week's worth of work. In the village there was only one decent restaurant, which was in the sole hotel. There for twenty dollars one might have a fish soup sprinkled with cheese and croutons slathered in the reddish mayonnaise called "rust" (*rouille*). Followed by half of a roast chicken or three lamb chops. Then cheese and dessert and coffee. Delicious food. More than "correct."

The customers whispered. Even families with children. To speak in a normal voice would have been proof of vulgarity, a sign that one was badly brought up (*mal élevé*). The restaurant was owned and managed by a placid, watchful, evil woman who resembled the queen of England. She never enthused over her customers, not even regulars like me and my guests. Her shoulders sloped, she held one hand dangling bonelessly in front of her; she was *molle* (flabby, flaccid, soft). She'd nod coolly, condescendingly, at a slight angle. Her face relaxed into an unchanging expression of sleepy contempt. If she was nearly indifferent to us, the sole waitress, Marie-Louise, was always animated and attentive. Over the course of many evenings at the hotel, we learned that Marie-Louise had been in service all her life since she was fifteen, half a century before then, when she'd begun working at La Mère Poularde on Mont Saint-Michel. Briefly she'd worked in Germany "in order to learn the wines"—a biographeme that startled us since as good French chauvinists we just assumed French wines were superior to those of any other country. It was a bit like a Renaissance Florentine traveling to Zagreb to study art.

The hotel dining room had clean, gleaming tile floors and simple wood tables, crowned with pure white napery. The many windows were tall and let in the soft sunlight by day; at night the curtains, ugly orange and brown hunting scenes, were drawn against the perpetual winter fog. When my writing or my life was going badly I dreamed of living at the hotel upstairs in a room I somehow imagined was austerely platonic.

One day an aristocratic party of twelve came in for lunch after the stag hunt, but even they whispered—a decline from the days when duchesses barked at the servants and dukes audibly sneered at the bill after the tradesman or waiter presented it. Now the local nobility had taken up the same infernal mincing as their *roturier* ("commoner") neighbors. Eleven of the group ordered the same dessert, but a twelfth woman chose the *feuilletines au chocolat*, justifying her supposed eccentricity by saying "I'm plunging into an adventure!" (*"Je me lance dans l'aventure!"*).

One day we'd eaten so heartily that I told Marie-Louise I thought I would skip the dessert. We were the only customers. The queen of England was nowhere in sight. Marie-Louise leaned slightly in my direction and whispered, "Then would you possibly be willing to order the dessert with the chocolate leaves?"

"Sure. Of course. But why?"

"You could leave it for me. I've never tasted it."

"You've worked here how many years?"

"Twenty-five. Madame never lets the servants taste the desserts."

Another day Marie-Louise had obviously been weeping. She wasn't her usual brisk, tidy self wearing her fake pearl necklace and with her hair up. Her eyes were smaller and her voice subdued, and I said, "Is anything wrong, Marie-Louise?"

"My brother died yesterday and he's to be buried tomorrow in Brittany. I asked Madame for the day off. I could make it there and back in a day by train but she said no. *'Mademoiselle, je ne peux pas vous épargner.'* [I can't spare you.] It was the first time in twenty-five years I'd asked for a day off. I'd even found a young man in the village to fill in for me."

This sounded to us like something out of Mauriac's *A Nest of Vipers*. Marie-Louise had only two consolations. One was that she was about to retire. The other was that Madame let her choose the busboy every summer when things got busy, and Marie-Louise always chose the most handsome. This year it was a tall blond who had bad teeth and never smiled but who blushed easily and sometimes, very rarely and improbably, laughed at Marie-Louise's wisecracks and instantly covered his ruined mouth with his hand. He surely lived at home with his parents where he had rural chores to do, for the layer of urbanism in the village was literally only one street deep and the burghers' houses—even those built around the town square with its band kiosk and town hall—opened up in the rear to fields and barns. One night my lover Hubert, who was very ill, couldn't finish his meal. Marie-Louise sniffed, *"Une petite nature."*

We invited the "peasants" who lived next door (I could never get used to calling them *paysans*) to visit the house sometime, and Hubert bought a bottle of aperitif, Suze, popular in the French countryside. I don't drink, but I admiringly smelled the bitter medicinal yellow fluid (a cordial made from boiled yellow gentian roots) in its tall, narrow bottle. The invitation we'd extended was understood to be flexible and open-ended and we didn't know when to expect the neighbors, yet two Sundays later all of them showed up, parents and grandparents, the two little girls and their handsome, effeminate teenage older brother who was being sent off to hospitality school to become a waiter. He'd straightened his blond hair and his clothes had sophisticated, stylishly useless buckles and straps.

The conversation was ponderous, the dialect (reputed to be the best, purest French) nearly incomprehensible to me—and I fled into an adjoining room and waited for it to end. From what I could understand, they were telling dull local stories involving the weather, much as my Texas farming relatives might do, except that my relatives would also include the mileage they'd gotten and the route they'd taken and the dust storm they'd seen. When my born-again cousin Dorothy Jean came to Paris, I took her to a museum entirely devoted to the work of Gustave Moreau and pointed out a painting of Judith cutting off the head of Holofernes. "It's a biblical scene," I said optimistically.

"That's not in my Bible," she scoffed.

One night Hubert and I, as we drove home from the hotel, saw a car that had gone off the road into the ditch. We hopped out and peered into the driver's side, where a young woman was slumped over the wheel, her ear running with blood. The headlights blazed into the tall, uneven grass. A little dog was yapping soundlessly in the backseat behind a closed window. The only noise was the creaking and ticking of the still-warm automobile. Since we didn't have a phone in our house, we rushed up the nearest drive to the peasant's house and knocked. The farmer answered the door, blotchy-faced and reeking of cheap brandy, his trousers unbuttoned.

"Who is it?" he said, referring to the victim.

"What difference does it make?" cried Hubert. "She's hurt! Call an ambulance!"

"But who is it?"

"We can figure that out later. Whoever it is, we need to get her to the hospital."

The entire family, even the grandmother, wanted to know who it was before they would bother to call the ambulance. It was raining slightly as we all trudged down to the still-illuminated car in the ditch. If I'd been able to communicate with them more readily, I might have reminded them their hesitation could very well end up being partly responsible for the woman's death.

"Oh, it's Hélène!" said the farmer. "She and her mother are both big drunks. This is the second accident she's had in a month." And he went on and on filling us in on the sad case of Hélène as the dog barked silently and climbed up on the backseat to look at us through the window and left a breathy ghost of his nose on the glass.

I couldn't quite see how French city dwellers could idealize the *paysan* unless it was just one more strategy for despising the bourgeoisie. I can still picture Hubert and me walking down a country lane with tilled fields on either side discussing the word "peasant." The fields were full of sunflowers taller than us that had been starved of irrigation and allowed to brown, wither, and die so that their seeds could more easily be harvested, and I felt that *paysan* must be a derogatory word for anyone except a royalist like Hubert. Finally, a little to my relief, we decided that their word *paysan* didn't quite carry the same meaning as our "peasant," and that no French Hamlet would exclaim bitterly in an excess of self-hatred, "Oh, what a rogue and peasant slave am I!"

Chapter 4

Of course, I'd lied to the editors of *Vogue* and told them I spoke perfect French.

My first assignment was to interview Éric Rohmer, the most intellectual of all French film directors, an elderly genius obsessed by *midinettes* (shopgirls). And yet in 1984 he was only sixty-four, which naturally seemed ancient to me then. Someone had said that seeing his movies was "kind of like watching paint dry." I preferred what my friend Jacques Fieschi had said, that Rohmer was "this sensual intellectual."

Rohmer had been born Maurice Henri Joseph Schérer. I'd admired his talky films *Claire's Knee* and *My Night at Maud's*. I'd rehearsed my questions carefully with Gilles Barbedette, who'd translated my novel *Nocturnes for the King of Naples*. I had to tape Rohmer's answers, since I had no idea what he was saying—which of course meant that I couldn't pose any follow-up questions to the provocative and original things it turned out that he was saying. In Hollywood movies the star absorbs and perfects the foreign language seamlessly, and in a matter of days, since language plays no part in the plot. But my fear of daunting linguistic encounters only added to my mounting agoraphobia: I seldom left the apartment. I'd sit in a chair and rehearse what I might say, what Rohmer might say, and how I'd answer, and hours of invented conversations would play out in my head. I'd think something in English and immediately try to translate it into French. I'd practice translation so much that I could say many things, at least the sort of things that typically I'd say in my own language. Comprehension, however, was another thing altogether. After I'd present my own carefully displayed sentence like a diamond necklace on black velvet, the other speaker, the French person, would throw his sentence at me like a handful of wet sand. It would sting so badly that I'd wince, and an instant later I would wonder what had just happened to me. Perhaps worst of all, I'd failed to grasp little nice things shopkeepers or neighbors were saying about the weather or the wild strawberries, pleasant comments I was unable to acknowledge or engage with. John Purcell couldn't speak but could understand, and together we made up an inept sort of team. What I could do was read French books and look up the words. Sometimes now when I glance over the novels and nonfiction works I was patiently annotating in those days, it astonishes me that there was ever a time when I didn't know those words.

I'd lie on the couch and read and read. Marie-Claude, who knew the publicity girls at all the publishing houses, had put me on every list for freebies; in addition she'd call to nudge them along if she was excited about a particular title. She'd say, "But Monsieur White *is* American *Vogue* in Paris," letting them imagine I might write up an obscure first novel and start a bidding war for it in the States.

What I learned soon enough was that American magazine editors weren't interested in anything happening in France unless it was happening to other Americans: a hit play where the audience had to vote every night whether to behead Marie Antoinette or not? No interest. The reopening after many years of the Musée Guimet, one of the great collections of Asian art? No interest. Fashion was interesting, since anyone could buy it and everyone would eventually be affected by it. A lawsuit by Margaret Mitchell's heirs against Régine Deforges, a French woman who'd adapted the plot of *Gone with the Wind* to France during World War II (the Nazis were the Yankees), was interesting since it dealt with an American classic and an American legal victory, though it was shortlived as Ms. Deforges later won her appeal.

Fortunately I didn't understand the limitations of my role as American cultural reporter in France until after I'd read through hundreds of books and looked up thousands of words—many of them time and again. At one point it occurred to me that I had to look up the same word five times before I'd learned it. And of course I nearly always got the gender wrong. Jane Birkin, an English actress who sang in French in a high, squeaky voice, in interviews always confused the *le* and the *la* and French comedians impersonating her always used this habit of hers as the basis of their send-ups. I remember once saying *la mariage* and a five-year-old corrected me, "But it's *le marriage*." Quickly, her mother, blushing, whispered to the little girl, "Don't correct Monsieur. He's a professor."

In the winters it was gray and would rain every day, but my apartment was snug and had good heat. I lay on my couch, actually a daybed, and read. I had just two rooms. My bedroom was twice the size of the double bed with tall French windows looking out on the slanting roof of the Saint-Louis-en-l'Île church with its upended stone volute like a colossal snail that had broken through the rain-slicked tiles and was inching down toward the gutters at geological speed. The sitting room was larger, with two windows, a desk, a basket chair, a dining room table, and the daybed in an alcove. The apartment had been the study of the landlady's deceased husband, an epigraphist, and on the walls held up by metal brackets were ancient stones inscribed by the Romans, marble fragments he'd excavated in Algeria.

Language problems guided me in my choice of friends. Women, especially old bourgeois women, spoke more clearly than their male or younger counterparts. The very speech patterns (emphatic, precise) I might have found annoying in English came to me in French as a blessing. My favorite old woman was my landlady, Madame Pflaum, an Austrian who'd lived in Paris since the 1930s. She had me to tea with her best friend. The two women had known each other for over forty years but still addressed each other as *vous* and referred to each other as "Madame Pflaum" and "Madame Dupont." Perhaps because she was a foreigner, Madame Pflaum spoke her adopted language with unusual care.

At the gym I met Barbara, a girl with a pretty, chubby face and an almost neurotic level of curiosity, and I cherished her for her clear enunciation, her avoidance of slang, and her linguistic patience. Like any good teacher, Barbara took my cloudy, twisted sentences and reworked them into model phrases out of a textbook. "Do you mean . . ." she'd say in French, and then rephrase my hazy remark in crystalline language.

Barbara had divorced parents—an architect father who worked in his spacious studio overlooking a garden and a batty, out-of-work mother who lived in a project for the poor, an HLM (*Habitation loyer modéré*, or medium-rent housing), though hers was located in a sleek skyscraper that Pompidou had thrown up in La Défense in the 1970s to modernize the capital, rival New York, and ultimately destroy the Parisian skyline. Fortunately for many Parisians, Pompidou would die before he could commit more mischief.

Barbara had sex on the brain and always wanted to know what different boys in the gym looked like naked in the locker room. She either was slightly dim or pretended to be. Over and over she'd ask me her slow, precise, primary questions about homosexuality.

"Now tell me, Edmond, have you ever tried sex with a woman? Are you afraid of the vagina? Do you think that there are teeth in there?"

But no matter how irritating her questions might be, she spoke clearly and slowly and always corrected my French in an inoffensive and automatic way. For instance, I had a habit of interchangeably using the adjectives *immense, grand*, and *gros*, yet Barbara had assigned a different nuance to each word. She was also a stickler for the progression of tenses—only a pluperfect could be nested inside a past clause. Despite her careful and kind ministrations, I never mastered these nuances. Barbara suggested I buy the *Grévis*, a thousand-page grammar text with which every French person is familiar. That this pedantry coexisted with an unhealthy or obsessive sexual curiosity should not have surprised me. What is certain is that if she were a mumbler, as many of us Americans are, I'd never have had anything to do with her. I envied her because she dated a slender young German with a mild, gentle manner and a large, uncircumcised penis, which he would towel-dry at length while chatting affably with me in the locker room. Then again, there was always a bit of seduction in the air.

At the gym I only met ordinary French office workers who like people everywhere led a treadmill existence called, colloquially, *Boulot-Métro-Dodo*—Parisian slang for "Job-Subway-Bed."

A bit infuriatingly, at Marie-Claude's dinners no one spoke in any predictable way. They were all intellectuals and writers who I learned had to show how ironic they could be, how droll, how quickly and easily they could anticipate every objection their interlocutors might make. The advancement of a simple idea or piece of information was not the object. The task was to show they were civilized beings who caught every allusion. They were capable of enclosing linguistic brackets inside conversational parentheses.

Moreover, they interrupted constantly, which, it amazed me to learn, was not considered rude in Paris. Madame de Staël, in her book about Germany, had written that German was not a proper language for intelligent conversation since you had to wait till the end of the sentence to hear the verb and couldn't interrupt. I found interruptions especially irritating because I needed my full allotment of airtime in order to stagger toward my point.

But France, more than any other culture, is a tight, silver skein of names and references and half-stated allusions. Whereas America is so populous that even the writers don't know all the names of the other writers, in France the members of the general educated public recognize the names of all French writers, whether they've read them or not. Of course it helps that writers are so often interviewed on television and by the press. What is true of writers is true of every other category of civilized experience; everyone knows the name and address of the best pastry maker, the best source of bed linens and napery, the best caterer, the best saddle and harness maker. They're listed in every middle-class person's mental collection of *les bonnes adresses.* Pourthault for sheets. Hédiard for food. Berthillon for sherbets and ice creams, so confident of its status that it closed for the entire month of August. Furthermore, failure to know any one of these names can even suggest inferior social origins.

This little world is a ball that is always in the air, bounced from hand to hand. Maybe it aids the native speakers that French (not Spanish, as everyone says) is spoken more rapidly than any other tongue, facilitating an unequaled density of reference and qualification. The composer Virgil Thomson, who lived a third of his long life in France, once pointed out that the French never grope for a word or stutter or go blank and say, "Uh . . ." He suggested that the French, unlike us, have what today we'd call a social GPS, an instant device for orienting themselves and navigating their way through their own culture, whereas we are not only often at a loss for words but also for opinions. The maddening confidence of the French (about the sequence three cheeses should be eaten in, from mildest to strongest, about exactly when to arrive at a party and when to leave, about how to sign off in a friendly but correct formal letter) fills in all social, and verbal, blanks.

I quickly learned that for a linguistic neophyte like me, the most difficult encounter to deal with was a party attended by a group of friends who'd all known each other forever. They'd be hard enough to cope with if they were speaking English, since even then they'd all be talking in shorthand. In French, they became incomprehensible.

The easiest social situation, I found, was talking to one person who was in love with you, someone who was studying your face for the slightest frown of confusion. The eyes, I figured out, always betray a failure to understand. If I didn't want to flag my distress in a small dinner party or provoke a tedious explanation made merely for my benefit, I lowered my eyes like a Japanese bride. A *diner à deux* is the easiest exchange because we quickly become accustomed to a lover's accent, turn of mind, range of reference and vocabulary—and *he* instantly gears his words to our level of comprehension.

I never failed to understand MC's French. (We called Marie-Claude by her initials, pronouncing the letters in the English fashion and not as "Emm-Cay" *à la française.*) But the same person becomes more difficult to understand on the phone, where one has none of the same visual cues. After a party the most difficult event is a narrative French film, in which the actors usually speak more carelessly than random individuals on the street. Mumbling is proof of artistic verisimilitude. A television newscast is the next most difficult occasion, since it usually depends on a vocabulary and metaphors peculiar to itself. As a foreigner I realized what a closed world the news is for all but the initiated, an obscurity that is obviously worrying in a democracy.

Some American or French friends who were bilingual wondered why I was spending so much time with kids from the gym. I was too embarrassed to admit that I had chosen these particular kids for the slow, clear way they spoke French. When the great writer Emmanuel

Carrère and his wife came to dinner, they teased me for my "adolescent evenings" (*tes soirées ado*).

I'd always been a bit arrogant about my lack of a need for intellectual stimulation. I had a scholarly, researcher's side, which reveled in reading up on difficult subjects, but I also had a silly, social side that found it more relaxing to chatter about nothing, as if I wanted my "artist" side to prevail over the "intellectual" role. I suppose I thought an artist shouldn't be too cerebral. Camus said that American novelists were the only fiction writers who didn't think they also needed to be intellectuals. Whereas a French writer such as Gilles Barbedette, my translator and friend, wrote novels and essays and read only serious things such as Montaigne and Nietzsche, in America a friend such as Brad Gooch could listen to rap, read theology, dress in drag—Brad was closer to my sensibility. Even the range of Brad's biographical subjects—Frank O'Hara, Flannery O'Connor, and the Persian mystic Rumi—showed his mix of piety and camp. That he was also an Armani model further broke the mold of the intellectual.

And yet it was arrogant of me to think that I was self-sufficient, that I didn't need to be with smart people since I was smart enough all on my own. I always found my evenings with creative, analytical people especially enthralling, but something perverse made me not seek them out. Albert Dichy—who is funny, observant, and subtle and has a great memory and vast levels of information—always made me laugh hard and sent me off into a paroxysm of serious reading. Fortunately, we worked together researching my biography of Jean Genet; given how contrarian I am I might not have befriended him otherwise.

Albert was a dapper middle-aged Jew from Beirut who'd grown up speaking French because it was the only language his parents had in common. His mother, from Turkey, spoke Ladino, a form of medieval Spanish, and his father was an Egyptian whose first language was Arabic. Albert was sent to a French Jesuit lycée in Lebanon—which he hated because all the students were boys and he didn't like males. In the streets Albert and his brother spoke Arabic, which eventually Albert's brother taught in a French university; much to the dismay of his Jewish parents, the brother converted to Islam and married a second-generation Arab woman. Albert's grandfather had been a rabbi.

When the Lebanese civil war started in 1975, the family took refuge in Britanny. Albert, his mother, and his brother were all French citizens since one of Albert's maternal ancestors had taken French citizenship, and after that every succeeding generation had been careful to register at the French consulate. Only Albert's father—who'd lost his Egyptian citizenship when Farouk was deposed and then lost the Iranian passport he'd bought when the shah was ousted—had had to wait to emigrate to France.

Albert's first job in France had been going door-to-door and doing customer interviews for an electrical appliance company. Milan Kundera, who'd recently left Czechoslovakia and arrived in Rennes, was still so intimidated by "officials" asking questions that when Albert showed up at his door one day Kundera docilely submitted to Albert's lengthy and detailed interview about his sweeper. Albert used to say he had in his possession one of the few unpublished interviews of the great Kundera.

As a youngster, Albert had met Genet in Beirut. Perhaps partly because of this encounter with the charismatic writer, Albert had become the world's leading expert on Genet. Although he worked on many other writers (including Marguerite Duras; Georges Shéhadé, the Francophone poet from Lebanon; Pierre Guyotat; and Kateb Yacine, the Algerian nationalist writer), he published at Gallimard a collection of Genet's political writings and prepared the Pléiade definitive edition of Genet's plays. And I was supposed to be writing Genet's biography. Genet had died in 1986, the year before I was commissioned to write the book. I kept trying to pry information out of Albert until I realized it would be simpler to hire him using some of my advance money. At the time, Albert was working part-time for IMEC (L'Institut Mémoires de l'Édition Contemporaine), a private library that housed the archives of publishing houses and contemporary writers. When he wasn't at IMEC, Albert was making a living as an advertising copywriter. Once we started collaborating, he was able to quit his advertising work.

I took seven years to research and write my biography of Genet. Albert helped me at every step—writing summaries of interviews he conducted with people who'd known Genet, finding me relevant texts and photocopying them, establishing dates in a clear chronology, fact-checking everything I'd written. We went together to Alligny-en-Morvan, Genet's village in Burgundy, where we visited a dozen people who'd known him, including his godmother—who was over a hundred years old and spoke to me in the dialect of the region, which her granddaughter had to translate into French. Even though the wife of my French editor, Ivan Nabokoff, was the sister of Pierre Joxe, the minister of the interior in Mitterrand's government, I couldn't convince Joxe to open Genet's adoption dossier. But Albert found plenty of other details: that one of Genet's childhood friends was named Querelle (the name of one of his later novelistic heroes); that one could still visit Mettray (Genet's penal colony when he was an adolescent); that one could read the very literary letters Genet wrote to a woman he'd met in Czechoslovakia, a German Socialist refugee; that the widow of his doctor was still alive, a woman whose husband had prescribed Genet his massive doses of Nembutal (she'd helped Genet prepare the final draft of his longest play, *The Screens*, and she even showed me X-rays of Genet's kidneys). Albert tracked down Genet's record of arrests for petty crimes (for stealing a bolt of fabric from a department store and the autograph of a French king, and for doctoring a train ticket). We met a former convict from one of his prisons; an actress who had played the Madame in *The Balcony* and who shared her letters from Genet; the Swiss translator who accompanied Genet among the Black Panthers in America; the adopted son of one of his lovers and his principal heir; his obstructionist agent in London; the two high-born Palestinian women who'd played such a large role in his old age, and so on. Our interviews took me to Damascus and all over France and the United States.

Albert had a very precise manner—the product of a good French Catholic education. He loved to clarify his terms, nail down a fact, take notes in the hour after an encounter, annotate his reading. At the same time he was quick to see his own absurdities and those of others. And he was affectionate. I guess I define intelligence as the power to make new, surprising, wide-ranging associations and never to rely on automatic, untested generalities. With Albert I felt that I was in the presence of someone like Wittgenstein who was actually thinking out loud, thinking right in front of you, thinking a thought for the first time.

He was a great womanizer. Perhaps he was aided by the catholicity of his tastes. Although he had a beautiful, cultured wife who was a nonstop reader, an art dealer, and related to Georges Shéhadé, the Francophone poet from Lebanon, Albert had many adventures and affairs. The other day my French scholarly friend Alice Kaplan had dinner with Albert and a new girlfriend—who turned out once to have been his shrink. He was the male version of Catherine Millet, the author of *The Sexual Life of Catherine M.*, which details her thousands of conquests. I've always been fascinated by libertinism and promiscuity, particularly the often philosophically self-assured French variety, and when I reviewed *The Sexual Life* I called it "the most explicit book about sex ever written by a woman." I interviewed Millet at the literary festival at Brighton before a packed crowd, translating back and forth from English into French. I also spoke about her on the BBC. She was a very courteous, intelligent woman, an art critic who's written a study of Salvador Dalí.

I'd met Michel Foucault in New York when I ran the New York Institute for the Humanities. Foucault was like me in one regard—he hated to talk about ideas during social evenings. (Richard Sennett, the sociologist and the founder of the Institute, once said to me, "You'll tell everyone about your sex life; your only secrets are your ideas.") Foucault's partner, Daniel Defert, had given a fascinating seminar on how the Spanish colonists had classified the Aztecs according to medieval rankings based on clothes, the *habitus* (as in "The habit makes the man"). Foucault conducted a seminar on the last volume of his History of Sexuality, which was to be about the difference between the late pagan emphasis on which sex acts were permissible if committed between masters and slaves, or masters and masters, with little regard for the gender of the participants (e.g., a free man must never be the passive partner with a slave) and the early Christian obsession with sin, buggery, and fornication, not just in deed but in thought.

Foucault spoke English through an act of will—I don't think he'd ever studied it and he wasn't worried by his very strong accent. I thought that anyone as smart as he would of course speak English—or any other language he set his mind to. He was surrounded with beautiful ephebes such as Hervé Guibert, Mathieu Lindon, and Gilles Barbedette, but sexually his type was burly and macho.

But he never thought the sexual identity of someone was all that revealing, and as his disciple I mustn't pretend I'm saying something profound about him by talking about his kinkiness. He was both fiery and sweet, a rare combination of traits. He showed me that you can be passionately aggressive about advancing your views, arguing your position, but in the bosom of your friends mild and even humble, certainly sweet. Maybe that explains his aversion to discussing ideas except in the classroom; he was deeply engaged in intellectual discourse, was quick to the point of paranoia in defending his theories, but he didn't want combativeness to poison his social evening. *Ce qu'aimer veut dire* by Mathieu Lindon (the son of Beckett's publisher) is an extended, intimate view of Foucault by a real friend.

Toward the end of his life Foucault thought the basis of morality after the death of God might be the ancient Greek aspiration to leave your life as a beautiful, burnished artifact. Certainly in his case his gift for friendship, his quick sympathy, his gift for paradox, his ability to admire left his image as a man, as an exemplary life, highly burnished. The people who said his promiscuity or his death from AIDS diminished him were just fools.

Marie-Claude would not countenance my complaints about the French language.

"But your French is perfect!" she said in English.

She and I spoke English all the time except at her dinner parties, where she'd invite the latest literary star to bask in our short-lived adoration. I'd been put through similar paces when *A Boy's Own Story* had come out in France (*Un jeune Americain*). I'd assumed that one charming older gay man, the editor of *Science et Vie*, was actually interested in me personally and would want to see me often in the future. In fact, I'd made a modest little splash, and the editor as a true Parisian needed to know everyone and everything *dans le vent, à la page, au courant*—all ways of referring to what's new, the latest manifestation of *l'air du temps*.

Of course journalists back in New York had to keep up with the latest trends, but they wouldn't have invited the trend to dinner. New Yorkers were always exhausted after their twelve hours at the office and two hours at the gym and hour at the shrink's; when they got home, they would crawl into a hot bath, and from there to a huge immaculate bed where they ate their plate of take-home lobster ravioli and watched a talk show until they sank into restless, clamorous sleep. They couldn't be bothered seeing their oldest friends, much less a total stranger. A friend in New York was defined as someone you never needed to see, who would never get angry at you for ignoring him.

In Paris, however, there were still rituals in place for promising new people, new ideas, new trends (which a bit later, in the nineties, would eventually be colloquially labeled *tendance*, or "tendency"). Something new was said to be *très tendance*. If you were a mere trend, no one wanted to be stuck with seeing you more than once; the host expected you to stay on message during your single visit and communicate clearly what was new about you and your work.

I'd written a novel about my life as a tormented teen in the Midwest in the 1950s. It was hailed in the English-speaking world because it was well written, at once a breakthrough thematically and an "instant classic." The French couldn't quite grasp the novelty or the importance of my accomplishment. After all, France was the country of Proust, André Gide, Jean Genet—all three among the most celebrated innovators of the twentieth century and all three writers who wrote quite openly about being gay: Gide's journals and his memoir, *If It Die,* as well as his early novel *The Immoralist;* Genet's *Our Lady of the Flowers* and his four other novels; Proust's entire oeuvre, in which so many of the men and women turn out to be homosexual. How could my slender volume compare to this massive achievement, which had preceded it by fifty, seventy, eighty years?

Nor did the French like the whole idea of "gay fiction," though they'd invented it. France was opposed to the notion of identity politics and even more so to the literature of special interest groups. In France there was no black novel, no Jewish novel, certainly no gay novel. To be sure, Jews wrote about being Jewish but everyone, Jewish and gentile alike, regarded with horror the category of "the Jewish novel."

If specific identities were rejected in France, it was in favor of "universalism," a concept so dear to the Enlightenment and the Revolution, the ideal of the abstract citizen, stripped of all qualifications, equal to everyone else before the voting urn and the court of justice. In the arts it meant that the individual with all his quirks was thrown into high relief but the group he belonged to was pushed into the background. French schoolchildren in history class did not learn about Napoleon's Corsican heritage, just as in literature class no one mentioned that Proust's mother was Jewish (nor had Proust himself mentioned it). Proust made his narrator heterosexual and his family Catholic so that against this gold standard of propriety he could describe in detail his lesbians, his intergenerational gays, his gay sadists and rent boys, and more broadly the secret world of homosexuality that interpenetrates the visible world of class and age distinctions. His contemporaries congratulated Proust on his "courage" in exploring the twisted world of homosexuality, since he said nothing to enlighten them about his own orientation. The only trouble with universalism was that if it had been progressive originally, now it had become conservative.

Translation is always difficult. The lush metaphors of my *Nocturnes for the King of Naples*, so slippery in English, had to be sorted out in French. Time and again, of a figurative conceit I'd carefully crafted, I was told, "But you can't mean *both* things in French." Even the word "boy" (*garçon*) was suspect; it sounded too much like a waiter or a pedophile's delight. That's why *A Boy's Own Story* was translated as *Un jeune Américain*. I wanted it to be called *Signes de Piste* (a 1930s collection of Boy Scout novels) or even *Feu de Camp*, but I don't think any French person understood what I was getting at.

Not that the French were impervious to the allure of the exotic, but they preferred to locate the Other elsewhere. Within France they wanted everything to be uniform, starting with themselves. No wonder those French living in the capital resented the question, "Where are you from?"

"Paris, why do you ask? I've lived in Paris all my life."

"And before that?"

"Marseilles. Surely you can't hear the accent?"

"Not a trace."

"But is there anything I do differently from all other Parisians?"

"Of course not. You wear the same dark clothes and are just as skinny and murmur just as softly and take the same group tours to the same places like Vietnam or Anatolia or Egypt and have never toured France itself. You know the canals of Venice better than your own medieval monastery of Moissac or the chalets of Franche-Comté—though your grandparents still vacation close to home."

Reassured, your friend smiles and says, "I still don't understand."

"In America, we're proud of our regional and national differences. We say, 'What are you?' And the answer is 'Irish' or 'Italian,' though our ancestors came over from Galway in the 1840s. We say, 'Where are you from?' and the answer to that is, 'Arkansas, my mother never wore shoes till she was ten,' and we're proud of this."

Your interlocutor will then say, "In France we have no class differences in our way of speaking and only four slight, very slight, regional accents, impossible for a foreigner to detect."

"The Provençal accent is easy enough, like when they say 'vang' for *vin* or 'pang' for *pain*."

"But no one says 'pang'!"

I can remember when Hector Bianciotti, an Argentine novelist living in Paris, interviewed me for a two-page piece in the *Nouvel Observateur*, a weekly left-of-center glossy that's roughly equivalent to the weekend magazine of the English *Guardian*. He and I met in the downstairs bar at the Montalembert, a few doors from the offices of Gallimard, the premier publisher. With its brown velvet walls and heavy leather club chairs, the room had been a meeting place for writers since the time of Sartre and Beauvoir, who'd more famously also liked the Café Flore three blocks away. I had seen photos of Sartre taken here with his followers, including his handsome secretary Jean Cau. In another photo Jean Genet was being introduced to the author of *La Bâtarde,* Violette Leduc. She was upset that day because Genet said, "I've been enjoying your *Asphyxie,*" though the book was named *L'Asphyxie* and Genet's way of saying the title suggested he was enjoying the feeling of moral and mental disarray in the work—or so she imagined in her hysterical, paranoid way. Like Genet, she was a father-less child, as was their wealthy patron, Jacques Guérin—another "bastard." (Ironically, later the three bastards would collaborate on a short black-and-white film, now lost, about a baptism in which Genet played the baby.)

Hector asked me a few random questions about my *enfance dans le Ohio*, but rather than tossing off a witty remark or two, I started giving a complete report: ". . . then, at age seven, I moved from Cincinnati to Evanston, Illinois." At last I noticed the look of panic and even disdain crossing Hector's face. "I don't need to know all that. It's just an article, not a hagiography!"

When the article appeared in print, it had several mistakes in it and my friend Gilles said,

"It's of no importance. No one will remember. No one will even finish reading it."

I mentioned that in America we had fact checkers and that we had to put red pencil dots over every statement after we'd verified it from three sources. Gilles merely waved a hand as if driving away an annoy-ing insect. When I went on pointing out the mistakes, Gilles said, "My poor Ad." He pronounced my name in what he believed was the usual American way, *Ad*. "I think you have no idea how important Hector is. He will probably win the Goncourt this year and soon he'll be a member of the French Academy. He's done you a tremendous honor."

Hector had begun to write in French, not Spanish, only a few years previously. People said he was helped by his lover Angelo Rinaldi, a Corsican novelist and the extremely acerbic critic for *L'Express*. (Hector wrote one terrific book about his coming out in the Pampas, *Le Pas si lent de l'amour.*) In the years to come, Angelo would like every other book I wrote and hate the alternate ones. His vitriol in general won him lots of attention, since most French critics were routinely positive. An older writer explained to me that during the Vichy years of the Nazi occupation, right-wing critics had been so brutally nasty that ever since, the left-wing style had been pleasantly anodyne; the slightest reserva-tion was read as a violent dismissal. Gilles had been right about Hector, who was invited to join the Academy, and a few years later so was

Angelo. I would often see Angelo, always grimacing, each time his hair a color never encountered in nature, headed to his *chambre d'assignation* on the Île Saint-Louis, usually in the company of a teenager he'd met at a gym during wrestling practice.

I can't remember how, but in some way Milan Kundera became aware of me. He wanted someone to translate two of his political essays from French (which he'd recently begun writing in, too) into English. I told him I could not even translate a French menu in restaurants—was *confit de canard* "duck preserved in its own fat"? And did a *financier* have something to do with cake or a pastry? Kundera said he didn't want anyone too sophisticated. *Sophistiqué* had kept in French some of its original sense of sophistry, of an ingenious playing with words, and I took it that what Kundera hated was what Fowler in his *Modern English Usage* calls "elegant variation"—the pointless and confusing interchanging of near synonyms so that the reader thinks something new is being discussed.

At the time Kundera was very paranoid that the Czech equivalent of the KGB was trying to bump him off, so I had to buzz him precisely at noon, neither a minute before nor a minute later, and I'd be accompanied by his wife Vera up to the first landing of his rue Littré apartment. Then he would walk with me up the last flight of stairs. If he was famous as a wrestler, he must have been a featherweight, because he was very frail, though his pictures made him look big and powerful. He didn't know English very well. He knew that *about* meant "more or less" but he didn't know it was also a preposition, as in "about love." We wrangled over many words in that way. His essays, as I recall, were about the spurious idea that Prague was closer culturally to Paris than to St. Petersburg. His own father had been a musician for Janáček in Brno, and I wanted to point out that Janáček had adopted a Russian play (Ostrovsky's *The Storm*) in *Kát'a Kabanová* not a French one, but I didn't dare. Yet he was very sweet and played a record for me of one of Janáček's chamber works and gave me a running commentary on its secret plot: "Here he sees her again about to board the train." His wife fed me a treasured Czech recipe which was so garlicky that the next day Marie-Claude wordlessly gave me chlorophyll gum and at the movies the couple in the row in front of us got up and took different seats when MC and I sat down behind them.

My early, brief moment of Parisian celebrity came and went. Afterward few people in France could place me but some gave troubled little smiles of recognition when my name was mentioned. *"Mais bien sûr,"* they whispered politely. This French system of making a fuss over whatever was new and then promptly forgetting it meant that many young innovators had their moment in the sun right away, without having to wait years as they would have to in America. But it also meant that new ideas—feminism, say, or gay liberation—weren't revolutionary or very interesting, since they were treated as this year's fad, no more, and quickly were cycled out of sight. In America an idea was accepted only after it was judged to be of real, lasting significance. Then it stuck around forever, especially if it became a department in American universities—gender studies or queer studies. If I'd introduce an American intellectual to French friends in the mid-1980s, and say, "She's a leading feminist who's queering the Renaissance," they'd make a face and say, "Feminism. You mean that's still being discussed in America? We had that here in the early seventies, but it's hopelessly *vétuste, démodé*. No one ever mentions it. No more than any woman now would wear Berber jewelry or a tuxedo or a hoop skirt."

Chapter 5

My great love during those years was from Zurich, the manager of a small chain of Swiss cinemas, whom I met in Venice. I'd been spending several weeks every year in Venice with my best friend, David Kalstone, who lived in New York, taught English at Rutgers, and in the summers lived in Venice. David spoke Italian and loved Venice, a great pedestrian city if you were a good walker, and he was. He was nearly blind, but Venice's walkways were well lit and the steps over bridges were clearly outlined in white pebbles. It was a city without cars and, though it was awesomely labyrinthine, David knew all its byways. He was a great friend of Peggy Guggenheim and we spent many evenings in her historic, if tedious, company, always accompanied by her little dogs. In her garden (a garden was a rare feature for a Venetian palazzo), Peggy had a white marble Byzantine throne and around it her various shih tzus were buried. Sometimes Peggy herself would sell tickets to her museum and if tourists asked her if Mrs. Guggenheim was still alive, she'd assure them she wasn't.

Every artistic or political or entertainment personality who came through Venice felt obliged to contact Peggy, and if the dignitary was sufficiently important she'd give him or her a cocktail party. That's how I first met Gore Vidal, who in those years lived full time in Italy. He blurbed my second novel, *Nocturnes for the King of Naples,* but later, toward the end of his life, he turned against me because I wrote a play about him and Timothy McVeigh.

I met my Swiss cinema magnate one night on what we called the *molo nero*, a "dark dock" for cruising, a pathway between the Piazzetta

San Marco and Harry's Bar—by day a major thoroughfare for tourists heading to the vaporetto stop but at night a byway where gays could be found milling around, to the extent that they congregated anywhere in this least gay of all cities. (In those days, they also went to a gay beach out on the Lido, to Haig's Bar across from the Gritti Palace hotel, and to the public toilets on one side of the Rialto Bridge.) There, on the *molo nero*, around midnight when the crowds had dissipated (most tourists were day trippers, since hotels in Venice were so expensive), a few gays would linger, though they could be scared off by the glare of approaching boats. One evening, sitting on a fence all dressed in white was a tan, smiling man not in his first youth, closer to my age—a decade younger, as it turned out.

As I approached he said in accented English, "You must be American."

"I am. How could you tell?"

"The way you smiled at me even though I'm a stranger."

Later, I thought it must have been my sloppy appearance that gave me away, the fact that my shirt wasn't tucked in.

I couldn't imagine why this handsome man would be interested in me, so I said, "You should come back to the palace where I'm staying. It's pretty spectacular. The kitchen was John Singer Sargent's studio, and Henry James slept in the library in a sort of medical metal bed."

I'm not sure he knew who James or Sargent was; the past interested him not at all.

When we were standing in the middle of the immense marble floor of the library, he took my glass from my hand and put it on the floor, then he kissed me passionately.

It turned out that he had my novel *A Boy's Own Story* in his bag. His longtime lover, the art dealer Thomas Ammann, who had just broken up with him, had brought back from New York the new gay book everyone was talking about, so I think it pleased This—short for, Matthias and pronounced "Tees"—to have the author of the new vogue book in bed. Thomas had left him for George, a beautiful young Greek man who was a model and who'd just had an affair with Rock Hudson (Hudson's AIDS had not yet been made public). This was disease-phobic, and used not one but two condoms. ("I'm Swiss," he explained.) Within a few years both George and Thomas would die of AIDS.

This asked me if I'd been "careful" and of course I said yes, though just the night before I'd slept with a young Spaniard who'd worked my nipples so hard they were still aflame and I winced whenever they were touched. But at that time, in the early eighties, there was no test for AIDS and no one knew exactly what caused it. We suspected it was caused by sex, but how? It seemed too unfair to us that a single exposure could infect someone; in our guilt-ridden way we wanted the disease to be the punishment for a long life of vice.

But even by those standards I'd been what the French called *vicieux* (a compliment in the world of gay French small advertisements). I'd slept with some three thousand men, I figured, and big-city gay men of my generation asked, "Why so few?" My figures were based on the rate of three a week for twenty years, between the ages of twenty-two and forty-two in New York, but many of my coevals "turned" two or three "tricks" a night, using the whore's slang of the period (a "trick" was a once-only encounter, a word I had to explain recently to gay grad students). Truth be told, I would often go to the sauna, where I'd meet a dozen men a night. But to This I pretended to be far more innocent. He was reassured and thought of me as a sort of responsible gay leader thanks to my work with Gay Men's Health Crisis.

I wasn't ready to change my ways. I was so used to undressing mentally almost every man I met (and often went on to do so literally) that promiscuity was my first response to the least sign of reciprocity. I loved sex, but I never experienced it in its "pure" state; to me, it was always blended with at least some shred of romantic fantasy.

Soon I began to visit This in Zurich every other week and he came to Paris occasionally. When he traveled to my city we stayed on the rue du Cherche-Midi in the beautiful apartment belonging to Andy Warhol and his business associate, Fred Hughes. It was reached by crossing a formal French garden, mainly of gravel, that was dominated by a sphinx with the head of an eighteenth-century female courtier. Inside, in the salon, there were a newly upholstered Second Empire couch and a huge circus painting by José María Sert resting on the floor. The kitchen was the latest in stylishness and efficiency, designed by Andrée Putman, a French woman who looked like a man in drag ("More man than *pute*," people said). In her store in the Marais, Putman was recycling designs from the past by Charlotte Perriand and Jean-Michel Frank. Warhol's apartment looked as if someone with money and taste hadn't quite moved in.

I wasn't used to going out with mature men who already had strong opinions and spoke confidently of their defining life experiences. The boys I usually dated tried to fit into my crowded world because they had only the smallest, thinnest world of their own. Their feelings were often hard to sound because they themselves didn't know what they felt. This knew how people should live and in what surroundings. He had opinions on everything that interested him, and what didn't interest him he shrugged off. Maybe because he was involved with two visual arts—he exhibited and sometimes produced films and he collected contemporary art—he was very concerned about how everything looked. We spent a whole day at Puiforcat in Paris choosing silverware for his table. He cared how I cut my nails. He didn't like me to be thirty pounds overweight, so we went to a Swiss spa and ate nothing for ten days. Clothes were important to This. His ex, Thomas, was regularly listed among the ten best-dressed men in the world. Thomas would fly the king of Spain's tailor from Madrid to Zurich for fittings. They both pioneered the beautifully cut blazer-with-jeans look. Thomas's cook/maid, who had worked for a Spanish ambassador and knew how to iron shirts expertly, gave ironing lessons to This's maid. Once when I suggested we go to the Canary Islands for a vacation, This said the only snobbish words I ever heard from his lips: "Oh, that's where we send our maids for their holidays—Putzfrau Insel, we call it."

I got an assignment from Lucretia Stewart, then the editor of *Departures*, the American Express travel magazine, to write about Egypt, and I invited This along as the photographer. It thrilled me to be able to offer him the trip, since I was so much poorer and was always so self-conscious about my gifts to him. He took the assignment very seriously and was up every day before dawn, since the early morning light was the best. We traveled slowly down the Nile from Aswan to Luxor in a Hilton boat, the *Osiris*, which served wonderful international food and provided us with a luxury cabin at water level. We'd look out our cabin at dawn at the ibises and hoopoes in tall reeds. This had never been to the Third World before and he'd agreed to come along to Egypt with much trepidation. Travel for him had always been traumatic. When he was a child, the first time he'd crossed the Alps into Germany in a car with his father, he'd fainted, so frightened was he to leave Switzerland for Germany.

This knew a woman who worked for the Swiss embassy in Cairo who managed to get us a hotel room looking out directly on the Great Pyramid. And in Luxor, she put us up in the old Winter Palace, King Farouk's former palace, in a room with a big, dusty balcony overlooking a huge, scraggly garden complete with monkeys. Outside our door, a servant slept on the floor, ever ready to serve us. Servitude of that sort bothered me, but I didn't want to object lest the man be dismissed and plunged into total poverty. In Aswan, we stayed at the old Cataract Palace, with its louvered wood shutters, ceiling fans, and balconies facing the Nile. We felt we were in an Agatha Christie novel, and we pitied those tourists who'd ended up in the new, Stalinist-cement Cataract Palace.

This had an exaggerated respect for me as "an artist" and would never let me pay for anything: "Because you are an artist—artists should never pay!" He also had a Swiss respect for work and he exaggerated how hard and long I worked on my books; I had an equal but opposite Anglophile adherence to my amateur status and a corresponding disdain for work, and I exaggerated how easy it all was: "First drafts only!" In fact, I labored over my manuscripts and walked around town sounding out phrases in my head, but I wanted to pretend it all came effortlessly to me; that was my myth of myself.

He seemed torn between his cult of friendship and sincerity and his pursuit of celebrities. He wanted to keep up the valuable friendships he'd made through Thomas. Valuable to Thomas, who said it was easy to sell paintings by famous artists but hard to find them. That's where the celebrities came in, since they often knew collectors who needed to sell. At the same time This didn't want to admit he was motivated by feelings other than natural affection and admiration.

As a result he spoke with heightened affection, even love, of even the celebrities I found the most vacuous: "Oh, I *love* Bianca. She is so intelligent, fighting for her little country at the UN. And she's so warm, like a sister to me—she sleeps in bed with me, hugging me!"

Everyone famous he approved of, usually in ecstatic terms. "He's the most wonderful man on earth, so kind, so generous." His unrelenting esteem for everyone rubbed off on me, and my friends said that suddenly I was a bit Pollyannaish and no longer so tart tongued. The French weren't sure they approved of so much enthusiasm. But it wasn't really a matter of national character but of class. This and his successful friends were confident enough to be able to approve of people; my loser friends (except the ones in AA) only rose in their own opinion if they denigrated everyone else.

This went with Thomas every Christmas to Gstaad, where he and Thomas were among the few Swiss who rented a chalet. Most of the real Swiss millionaires were too tight-fisted to spend a hundred thousand dollars a month on a rented chalet. The old women, the real Swiss gnomes, did their own housework, drove a ten-year-old Mercedes, ate at the local vegetarian cafeteria and had the biggest savings accounts on the planet. They wore brown woolen stockings and black sensible shoes. In Gstaad This and Thomas hobnobbed with Valentino and Elizabeth Taylor and Gunther Sachs, a German playboy they knew, as well as with a Belgian banker-baron I'd had sex with. Gunther Sachs had been married to Brigitte Bardot and was the iconic playboy of the 1960s. He committed suicide at Gstaad in 2011 when he discovered he had Alzheimer's. My Belgian baron was an ugly but sexy and intelligent man who died of AIDS early on. His sister-in-law remained my friend, as did her husband, my friend's brother. He, the brother, was very handsome and had once been the lover of Rita Hayworth, but he was a bit dull. The sister-in-law said that as long as the fascinating gay brother-in-law was alive she had someone in the family to talk to. After he died she had to make do with her beautiful but dumb husband.

Although I make the eighties sound lighthearted and frivolous, I was haunted by AIDS, as were most gay men. I was diagnosed as positive in 1985. Although a diagnosis has galvanized many writers, I just pulled the covers over my head for a year. I was very depressed. I felt so isolated and read about ACT UP in America with envy. I belonged to no AIDS community in France. Larry Kramer attacked me for devoting seven years of my post-diagnosis time to Genet. Larry felt every gay writer must write about AIDS alone. I wanted to remind readers that there were these great gay contemporaries (Genet died in 1986) who had nothing to do with the disease. Our experience couldn't be reduced to a malady. I didn't want us to be "re-medicalized."

I survived because I turned out to be one of those rare creatures, a slow progressor: someone whose T-cell counts fall steadily but very slowly (nonprogressors are those even rarer men and women who never get sick). I didn't know that when I was diagnosed; I thought I'd be dead in a year or two. I'm not a mystic and I don't meditate, but one day in 1986 when I was meditating, in my amateurish, mud-pie way, I interrogated my body and it told me I was going to survive. It was not until ten years later that my doctor explained to me why I'd survived. People tried to ascribe my longevity to my Texas genes or my newfound sobriety, but I knew it was just a freak of nature and I could claim none of the merit just as the victims couldn't be blamed.

This insisted we be tested in the mid-eighties. The test had just become available and a blood sample had to be sent all the way from Zurich to San Francisco, then the results had to be mailed back—a three-week procedure. Nor would the doctor, an arrogant young heterosexual who'd interned in San Francisco, give the results over the phone. I had to make the trip from Paris to Zurich to have a consultation in person. As we were going up the snowy path to the university hospital, This suddenly chickened out. I was the one who insisted we keep our appointment. I already knew in my heart that he, with his two condoms, would be negative, whereas I, with my thousands of tricks, would surely be positive. I said that to This and added, "I'm a good enough novelist to predict you'll be very tender and kind with me and within a year you'll break up with me."

Sure enough, the beautiful young doctor leaned back in his office chair; he'd crossed his legs and now pointed at me with one of his expensive, light tan lace-up shoes and said, "You. You're positive."

Then he swiveled and indicated This with his shoe: "You. You're negative." He'd just delivered a death sentence to me, for all we knew, but there was no follow-up, no appointments made with a counselor.

For some time This and I had planned a romantic trip to Vienna. We went that afternoon. We stayed in the city's oldest hotel, the König von Üngarn, right in the shadow of St. Stephen's Cathedral. Of course it was all beautiful and we had time to visit Mozart's apartment around the corner, but that night I was in anguish and couldn't sleep, not because I was afraid of dying but because I knew my wonderful adult romance with This was doomed. I kept getting out of bed and going to the toilet, which was at the end of a long corridor. There, at a safe distance, I'd close the door and sob. I felt so bereft. On my third trip to the bathroom This woke up and padded down the hall and comforted me, though with my bleak "realism" (my most French attribute) I was profoundly inconsolable.

This invited me once to Gstaad, but since I don't ski and was in the throes of writing my best short story, "An Oracle," I shut myself away in the chalet and didn't even attend Liz Taylor's party. I do remember that Liz gave Pashmina shawls to all her guests. (I eventually met Liz and Audrey Hepburn when they were auctioning art in Basel for an AIDS charity.) The central piece of gossip that year was that everyone laughed at Valentino for thinking Tina Turner was going to come and be the guest of honor at his Christmas party. He declared her the greatest singer of our day, but when she turned him down he called her "a washed-up cow." Stories like this were endlessly repeated—as well as ones that pictured Thomas's new love, the beautiful George, as an idiot and a gold digger.

The jet set, I concluded, amused itself by attacking one member or another. They were led by "Zip," Nancy Reagan's friend and gay walker, the New York socialite and real estate heir Jerry Zipkin. Their conversation consisted mainly of their schedules—where they'd been and where they were going. If you weren't going to Gstaad or Venice or Marrakesh or New York or Paris, they lost interest in you. Many of them were interested in the *business* of art, and they flew to art auctions in various countries or to Art Basel in Basel or eventually to its sister exhibition in Miami. They thought collecting art somehow made them artistic and bohemian. After all, most rich people collected cars or houses or jewels or wives.

There was always a lot of drama at table. Once Thomas was seated next to the rich British Picasso collector Douglas Cooper. When Thomas bragged he'd just bought a Picasso from a dealer in Italy and described the canvas, Cooper stood up and said, "That painting was stolen from my château in France, and you must hand it over immediately or I'll denounce you to the police."

Ever so coolly, Thomas replied, "Please stop threatening me. Switzerland has no legal reciprocity or extradition agreement with France. If you don't ask for it nicely, I'll put it up for auction—with all the proceeds going to a Swiss orphanage."

Cooper backed off quickly and Thomas returned the painting at a tremendous loss.

In This's modern jewel-box apartment on the Zurichberg I always felt like someone from the Third World. I was so afraid of breaking something or smelling something up (from This I'd learned to light a match in the toilet after shitting to disguise the odor).

He had a little side table by Jean-Michel Franck that was worth fifty thousand dollars. His couch was by Jean Royère, the great French furniture designer of the fifties. The lights in their brightly colored canisters were fifties Stilnovo from Milan. Over the fireplace was a big Mao drawing by Warhol, which showed what a great draftsman he could be when he set his mind to it. On another wall was a Warhol hammer and sickle painting. I suppose these Communist subjects were less costly because less popular among the airhead rich. On the floor were beautiful rugs of sea grass bound with cloth at the borders. Above the couch was a huge beach scene by Eric Fischl. This often said this painting comprised his retirement fund. When he needed an extra million for his old age, he'd just sell the Fischl. He also had a disturbing Francesco Clemente in his bedroom, a self-portrait with a knife in his guts and bloody-looking Italian words. Up and down the staircase of his apartment were photographic portraits of contemporary artists, including the monklike Clemente by Jeannette Montgomery Barron.

This probably wouldn't like me describing his apartment, for fear of robbers or the Swiss internal revenue. When the French version of *House & Garden* described and photographed the malachite collection of one of my friends, burglars wasted no time stealing it, while leaving untouched other objects worth much more. No one in This's social circle wanted their house featured in a magazine spread.

Of course, This had many friends and entertained often. Like MC, he called up people all over the world and received them generously whenever they came to Zurich. His apartment with its bright colors, luxurious furniture, and many lights sparkled when guests arrived. There was a separate apartment upstairs for guests. His table always looked beautiful with its Hermès plates, Puiforcat silverware, and lots of small bouquets. The food, which he prepared himself, was always exquisite and often ended with a homemade kumquat sherbet. Around his table, I met John Waters; the photography collector Baroness Marion Lambert; Bice Curiger, a curator of the Kunsthaus Zurich; Jacqueline Burckhardt, an editor of *Parkett* and the granddaughter of Jacob Burckhardt, the art historian who invented the concept of "the Renaissance"—and many other beautiful and fascinating people. Bob Colacello, the Warhol biographer, regaled us with tales of his encounters with King Victor Emmanuel's aged daughters living in exile in Portugal. He, who'd grown up a poor Italian American in Brooklyn, was thrilled to be able to show his old mother pictures of the royal Italian princesses.

For Bice and Jacqueline, I wrote several articles for *Parkett*, including one on two Princes: Prince, the pop singer and composer, and Richard Prince, the photographer and master of appropriations.

This was my first and maybe only grown-up affair. It was a comfort and challenge to spend time with a mature, successful man, a fully formed personality, someone who could trace the contours of his personality, who was never undecided about his tastes, who understood his aversions, who had opinions. Most of my boyfriends had been twenty or thirty years younger than I and poor and dependent on me—very safe for me. I had always had the upper hand. This was sufficiently different from me to keep me enthralled. I'd known about contemporary art in the sixties, the heyday of Pop Art. While working at

Time-Life Books in New York, at lunchtime I'd gone to a gallery nearly every day. Then I'd lost track of all the new developments, though in the early 1970s, when I'd been the arts editor of another magazine, I'd learned a lot about contemporary painting from our art critic, David Bourdon, who'd previously been the art critic for *Life*.

Now, ten years later, I was catching up. Thomas had a beautiful series of self-portraits in pastel by Francesco Clemente, including one where he was exploring his own bowels, candle in hand; over his fireplace hung a powerful, iconic horse by Susan Rothenberg. He had a stenciled portrait of himself by Warhol. Thomas's idea was to *collect* paintings done since the early Warhol and to *deal* in paintings done from the Impressionists up to the Warhol "disaster" series and the electric chairs. That way he'd never be in competition with his clients to secure a prize painting.

As a novelist, I was intrigued by the economics of painting. Whereas serious novelists, even celebrated ones, could barely survive, the top painters were very rich. It was all because a painting was a unique object whereas a book was a multiple. No wonder so many writers turned to the visual arts—Burroughs to painting and Ginsberg to photography. That was the only way they could make money. (Ginsberg also got a million dollars for his archives.)

It took ten critics, two dealers, and twenty collectors to get an artist on the cover of *Time*, whereas a novelist had to convince eighty thousand readers to buy his book to win a comparable fame. For this reason, the painters could be more daringly experimental than the writers, who had to please so many more culture consumers, many of them with brows firmly in the middle. Painting—and heavily subsidized arts like ballet and poetry and "serious" music—were obliged to be avant-garde in order to seem flamboyantly original. Fiction and theater, which were expected to earn their own keep, had to maintain a broader appeal.

This knew both the painting world and that of cinema (which needed thousands of paying customers in order to survive). Certainly feature films were doubly cursed, since they needed a huge fan base in each city to fill those theater seats, whereas a novel could go out into the wide world and nab a reader here and another one there—no more than half a dozen in any one city.

This invited me to the Cannes and Berlin Film Festivals for many years in the eighties. They were completely different from each other. In Cannes, we'd stay at the Carlton, the chicest "palace" along the Croisette. Would-be starlets would hold bikini sessions on the beach nearby for amateur male photographers. Huge billboards all over Cannes advertised the newest films. The major films in competition would be screened in an ugly modern building accessible only by the red-carpeted stairs. Invited members of the audience in evening clothes would mount the two dozen stairs to the exhibition hall while velvet ropes and policemen held back the adoring crowds and busy photographers. Even though it was only May, the days were already long because France is so far north, and it was strange seeing all these heavily made-up female stars in strapless sequined gowns in broad daylight. The men had to be in tuxedos, no exceptions, though once a handsome young guy went nude with the tux painted on his body and he got in—after all, it was all show business, feverishly in pursuit of as much publicity as possible.

A typical day at Cannes was at once somnolent and exhausting. Since This was the manager of five cinemas in Zurich and since his rivals, who managed national chains, got all the blockbusters, he had to run after all those "interesting" movies made by Belgians or Taiwanese, films that would presumably receive good reviews. We would see as many as five films during the day in what was called the marketplace. He provided me with full accreditation as his assistant. My parents had not permitted me as a child to see many films, no more than one a year, considering them an unhealthy influence. As a result now I was overly sensitive to anything occurring on screen and would scream bizarrely if a close-up showed an actress breaking a nail. Anything sad made me cry and when it was all over I said to This that I felt like a Japanese court lady out of Sei Shōnagon; I'd spent five days in dark rooms weeping.

I suppose the two biggest evenings I had at the Croisette were both in 1985: *Rendez-vous*, with Juliette Binoche in her first leading role— everyone knew right away that a star was being born—and Paul Schrader's *Mishima*. Schrader and his wife, the actress Mary Beth Hurt, were friends of This and had been traumatized because they'd just been held up by thieves while they were looking at the view from a turnoff near the French-Italian border. The sets and costumes in *Mishima* were sumptuous, the whole film was beautifully conceived, and it won the Palme d'Or.

We would dash from seeing two or three films in the morning (This would often fall asleep in his seat) to the beach, which was partitioned into expensive cabanas with lounge chairs. We'd take the sun and have our lunch while tall, elegant Africans threaded their way among the bronzing white people offering for sale African carvings and jewelry no one bought. After lunch, we'd go see more films—at the old competition palace, where there was a director's festival, or back to the marketplace scattered among the city's various commercial cinema theaters. In the evening we'd don our tuxes and head for the red-carpet events or we'd grab a drink in the lobby and bar of the Carlton, which was thronged with propped-up cardboard promotional cutouts. Dozens of paparazzi clustered around the entrance on the lookout for stars. We had drinks with Spike Lee, who was just beginning to be known. I wasn't really used to being the quiet little sidekick. It's a very tiring role, and of course no one knew who I was. It gave me a new appreciation of what John Purcell must have felt all the time, although John seemed suited to his role as sidekick/son/wife/kid brother. And yet I wondered how happy anyone could be playing second fiddle. No matter how wifely his fantasies, every man is brought up to be the first violin.

No one lingered long because everyone was looking for producers and distributors. It struck me that although a movie required hundreds of thousands if not millions of dollars to make, most of the actual filmmakers were poor and perennially broke. In this crowd at the Carlton bar, everyone was trying to put together a deal. In Europe a film typically received a third of its money from distributors in the form of an advance against eventual receipts, a third from a TV channel, and a third from government subsidies or private producers. This last source of funding was the hardest to find, and all these half-shaved, half-bathed directors were scrambling around in search of money, their beseeching faces and politeness at odds with their bohemian backgrounds.

Late at night there were big parties in the area in the hills known as La Californie, in elegant rented villas. The Weinstein brothers and other moguls would be holding court. Metal torches were planted in the ground. Hundreds of Yugoslav or Greek or Taiwanese directors came out from under a log for funding or a free meal of hot hors d'oeuvres. Before Cannes, I'd assumed movie people were well heeled and that their money came to them in regular, foreseeable ways. I would never have guessed how improvised their financing was. Cannes (unlike the Venice Film Festival) was more devoted to wheeling and dealing than to pure cinema.

If Cannes could be symbolized by a white fur draped over a bikini, Berlin was cold and grimly serious, typified by dirty-haired intellectuals viewing a six-hour Bulgarian film about a failed businessman. Because This spoke German somewhat more easily than French or Italian or Spanish (though he was fluent in these languages as well), he felt more at home in Berlin—even though he'd been attending Cannes since the Sixties. In Berlin he had a secret language, Swiss German, which real Germans couldn't understand. He would discuss money or business with other Swiss friends in Switzerdeutsch and no one knew what they were saying. He did so only in an emergency. Normally he spoke his guests' language. I'd leave a table of Zurichois to go to the toilet and when I came back they would still be speaking in English. The French would never have been that polite. First, they wouldn't all have been fluent in English, and second, they wouldn't all have continued in a foreign tongue longer than a minute if they outnumbered the anglophones. Perhaps that's the difference between a big country and a small one—moreover one like Switzerland with four national languages. When This and I went to Egypt it was with a Swiss tour in which the guides repeated everything in both German and French. No one got impatient. We even traveled with a mother and her grown son from Basel; she spoke to him in German and he replied in French. I once had to wait for someone in the lobby of a grand hotel in Switzerland. The young woman concierge chatted amiably with clients in French, Italian, German, Swiss German, and English without any apparent transition or hesitation. Movies in Switzerland often had subtitles in two or even three languages, which ate up the bottom third of the screen. As a child, This had been sent every summer to French-language camp in the western part of Switzerland. The Swiss French only rarely spoke German, and only those Swiss Italians who actually lived in the north knew German, while most of the Swiss Germans knew at least English and French.

One year in Berlin, the self-created it-girl Pia Zadora astonished the German journalists when she gave them a bikini session in the swimming pool in the old Kempinski Hotel Bristol on the Kurfürstendamm in Berlin. She also summoned them to her glamorous airport arrival when she walked down the stairs in a chinchilla coat—Germans weren't used to stars of that magnitude. They were used to Tilda Swinton or Klaus Kinski talking about their roles as an English hermaphrodite or a suicidal Austrian homosexual. But Pia's diminutive, sunny disposition, delicious child's body and rich girl accoutrements were out of their range. Her very rich husband was an Israeli industrialist. He paid for billboards advertising her questionable talents as a disco singer and movie star along Sunset Boulevard back in Hollywood. She was made for John Waters.

The Berlin festival was in January, the coldest time of the year. It took me back to my adolescence in Chicago, my fear of freezing before I got home. I spent a lot of time alone and went to the Mövenpick cafeteria for my meals since the only German food word I knew was *Kalbsleber* ("calf's liver") and I quickly got tired of that. In spite of my nonexistent language skills, we went several times to the theater, where we saw plays I already knew and could follow (like Chekhov's *Three Sisters* in 1984). Occasionally I'd be stuck in a new four-hour German play in which the characters were crawling across a huge, bleak rock surface.

Three Sisters, starring Edith Clever and directed by Peter Stein, was a breakthrough in what I joked was a daring experiment called "realism." There were real birds on stage, confined by a nearly invisible wire net. The actors all left the stage to eat dinner in another room, not visible but audible to the audience. We could hear the clinking of silverware and plates and the shrieks of women's laughter and the murmur of conversation. This went on for a very long time.

Once in Munich we went to see the reclusive director Werner Schroeter, who was editing his 1986 film, *Der Rosenkönig*, starring

Magdalena Montezuma. We also spent time with the handsome, if drug- and AIDS-ravaged, film actor Dieter Schidor. Schidor usually played German soldiers in films like Sam Peckinpah's *Cross of Iron*. He also produced and played in Rainer Werner Fassbinder's last film, *Querelle*, based on Genet's novel, in which Brad Davis, Franco Nero, and Jeanne Moreau also acted. Apparently he'd had sex with the American writer Gary Indiana in an oven at Dachau while they were both tripping. Gary wrote about it in his 1993 novel *Gone Tomorrow*. When Dieter found out he had AIDS, he sold an expensive painting and traveled extensively. At last he was ready to commit suicide and took tranquilizers and sat in a tub full of hot water. The idea was that he'd doze off, sink under the surface and drown. A woman friend discovered him still alive days later and "saved" him, so that he could die a horrible death in a hospital ward weeks later, his body still recovering from the hot water burns he'd sustained over three days in the tub.

There was something perverse and eccentric about all the people who'd once surrounded Fassbinder. Although he was gay, Fassbinder had a wife, Ingrid Caven, to whom he was married from 1970 to 1972. She told us that once when she was in the States, she was broke and got a gig through the actor Peter Chatel to dub *Deep Throat* into German.

"I knew Rainer disliked porno and would never see it, and since I needed the money, I went ahead."

Then one day, stopping in front of a cinema in Munich, Fassbinder had said, "This is that movie everyone's talking about. Let's go in and see it."

"Oh, no, darling, it will be boring," Caven said modestly.

Fassbinder insisted, and according to her the minute Caven's first groan was heard he turned in his seat and slapped her and said, "Slut!"

We saw Caven in a strange ragtag evening onstage put together by Rosa von Praunheim. Later, in 1989, I saw her in Paris singing Édith Piaf's repertory at the Plaza l'Athenée Theater. She was wearing a backless floor-length dress that Yves Saint Laurent had designed for her.

I once spent an evening in a garden in Paris with her and Maria Schneider, who was no longer the curvaceous teenager of the 1972 Bertolucci film, *Last Tango in Paris*, in which her character was sodomized by the much older Marlon Brando character using butter as a lubricant. I'd seen the film in Italy, and when the now-infamous scene began everyone in the audience was exclaiming *"Burro, burro!"*

Schneider felt traumatized by the movie and her fame and had turned to drugs, which had left her once-beautiful face ravaged. That night she was with her female lover, Pia, whom she credited with saving her. Caven was with Jean-Jacques Schuhl, a French writer who in 2000 won the Prix Goncourt for his novel *Ingrid Caven*—not a biography but a highly fragmented novel. Both Ingrid Caven and Maria Schneider had been in scores of films and survived decades of being sex goddesses.

Caven was often with Rosa von Praunheim, who, in spite of his name, was a man and a very sexy one at that in black leather pants. He'd defiantly assumed the name "Rosa" to recall the pink triangles that homosexuals had been forced to wear in the Nazi death camps. He, too, had made scores of underground films, most notably his 1973 hit *It Is Not the Homosexual Who Is Perverse but the Society in Which He Lives*. In 1992 Praunheim made a documentary about Charlotte von Mahlsdorf, an elderly drag queen who'd survived the Nazi and the Communist regimes, although it later came out that she'd collaborated with the Communists. Mahlsdorf lived in the Gründerzeit Museum in East Berlin, which she'd built to house artifacts of everyday life from around 1900 that she'd found at the dump and flea markets. The owners of the gay bookstore Prinz Eisenherz in West Berlin drove me there so I could meet her. She greeted us in a maid's uniform at the entrance. The "museum" was filled with the conventional middle-class trappings of the period. There was a huge Swiss music box that played yard-wide metal disks. On the landing leading to the basement kitchen and a detailed recreation of an old Berlin gay bar, there was a vitrine filled with Charlotte's sadistic leather accoutrements. Years later, in 2003, after she was dead, I saw the Pulitzer Prize–winning play about her, *I Am My Own Wife*, starring Jefferson Mays and written by a Texan, Doug Wright. From the play I learned that after the Berlin Wall came down and the Stasi files were opened, it was revealed that Charlotte had denounced people she knew in the antiques world. I thought anyone who survived the Nazis and the Communists as a transvestite must have made some serious compromises.

My This, with his beautiful clothes and kindness, *gemütlich* manners and eternal smile, was a striking contrast to these weird Germans with their perversions, drugs, and conversational directness. Once I asked Thomas, who'd grown up in Switzerland on the German frontier, if he'd ever run across the border to play with German kids, and Thomas shook his head and said, "No, my parents thought they were too dirty." This often made fun of himself (while, it occurred to me, half bragging) by referring to himself as a simple peasant boy from the mountains, and I gather that in Swiss German he had a comically rustic accent. But in a way he seemed as pure as a mountain stream.

The Germans always seemed to rub the French the wrong way, all the stranger since the French liked to act awestruck by the monuments of German philosophy, art, music, and literature.

A beautiful young woman who was a Berlin journalist and looked like a boy came to dinner in Paris. Ina worked for a left-wing Berlin journal. At the time, I was still researching my Genet biography, and my other friends were all French Genet scholars. Ina also wrote about Proust, Musil, and Jelinek. At a certain point in the evening, Ina said, "Now let me understand. All the men here are gay and all the women are straight, is that right?"

You could almost hear the deflating horns descending, *wah wah wah*. Her question put everyone out of sorts, since French life is built on the possibility of seduction, on the unsaid (*le non-dit*). By spelling everything out, she'd threatened to end the game of flirtation. Of course an American—at least one with enough self-confidence—might have blurted out the same question, too, since we don't like the murk of sexual ambiguity either. I suppose the Americans and the Germans are more alike than the French and the Germans.

Sometime in the mid-eighties, I made a trip to Berlin for *Vogue* with the photographer Dominique Nabokov. She was the widow of the composer Nicolas Nabokov, the great writer's cousin. For years Nicolas had organized the Festival of Europe, which had turned out to be a

CIA scheme for promoting a non-Communist left wing in Western Europe. Because of her husband's old connections, Dominique knew "everyone" in Berlin. We interviewed Aribert Reimann, who'd written the opera *Lear* for Dietrich Fischer-Dieskau. I also spoke to Otto Schily, a founder of the Green Party and a member of the Bundestag. Schily predicted the imminent reunification of East and West Germany, which no one else was talking about. He said that the sense of everyone being German, East and West, was stronger than the Communist/capitalist divide. I was further shocked when he assured me reunification would come soon. All the more so when one of This's friends, Karsten Witte, a film critic, arranged for me to go to East Berlin with two doctor friends of his, husband and wife, who drove me around the city. I was sitting in the backseat and within a few minutes the doctors pointed out that someone official was tailing us. The authorities stopped us and asked me why I was taking notes. I said it was for *Vogue*, just some banalities about the city, and they let us go.

This and I went to a beautiful, newly refurbished neoclassical theater in the East that had been run by Bertolt Brecht when he was alive. We saw *The Threepenny Opera* performed there by the Berliner Ensemble in a very scanty, impoverished production that brought out the plight of the poor, spunky characters. Near the theater was one of the few gay bars the regime permitted to stay open. The people there were shabby, friendly, and alcoholic, and many of the clients were women. No wonder people said the East was more genuine and "real" than the West, though few elected to live there, except the *Mauerspringer* ("wall jumper"), who'd confounded everyone by jumping the wall from the West to the East, then written a book about it.

Years later, after the Wall came down (on November 9, 1989), This and I ate at a trendy restaurant facing the splendors of the French Cathedral, the neoclassical Huguenot church on Berlin's most beautiful square, the Gendarmenmarkt. I went to the nearby flea market where hordes of Eastern Europeans were selling off their most treasured belongings for relative pennies, and the whole thing was terribly sad. Wanting to help one Russian man, I bought an icon from him. It was smoke-blackened from centuries of votive candles. The history of

Europe and, it seemed, of my time in Europe was turning another terrible, irreversible corner.

We were always there in the winter, which was so much more severe than in Paris, where it rarely snows. But for me, Berlin was epitomized by old women in galoshes crowding into one of the many concert halls. The novelist Jeffrey Eugenides, who lived there for many years, told me that his Asian wife was repeatedly kicked by these old ladies in the bus. Since she was beautiful and young and Asian, they assumed she was a prostitute.

When I'd spoken to students in English in an old-fashioned wooden amphitheater, they'd all drummed their feet on the hollow-sounding floors instead of applauding. When I read to them from my complex, not entirely successful novel *Caracole*, a pimply male student attacked me for writing in a cultured "Thomas Mann style," as if that were a terrible sin, and for recording painful events that had happened to me when I was much younger rather than reporting my current angst.

I knew from Nabokov's novel *The Gift* that Berlin could be a summer paradise of interlocking lakes and nude swimming, but maybe Berlin was no longer entirely like that. I'd seen nudism in Munich's English Garden, where there is also a perpetual cataract of cold water along the Eisbach, in which boys surfed in their wetsuits atop an up-gush—sometimes frozen in the hang-ten for minutes, their bodies tense and bulging beneath their Neoprene skins.

This had a social energy that astounded me. Whereas writers must guard against too much socializing in order to work, for This work *was* socializing. He was tirelessly cheerful, never moody, always perfectly turned out, always "on," though later he treasured his solitude in his mountain ski house in the Engadine; often he'd stay there with just his dog, Lumpi, for weeks on end. I could be social and most people considered me gregarious, but too much chitchat left me exhausted. This liked to sit alone and work his way through hundreds of cinema magazines in an effort to keep up.

Later, in my sixties, I became grotesquely fat. Although everyone in his world was slim, This wasn't embarrassed by my looks, since I was no longer his lover and didn't reflect badly on him. He turned me into a mildly comical character, "Professor Bear," bumbling and bewildered and endearing. But at the same time he continued to buy industrial quantities of my books and give them as Christmas presents to his often confused friends, who were uncertain what to think of these "gifts." Poor This lost both the great love of his life, Thomas, and Elisabeth, the woman he lived with for years (he was living with her when we first met). Waiters in Zurich called her his wife (though maybe *frau* is more ambiguous). She was a glamorous blonde but did so much cocaine that she drove her dress shop into the ground; This lectured her, which only alienated her. She moved out. In Cairo we had a green satin bedspread made for her; This thought she'd look like a Hollywood star lying on it with her long blonde hair. Once I brought her a new, light, flowery perfume from Paris. Since she was "known," she told me, for wearing Chanel No. 5, she said she'd wear the new perfume to sleep in. Eventually This talked of her less and less often. She had a shiftless lover This didn't approve of. And then one day he told me she had died.

Though he had what seemed a sun-drenched life, his childhood with a tyrannical father and an unloving stepmother had been so grim he seldom spoke of it, and even his adulthood was marked by these unexpected deaths of his intimates. There was something steely inside him that had been forged out of his abusive childhood; I recognized this cold, untouchable core because I had it, too, underneath my amiability. We were both survivors.

After I was diagnosed with HIV, This was afraid of me. We grew apart, as I'd predicted. I wept often over my lost love and felt abandoned. Death was my constant shadow. My mother said to me, "It's normal for someone like me in her eighties to lose a friend every month, but it's strange for someone like you in his forties." I was attentive but not devoted to my dying friends; I thought, My time will come. I can't suffer through this repeatedly.

Chapter 6

Marie-Claude would invite new French novelists or philosophers of the moment to dinner, and these young men from the provinces, who now taught in Paris high schools and lived with women in the twentieth arrondissement, would appear intimidated but also puzzled and surprised by what they were encountering. Who was this aging American fag barely able to speak French? Here was this slender woman in her sixties—with her short pearly gray hair, the floating ecru and beige panels of her layered Japanese clothes, her lacquered red shoes, her ivory cigarette holder, her slightly weary graciousness— offering them some of her famous tapenade on toast ("famous" like all the rituals of this woman's life, at least to the faithful). She was perhaps most famous for her low, smoky voice, though in fact it was someone else's, Jeanne Moreau's. On the phone MC was often mistaken for Jeanne Moreau and immediately put through, an error she relished. One of my naïve girlfriends from the gym thought Marie-Claude couldn't possibly be French: "Is she English, German?" I wondered what sounded foreign—her timbre? Her articulation? Her slow speech? When she was diagnosed with cancer the first time she did consider giving up smoking, but her doctor assured her that stopping would be too much of a shock to her system. (Another friend thought not smoking might destroy her lovely, distinctive speaking voice.)

To me MC seemed completely continental. She even had a very European way of being tired. She would say, "But we're all terribly tired. Everyone is worn out." It wasn't quite clear if she meant that the troubled politics of recent weeks had exhausted everyone, or whether in these impoverished latter days everyone we knew had to work like coal miners to stay afloat. I knew that if, in my empirical Anglo-Saxon way, I proffered these possibilities of what she meant by general weariness (since in English we craved examples), Marie-Claude would vaguely reject them, saying, *"Non, c'est pas ça,"* without elaborating on what she meant. "Everyone is terribly, terribly tired." I found that the French rarely descended to the indignity of an example. They couldn't think with them, and we couldn't think without them.

For years Diane Johnson, the American novelist and author of *Le Divorce*, was my expat pal and coconspirator in noticing and simultaneously scorning and admiring French foibles. Researching her novels, which she increasingly set in Paris, Diane frequently consulted with MC about French manners and morals and expressions. Since the death of Mary McCarthy there had been surprisingly few American novelists living in Paris, where the dollar was becoming weaker and weaker against the franc. Younger American writers were living in Prague or Budapest and would soon enough be moving to the still more affordable capitals of Latvia or Lithuania. This push toward Eastern Europe seemed likely to be less fruitful, since even fewer Americans would ever learn Slavic or Baltic languages or Hungarian, and so would have less of a chance for a real intellectual exchange with the people of these countries. At least in the twenties and thirties a few of all the American artists living in Paris had learned French and were influenced by contemporary French painting and literature.

Now Americans didn't like feeling intimidated by a superior culture but enjoyed dipping randomly into Czech or Hungarian cuisine, folklore, or even politics in a lightly condescending, neocolonial way before running back to their enclaves in bookstores and reading their copies of English-language newspapers and attending concerts by American or British music acts. That's probably why so many young Americans scorned France and believed the French were rude or snooty; they weren't used to dealing with their equals or their more intellectually and artistically refined counterparts in other languages. Whereas the English expats, mostly painters, I'd met on Crete intended to stay there if they could (their lives were better in Chania than they'd ever been in

Liverpool), no American I knew intended to die outside the United States. We all assumed our culture was the best—since our disillusionment with our culture had not yet had time to set in.

David McConnell, an American novelist (*The Silver Hearted*), was one of the very few Americans I knew in Paris. He rented Dominique Nabokov's apartment and, most generously, had a brief affair with me. (I say "generous" because he was young and beautiful, way out of my class.) But then he became besotted with a tough little garage mechanic—as who would not?—a guy with a motorcycle and a pretty face and an indeterminate sexuality. David was one of the few younger people among my countrymen who seemed to be as much a culture vulture as were those of my generation. And to retain a sparkling, eccentric sense of humor as well.

I'd interviewed Mary McCarthy, who was nice enough, a diplomat's wife, but then she'd become very nasty because in my rapturous article about her I'd called her slipcovers "chintz" instead of "sprigged muslin" or something. She said I'd never be a successful writer because I paid no attention to details. She was always cross, as if permanently enduring a bad hangover (*une gueule de bois*, a "wood muzzle"); her American husband, Jim, deserved his reputation as "the nicest man in Paris."

Diane Johnson was married to a noted American pulmonologist who tirelessly flew to Africa to treat AIDS victims with lung ailments, and she and I often laughed at Marie-Claude's announcement, not infrequent, that everyone was exhausted.

"How could everyone be exhausted at the same time?" Diane asked, with her infectious laugh bubbling just below her speech and sometimes drowning it. "And besides, in America if we're tired we take a nap, don't we, or have a good night's sleep, don't we, and then we wake up refreshed, right? We don't have this *condition*, do we, this existential condition of being weary? At least I never heard of it back in Illinois." And yet it seemed like an odd peccadillo of Marie-Claude's until I read in Zeldin's *The French* that *most* French people claimed to be exhausted.

If we laughed at two or three of Marie-Claude's foibles, we did so because we adored her otherwise: she was our point man for understanding all things French. In her novels *Le Divorce, Le Mariage,* and *L'Affaire,*

Diane dealt with the sometimes calamitous encounter between French and American laws, customs, and attitudes. And language. MC understood all these fine points of her own culture partly because she was a French-born Jew who had been raised in Mexico. She knew every out-of-the-way French expression and took a connoisseur's delight in them. Her father, a watchmaker named Bloch, had had the means and the wit to move his entire Jewish family—his wife, his two daughters, his mother-in-law, and her sister—from France in 1941 to Mexico City, where the girls were enrolled in French schools. There the whole family survived the war, and there MC had not only learned Spanish but "American." She'd met American soldiers and dated them, on the sly, when she was just fifteen or sixteen, learning their slang. She made some little mistakes in English but was so at ease in all three of her languages that if I complained I was tired and couldn't go on speaking French anymore she'd blink and say, "But I thought we were speaking English. Sorry."

Finally, after I'd been in France for a year and a half, she and I began switching from one language to the other without transition, and in midsentence. Harry Mathews, who had lived in France since the 1950s, would get irritated with us. "Either French or English, not both, please. If you keep that up, Ed, you'll lose your English—without gaining French." Somehow "gaining French," didn't sound right and he walked off with a quizzical expression on his face.

Harry lived with the French writer Marie Chaix, and they translated each other's books. My American friends and I were always testing each other: "Would you say that in English?"

I began to claim that trying to understand all those intellectuals with their qualifications and parentheses had made me appreciate simple declarative sentences of the subject-verb-object variety. The second book I wrote while living in France, *The Beautiful Room Is Empty*, was my most American, the leanest, cleanest prose I'd ever written, and without a single French expression in it. It was my sequel to *A Boy's Own Story*. Thanks to Roditi's warning, my career was back on track again. There were constant pitfalls in shifting from French to English. For instance, the French would say, "We passed a very funny evening with her," when they meant a fun evening—they'd *spent* a fun evening.

Or they'd say, "He's an excellent cooker," which to some English-language ears makes the subject sound like a stove. Or they'd say, "I know her since forever." There were lots of *faux amis* going back and forth. *Malicieux* means sly, not "malicious." *Actuel* in French means "present" and isn't used in our sense of "actual"; Henry James—who'd been educated in French—would refer to "the actual president of the United States."

At her dinner parties Marie-Claude's husband, Laurent, would sit at the table with a look of terminal boredom. As the French would say, *"Il est empaillé dans le coin."* ("He's stuffed in the corner," as a taxidermist's bear or antelope is stuffed.) Laurent made no attempt to hide it. His boredom was a form of narcolepsy he was always about to sink into. An onlooker might have guessed he was the one who didn't understand French, for after all it's impossible to look alert for long if no message is getting through. On his own, Laurent was a lively, playful, gentle man who liked to joke and whose eyes danced with merriment as he clowned around. He loved being a teaser. But at MC's state dinners, he appeared no more engaged than Prince Philip at royal events and a good deal less willing to go through the motions. He was very, very slender and carried not an extra ounce of fat on his body. Though he was already in his sixties when I met him, he was still taking yoga classes every morning. He and Harry Mathews both wore vests sewn with large pockets for pens and pencils that they bought at Hollington, a store near the Odéon. The vests were very well made, built to last, in a plain durable-looking fabric with subdued colors—artisan chic, you might have said. Laurent had a narrow, tall, Gothic face lengthened further by his bald head. Even his baldness, like Nabokov's, was distinguished, as if an excess of genetic refinement had banished everything hirsute. His unusual last name, de Brunhoff, with the aristocratic *particule*, could be traced back to Swedish ancestors; one of his female antecedents had been a Swedish king's mistress, although Laurent scoffed at such a claim and waved an impatient hand at it. I can still picture a nearly extinct Laurent, gray with ennui, wedged behind the round table between two vociferous, gesticulating writers. No one ever asked him anything other than to pass the grated cheese.

Marie-Claude's apartment was large by Paris standards but small by those of any other city. She had four modest-sized rooms. One in the back was her daughter Anne's bedroom, a space I never saw even by accident in my twenty-five years of visiting there. The other one in the back was Laurent's studio. The two larger rooms in the front were the "public" rooms. The sitting room/dining room had two couches forming an L, big, sunny French doors surrounded by plants and looking down on the boulevard St. Germain, and lots of exquisite shells and carved objects on the white marble mantel above the fireplace. On one wall was a small painting of a curious little man in an improbable flying machine and another small painting of superimposed tinted papers that looked Japanese and had, in fact, been bought at a Japanese art gallery on the place des Vosges. Marie-Claude loved the Japanese aesthetic and for years had studied the language. She had a computer that gave her Japanese and Chinese characters. She was friendly with Madame Tsushima, the daughter of the Japanese novelist Osamu Dazai (*No Longer Human*) and with the man who'd translated a part of *The Tale of Genji* into French. There were very few things here or in her perfect little summerhouse on the Île de Ré off the Atlantic coast, but each felt talismanic. I gave her a few expensive gifts that seemed to me to conform to her taste but after presenting them to her I'd never see them again.

Whenever I went to MC's in Paris for dinner (and I went hundreds of times), everything followed a ritual. I arrived at eight thirty and she was impeccably dressed in one of her pale, flowing skirts and layered tops, her body lightly perfumed with honeysuckle, always the same. When a woman always wears the same perfume, she does so to please the people around her, not herself. Honeysuckle, say, is her "brand," whereas on her own she might like to vary her scents. Because I arrived before everyone else, she usually invited me to go upstairs to her tiny studio in a maid's room to visit her latest Cornell-type boxes, though it was impolitic to mention Cornell to her, and there I could see what use she'd made of the model pillars I'd brought back from the gift shop of the Roman forum, the Fatima hand from Cairo, the tin ex-voto of a soldier in World War I uniform, or the one of a man on crutches I'd found in Crete. She decided to call her boxes *théâtres immobiles* in an upcoming gallery show for which I wrote the catalog essay (pretending to be Cocteau so I could turn out the glib, poetic words). Later René de Ceccatty wrote the brilliant preface to a book full of fantasias on her boxes composed by dozens of French, English, and American authors, including Richard Ford, a dear friend, and David Lodge.

Downstairs the other guests had started arriving and MC would serve them red wine—the French never seemed to drink anything else—and homemade tapenade on little squares of toast. Around ten o'clock, her shy, mannish, but beautiful daughter, Anne, would come in and help MC pull the round table out from the wall, remove the towering flower arrangement, and set the table.

The meal began with traditional bourgeois fare like a beet salad or stewed leeks or eggs cooked in red wine. But the second course was often a horrible surprise—one of Marie-Claude's famous inventions like chicken in a peanut butter and crème fraîche sauce, which she called *à la circasienne* for some reason. Whereas she was an unreservedly excellent cook in her house on the Ile-de-Ré, simple fresh fish and fresh salads and vegetables and fruits, in Paris she could be too "original," in the foreboding French sense of that word. Of course the wines flowed freely for everyone but me, and in any event people were too busy competing for airtime to notice what they were eating.

MC might have some of her English-speaking friends, such as James Salter's daughter, Nina, who was a book editor, or Diane Johnson and her husband. Diane was an animated, observant, kind woman. Her husband, John Murray, as tall as she was short, would fall asleep when the conversation wandered too far from his interests, yet he was a deeply compassionate man who visited our mutual friends hospitalized with AIDS; I know that Gilles Barbedette was comforted whenever John came to his sickbed. John had been decorated by the French government for providing free treatment to patients with AIDS-related TB in Africa. He and Diane collaborated on one of the first articles published about AIDS in the United States, in the *New York Review of Books*. Diane was as vivacious as her husband was reserved.

Often MC tried to mix people who didn't know each other. She wasn't the sort of managing, aggressive hostess who can draw people out and chatter confidently. She was really very shy except with close friends, so there were many silences (as the French say, "an angel is passing," *un ange passe*). With friends, especially on the phone, she loved to recount every detail of her life, often styled as "battles" to protect the rights of the children—her attractive, middle-aged daughter and her son who stayed in endless conflict with his mother. To the degree that MC was a fashion plate and *frivole*, Anne was imposing in her khakis and Brooks Brothers men's shirts. I've heard that since her mother's death she is alert, cheerful, and gainfully employed. I've known several butch daughters who were *cavaliers servants* to their girl-ish, self-dramatizing mothers.

Laurent, Marie-Claude's husband, had a brother named Thierry. Thierry had been a successful concert pianist, a piano teacher for soci-ety women, and the lover of the Mahler biographer Henry-Louis de la Grange, who had inherited millions from his rich American mother. One day Thierry threw it all over and became a monk. Worried that he'd commit the sin of aestheticism, he chose an ugly, modern cement monastery, and only reluctantly did he accept his abbot's moneymaking scheme of recording a monastery choir singing Gregorian chants. At the end of his two-year novitiate, Thierry's abbot gave him a lawn party to celebrate taking holy orders, where every other guest was a duchess and her lunch companion a smelly, toothless monk.

Thierry in his zeal found monastic life too worldly and easy and he became a hermit in a cave in the Pyrenees. He was looked after by nuns in a nearby convent who prepared his austere meals. He rose at 4 A.M. and began the day kneeling on stone and praying for several hours.

From time to time, he would come to Paris for a few days to see his mother, a former piano teacher, his other brother the doctor, and then, MC and Anne. He stayed with MC. In Paris he wore normal clothes, often slacks, shirts, and a warm down jacket he'd bought at Le Vieux Campeur, the vast sportswear emporium. Thierry was cheerful and a good listener to MC's rants about her battles to protect the worldwide Babar merchandising revenues from "La Dame"—Laurent's new wife, Phyllis Rose. In France, by Napoleonic law, Laurent would not be able to disinherit his middle-aged "children," but I pointed out to MC that now that her ex-husband was an American citizen living in America, he could leave everything to his cat if he wanted to.

MC went on red alert when La Dame dared to write a book in which she mentioned her friendship with Thierry the monk. "Oh no, this time she's gone too far. Her book will never be published in France, I'll make sure of it."

Since Phyllis's book was titled *The Year of Reading Proust,* I assured MC that it might not be translated anyway, since the French already had thousands of books about reading Proust, but it was important for MC and her amour propre to believe that she was powerful enough to thwart a French publication. Thierry just seemed bemused by the whole affair.

After dinner, her guests might leave directly from the table, full of promises to see each other very soon—or else retire to the adjoining library (secretly MC's bedroom, but for guests her second salon, the bed camouflaged by a red cover and a heap of black and gold pillows). There, people half-reclined and drank an herbal tea, a *tisane*—MC prided herself on the *tilleul-menthe*, a lime flower–mint blend she bought at a monastery shop on the rue Pont Louis-Philippe—and I wondered if I had to stay till the very end as a sort of man of the house.

Many French people were difficult conversationalists. Asking them not only where they were originally from but what they did in life was considered rude—I suppose because many of them did nothing (many Parisians are *rentiers,* people who live off the rents of their properties) or because they weren't proud of their jobs, which simultaneously supported and interfered with their intellectual and artistic passions. That did away with the top two American conversation openers. Americans aren't usually quite so paranoid, but the French are constantly alert to the possibility of a real or imagined slight. And being able to put someone down, even a complete stranger, is considered an admirable gift. That leaves the movies as a safe topic. A chatty but pointless anecdote designed to fill a silence ("And so we got completely lost around Vendôme") can elicit an *"Et alors?"*—which, depending on how it's pronounced, can mean "Then what?" or "So what?" or "Why are you telling me this?" Whereas Americans like to match anecdotes, the French at least try to make a general point. All the stories in Proust move from the specific to the general. Not only are the French, who are so protective of their families' reputations, mystified by childhood horror stories and confessions, they'd rather tell the kind of salacious sex stories that shock Americans—and, interestingly, the more sophisticated and international French people are, the more raw their stories can seem. Only strictly Catholic and royalist families are reduced to discussing the weather in great detail. It's a sign of "Parisianisme" to talk dirty—and it's proof that no matter how titled and aristocratic you are, in the 1960s you mounted the barricades and joined the student protests, too. Even the most resplendent countess can talk slang like a sailor (*"Ça me fait chier!"*: literally meaning "That makes me shit," a not necessarily racy way of saying, "How annoying!"). Or a bejeweled hostess might say something is *con*, literally "cunt" but figuratively "stupid." A child who is shy and won't come out to meet guests is called, half admiringly, *sauvage*—which means "shy," but literally, of course, "wild" or "savage." I once heard a very presentable French mother speaking faulty English and shocking the matrons of Houston: "My daughter is wild, very wild," when the girl refused to curtsy. On the other hand French children are brought up to kiss all the guests good night, even complete strangers—a touching, delicious custom when the child is a pretty, freshly bathed little girl.

While English speakers feel some team effort is necessary to keep a conversation going, the French don't mind if it founders completely. With friends they might make an effort but not with relative strangers, in case their loquaciousness might give some covertly hostile person the upper hand. Information can be used as a weapon and hostility is the default position. And too much laughing or whooping is considered vulgar.

All of which is not to say the French aren't good conversationalists. After all, they invented the art of conversation, and when someone has a good, scurrilous, fairly shocking story to tell (usually involving someone else), everyone is amused and the rejoinders are fast and clever. I read once that Americans talk about money so they won't have to talk about sex, whereas the French talk about sex so they won't have to talk about money. Milan Kundera and Italo Calvino both treasured "lightness" in writing; I wonder if they would have esteemed it so much if they hadn't both lived in Paris. Long-winded explanations are deemed pointless and embarrassing and are abhorred; when I used to hold forth, Gilles Barbedette would say, in English, "Thanks, Teach." In New York, I was used to drawing people out on their areas of expertise, which of course was flattering to the person being quizzed and informative to the other guests. But in general the French resist personal disquisitions and resent pointed questions. Americans think it is polite to grill a stranger; the French think of it as an invasion and an affront. Because I was an American and, after all, a writer, the French would gamely answer my questions—mistaking my politeness for professional, Balzacian curiosity.

Proud Marie-Claude boasted that she'd never consulted a recipe, and every cookbook she received she disdainfully handed over to me, marveling that I could be bothered with them at all. (And yet she wanted to collaborate with me on a cookbook; I pointed out that successful chefs all had TV shows.) The best course was the cheese and we all tucked in, able at last to identify what we were eating. The dessert was often a cherry clafoutis, the custard dried out and cracking, the cherries unstoned and burnt on top.

No matter. The conversation was lively as long as MC remembered to pose constant if oblique questions of the stiff young high school teachers in their suits of green Socialist corduroy and their manners which switched, exactly on the third drink, from nervous, tight-lipped petit-bourgeois propriety to a "Normale Sup" style—referring to the École Normale Supérieure (the teachers' school which both Sartre and Beauvoir attended)—of table thumping. You could feel a nearly geographical transition from Sunday dinner with their families in the suburbs to a smoky Left Bank café. Usually she wouldn't invite the wife or girlfriend of the new true genius, but if MC was talked into it the young woman was even more paralyzed with fear than her lover by all these rich bohemian ways—the presence of all these foreign writers, the ghastly cold chicken the young woman tried to hide under her lettuce leaves, the robotic entrances and exits of MC's daughter, the oddly flirtatious manners of a celebrated French novelist with his ironic smile and monk's tonsure and his internationally acclaimed wife (MC's top-shelf, blue-chip acquaintances and summer neighbors in Ré, the novelist Philippe Sollers and Julia Kristeva, the famous philosopher and scholar).

Of course I spent a lot of time alone in Paris. Most foreigners write about having been unbearably lonely in Paris. I wasn't, thanks to MC and Gilles Barbedette, both of whom I'd met in the States, after all. True, I seemed to have more free time in Paris than in New York. Someone said that if you're depressed in Paris, all you have to do is go outdoors and your spirits will be raised immediately. For me the transition felt more as if someone were lifting the lid and enabling me to float. I wandered idly, like a cloud, looking at the used books in the stalls along the Seine, the *bouquinistes*. Paris was full of things an older person likes—books, food, museums. Years later when an American complained of Paris I said, "I like it. To me it seems so calm after New York. As if I'd already died and gone to heaven. It's like living inside a pearl."

Near me, just across the street from the Tour d'Argent and down toward the pont Sully, there was a *bouquiniste* who sold biographies and novels of quality. The biggest star of the bookstalls seemed to be the once popular but now ignored collaborationist Paul Morand. My ability to read French was improving week by week since I looked up so many words. Most of my day was spent on the couch reading and looking up words and listening to the rain. Strange to say, but soon my vocabulary was better than that of most of my French friends; I amused them with my growing vocabulary of far-fetched words. Mind you, at the same time I often didn't understand common expressions that used ordinary words in normal ways. *"Tu m'en veux?"* a friend asked—which literally meant, "Do you want me of it?" but colloquially signified, "Do you hold it against me?" It's an ordinary expression. Marie-Claude gave me dictionaries of odd and picturesque French words. She herself was a bottomless repository of them.

I liked to wander the streets and sit in the Café Flore and for lunch order toast and a slab of fois gras and a salad; or go to the Village Voice English-language bookstore and check out the new titles and chat with the proprietor, Odile Hélier; or stop by my favorite French bookstore,

La Hune, next to the Flore, and sort through the new philosophy works or the new French novels, all of them arranged on long tables. In America I'd never kept up with what was recently published, but in Paris I did. Partly because books seemed the mildest, most manageable entry point for French culture at large. Partly because everyone around me here felt it was important to keep up.

Here I was in my early forties starting out all over again. In New York I'd been shabbily dressed, but in Paris I became more and more smart. I shaved my mustache, which I'd worn for the previous ten years as an emblem of the gay clone. Overnight the French gays had shaved theirs off and my few gay friends mocked me for still having one. I didn't invest any importance in any aspect of my appearance, and off it went. I wore bright silk pocket squares. I bought suits from Hugo Boss and Kenzo and even Yamamoto and ties from Proust's favorite, Charvet, and Church shoes. I tried out different colognes and changed my scent every two or three months. For a while, it was Blenheim Bouquet by Penhaligon's, then finally I settled on Bois du Portugal by Creed, which I still wear. The idea of donning dress-up clothes every day and shaving and perfuming myself before going out would have been unthinkable in my roach-trap one-room apartment in the West Village. There I wore a leather bomber jacket, ripped jeans commando style, and T-shirts, no scent at all; cologne would have struck New York gay guys as effeminate, and some gay bars banned customers from wearing it or even scented deodorant. I'd seldom worn underpants under my jeans. Mostly I never noticed what I was wearing, though I had my hair expensively cut and kept my teeth as white as possible. When one of my old gay friends in New York passed me on the stairs, he got a whiff of my "sissy" cologne and grumbled, "Cologne! What's happened to you? Paris has ruined you. You've gone completely *Cage aux Folles.*" In Paris, I worried over how I looked and what I ate, and I went to the latest movies and operas, though I liked French theater no more than American. Nevertheless, I thought of myself as a "cultural reporter" and I felt obliged to attend plays directed by Antoine Vitez and to take Marie-Claude to Racine's *Britannicus* at the Comédie Française, directed by Klaus Michael Grüber, possibly the first German ever to work in that temple to French drama. Grüber had the actors crowd downstage toward the footlights and whisper their Racinian alexandrines with their arms around each other's shoulders. It was a very effective way of bringing out the beauty of the language. They looked like the statue of the conspirators outside San Marco in Venice.

To be honest, I loved to go to the theater in London but felt that most French stage actors shouted and that the plays were either classics served up with a bizarre new visual interpretation or adaptations from works of prose by writers such as Kafka or Musil. Jeanne Moreau appeared in a one-woman adaptation of *The Servant Zerline*, a Musil novella. People said that she'd only recently become sober after years of excessive drinking and she was doing this demanding role to prove how thoroughly she'd dried out. I'd seen Moreau appear not long before in a French version of *La Celestina,* the Spanish Renaissance classic about a prostitute and her madam, and her performance had been impeccable. For *Vogue* I'd phoned her to ask her to write an homage to François Truffaut, who'd just died, and within twenty-four hours she had turned in a brilliant reminiscence in English—her mother's language.

I became friendly with Jean-Marie Besset, a playwright and director who lived half the year in New York. He was always charming if a bit too world-weary, too exhaustively social (a phenomenon the French called *"M'as tu vu?"* which means "Did you see me ?"). Jean-Marie was from a village in the south called Limoux, where he staged a season of plays and where they produced a sparkling white wine they weren't permitted, for jealous geographical legal reasons, to call champagne. And for some reason the French didn't think of champagne as a "real drink." Friends who knew I was a reformed alcoholic still offered it to me. "What? Not even a little glass of champagne?" The French, otherwise, were more polite than Americans about not pushing alcohol, maybe thinking I was on a "cure" for my liver—a common occasional privation for the highly disciplined French.

I had lots of sex in Paris. Like everyone.

In mixed company, a French friend used to begin sentences with "My grandmother's lover . . .," not a phrase one often heard in America.

I had an American woman friend who had come to Paris with her nice but nerdy husband, and when they returned to America a little while later she wept bitter tears. She was forty-something and had a beautiful body but an unremarkable face, and in Paris she had tons of sexual adventures while her husband was off at work. In America, no one on the street would ever look at her.

I'd meet actresses at dinner parties, since Parisian hostesses felt they should mix and match their guests—a novelist, a general, a judge, a movie star, a decorator. Early on I became friendly with Nathalie Prouvost, a rich woman who entertained frequently in her little house in the courtyard of a great apartment building, first one on the rue de Verneuil and later another a block away in the building where Lacan and Bataille had lived. Nathalie introduced me to Jean Clausel, who did something in the department of honors, and who Nathalie relentlessly petitioned until the department made me a knight and later a commander of the French order of arts and letters—a rank I shared with Sylvester Stallone.

Nathalie had Asian servants who crept silently and expertly among the diners. That was the moment when many hostesses decided it was more *intime* for everyone to sit together and eat in the kitchen—an enormous kitchen that had been entirely refurbished at great expense—which meant that we ate a lot of cold meals, given the French horror of the smell of cooking food. *"Ça sent la graisse?"* an insecure hostess would inquire. "Does it smell like grease in here?" I'd try to assure MC that Americans liked cooking smells, which we found cozy and inviting, but I read that the French had always detested the odor of food, and that in fact the first French Rothschild, James, in the mid-nineteenth century had built an underground train to bring the cooked dishes from the distant kitchen to the dining room at his estate of Château de Ferrières.

Eventually, Nathalie eschewed the kitchen in favor of her dining room. She'd decorated all her rooms in the Gustavian style of eighteenth-century Sweden—which meant cabriole legs and fine carpentry but no gilt or velvet, and pastel colors and white slipcovers and pale silks and wood that had been "antiqued" nearly white. There was something summery and cool about her salon, with ceiling-high glass doors on two sides and more rustic, countrified Swedish versions of French ormolu. The slipcovers of shot silk matched the curtains perfectly. I brought an

English friend to meet Nathalie and later he asked me, "Who's your nouveau riche friend?" I said, "You only imagine she's nouveau riche because everything in her house is sumptuous and new and matches. But her mother is a countess, Anne de Maigret, tracing her noble lineage back to 1367, and Nathalie herself was invited years ago to the Proust Ball where she had to dress like her great-grandmother—who was a model for one of Proust's duchesses. She was in a salon scene in that Ornella Muti Proust movie, *Swann in Love*. And her son is married to the princesse de Polignac. Her own family, the Maigrets, are related to the Poniatowskis, the Gramonts, and the Clermont-Ferrand family."

(I was reminded of that Frenchman who visited the Duchess of Devonshire and looked at her magnificent but heteroclite rooms at Chatsworth and commented, "The usual *désordre anglais*.")

My friend made a face and said, "She acted in a *movie?*"

By now I was in a proprietorial rage.

"You don't understand—the French don't like your worn-out old antiques and threadbare carpets. They want everything to be new and to match, and what's broken down is shunted off to a museum or the flea market. And no wonder French flea markets are the best in the world. They want what's chic and they sell off their old furniture. Since France has been a rich country for a thousand years and always a slave to fashion, the *puces* are groaning with fine furniture of even the recent past. What's chic right now is a black-and-chrome kitchen and a salon in the manner of Gustavus."

All of which is to explain why the English often break out in hives in France. When faced with a formal garden or the severely pollarded trees along the Seine, my friend would exclaim, "This is frightful. Why can't they just let nature be? Why must every last stick be tortured?"

Once an Englishman said to me in a near whisper, "Edmund, you live with them. You hear them. What do they say about us?"

I laughed and said, "They never ever talk about you except when they're making a trip to London for everything that's what they call terribly British—and they say it in English: 'terribly British.' They want Peel shoes, and Turnbull & Asser shirts, and hats from Lock's."

I became so Gallicized that I couldn't even understand the point of one English billboard that pictured a despised tiny "nouvelle cuisine" meal as opposed to a hearty English dish. To me the French serving size seemed much more reasonable and appetizing. And I admired the French emphasis in cuisine on presentation. The only thing that puzzled me—after all, both my parents were Texans—was the chilly reception one would get in a three-star restaurant which the ratings books would single out for its *"accueil chalereux."* Really? A "warm welcome"? The French *could* seem rude. When you asked someone how he was doing, he couldn't just say, "Fine," but would cut immediately to a startlingly abrupt *"Et vous?"* ("And you?") Of course, this whole worn-out, standard exchange was nothing but empty ritual, but one Americans liked to treat as sincere.

My English friend and I once stayed in a huge château that had long ago belonged to a king but had since become a hotel. On the extensive grounds, the plantings were in geometrical patterns, which, as we strolled through them, had Jonathan frothing at the mouth.

I said, "But your English landscape artists like Capability Brown didn't exactly practice benign neglect. You'd have a ha-ha that was invisible from the house and separated the working pastures with the animals from the pleasure grounds, and the pleasure grounds, even though they looked natural, were carefully and expensively built with 'upper' and 'lower' ponds and hills that had to be either leveled or created, and had these different sections divided into vernal 'rooms' in which different flowers would bloom at different seasons. What could be more artificial?"

"Yes," Jonathan sputtered, "but it all *looked* natural."

I had first met Nathalie through Marie-Claude, who'd invited Nathalie to dinner with her lover, Marc Cholodenko, a novelist, screenwriter, and translator. Soon Marc was translating my own novels. Marc lived in a one-room apartment on the Left Bank, but he was usually to be found at Nathalie's house. He told me once that I shouldn't have bothered to bring a certain champagne since Nathalie owned the vineyard. He was handsome, with curly blond hair, pale blue eyes, and a well-knit body. His passion was polo and he owned two ponies, which consumed everything he earned. His best friend was a friendly, charming young duke who was Marc's age and had drawn Marc into the costly, glamorous world of polo. Marc's other passion, also expensive, was bespoke clothes from Savile Row. Since I usually went to London every six or eight weeks, he'd use me as a courier to carry his jackets from his Paris tailor (who'd marked the places where they didn't fit in soap) to his English tailor on the side street behind the Burlington Arcade, and from there to Paris again—back and forth through a series of adjustments. After the jackets and trousers had gone through several fittings, they were at last ready to be worn. To me the finished product looked pinched, although I had nothing to compare them to. The only other person I'd known to wear bespoke clothes was my father, who'd gotten his in Cincinnati.

Marc wasn't very tall, but he held himself erect and wrapped himself in his tight tweeds and struck graceful attitudes. He was friendly, if not very warm; finally I figured out that he didn't want to appear anything beyond pleasant and cool. I'd read descriptions in nineteenth-century French novels about young French aristocrats who held themselves aloof, looking down their noses at people with a certain *morgue* and *mépris*. At first, as the true son of my mother, the psychologist, I imagined that Marc must have been wounded as a child (he spoke with vague scorn of his father, a race-track tout). Or was he ashamed of being a Polish Jew among so many aristocrats? Nathalie confessed that Marc was like another son and resented her real son. Of course, Marc was above all a distinguished novelist, who'd won the Prix Goncourt for his *Les États du désert* and who titillated his many readers with his delicately erotic fiction. He was also a serious art lover and visited the Louvre at least once a week.

Eventually I saw that as a Jew Marc resembled Proust's Swann or Proust himself, and just as Swann was the only Jewish member of the Jockey Club, Marc must have been among the few French Jews who played polo. When I mentioned Marc's duke to MC, she sniffed, *"Noblesse de l'Empire"*—that is, a Napoleonic noble and therefore supposedly lower in rank than the nobility of the ancien régime. As a reader of Proust, I found these distinctions mildly interesting, but as an American I thought it was all a bit silly. It was hard to believe people took rank, origins, and tailoring so seriously. And I wasn't sure MC truly understood the fine distinctions between the older nobility and the Napoleonic one. Marc once said to me, with his most innocent-seeming expression, "So you really like Marie-Claude? Surely you can see she's extremely stupid."

I was shocked. MC had been so generous to me, inviting me to her table at least once a week, introducing me to *le tout Paris,* gently correcting my mistakes in French ("You go *chez le dentiste*, not *au dentiste*. You never wish someone a good evening, *une bonne soirée*—it sounds so vulgar. And you *offer* someone a drink, you don't *buy* them one like you do in America."). She'd read thousands of books in her three languages. Her job was to write reports on new French books for Knopf and on American books for Gallimard. She could also read and speak Spanish.

Occasionally, like the rest of us, she made a mistake. She failed to see how inflammatory Salman Rushdie's *The Satanic Verses* would be in the Muslim world, although few people in the West did until the ayatollah pronounced the fatwa. I knew Rushdie, and he himself was surprised. He was attending Bruce Chatwin's funeral with his wife, Marianne Wiggins, when the curse was suddenly cast. British secret service men accompanied the two to an armed vehicle and eventually to the first of many "bunkers," and they began a life of constant migration from one hiding place to another. Eventually Marianne Wiggins left him and for the next several years we'd see Salman and his new wife, Elizabeth, at literary parties in London. We always knew he was in attendance as soon as we spotted the crew-cut, burly plainclothes security men guarding the door with wires in their ears.

Marie-Claude had never been educated beyond the lycée level, but then most middle-class girls her age had gone no further. MC had traveled extensively and with her good English would help guide Laurent on his promotional tours in the States. They'd be greeted in Minneapolis by a Babar parade, say, and when Neiman Marcus celebrated Paris Week they had Babar as the star—no Americans appreciate Paris more than the well-heeled culture-vulture women from Dallas and Houston; and indeed the open-minded, intellectually curious MC was friendly with Stanley Marcus and his daughter Wendy. MC was a collector of literary gossip, remembering every name and anecdote from the past four decades of Parisian *commérages*. I sometimes thought of Ezra Pound's "Portrait d'une Femme" ("Your mind and you are our Sargasso Sea," if that meant nothing ever sank out of sight but continued to float on the surface for all eternity. I'm a bit like that, and consider myself an archeologist of gossip). MC had strong instincts about people and wasn't afraid to voice them. Sometimes she was completely wrong and would say, for example, of a completely lovely guy, "He's a real Jesuit!"—meaning not to be trusted.

Above all, she had a great gift for friendship. She'd spend long hours on the phone with her ancient friend Kitty in Geneva, or with James Salter's expat daughter Nina, or with her dear Peter and Amy Bernstein in New York, or with Koukla MacLehose in London—Marie-Claude had friends everywhere. Koukla was French but working as an agent in London; she'd developed an early, visionary interest in Scandinavian authors. Her husband Christopher was a Scot, and one of the last independent publishers in England, the head of Harvill Press, publishing many of the previously untranslated authors whose books (like the popular Scandinavian thrillers) are read in every corner and in every airport of the Anglophone world.

MC's friendships encompassed as well the children of her friends, whom she'd quickly integrate into the ongoing drama of her life. Koukla's tall, handsome son from an earlier French husband was a cinematographer who was dubbed by MC "The Grand Duke" for his patrician looks (the "title" stuck). The two shared friendly drinks and jokes and stories, and he was often incorporated into her dinner evenings. MC was always anxious to meet the Grand Duke's latest girlfriend, or to discuss his fledgling career in the competitive and bustling Paris film industry. Her throaty Jeanne Moreau voice never changed register according to her interlocutor's age—MC was at home with any and every drop-in. In later years, Benjamin Moser, a prodigious young literary critic from Texas (and the prizewinning author of a biography of the Ukrainian-born surrealist Clarice Lispector, who emigrated as a baby to Brazil and began writing in Portuguese), was one of her closest friends. Ben left New York, where he'd been working as an editorial assistant at Knopf, to live in the Netherlands with not one but two older men, one of them a famous author. Now he's writing Susan Sontag's biography. MC was never competitive with her friends, never valued them as mere contacts, always was fascinated by the details of their lives.

Many of the American literary people passing through Paris spent an evening or two with MC and me. Louise Erdrich—the author, most famously then, of *The Beet Queen*—had been my student in a literature seminar at Johns Hopkins; she would always be accompanied to dinner with us by her husband, the writer Michael Dorris. There was something noble and tragic about Louise, I thought. She was an Ojibway from Minnesota, tall and lithe, young and sweet, and she seemed very close to her husband, who was also a Native American. We'd eat out, then stroll back along the boulevard Saint-Germain to MC's apartment. It always seemed to be cool out but not cold, a breeze was always blowing, and there was often a drizzle. Before meeting Louise, Michael had adopted as a single parent several "special needs" Native American children. Apparently one of his children had become so attached to an older retarded friend that when Louise and Michael decided to move the whole family to a ranch out West, the despairing boy had stepped in front of a car, preferring death to separation from his friend. Another time, while on a lonely book tour of America, I tried to phone them at their Minneapolis home but somehow suddenly couldn't reach them. Later it turned out that they had changed their phone number because another of the adopted kids was now a grown man who'd begun threatening and stalking them. Paradoxically, Louise and Michael seemed not only tragic but also blessed. In Paris, they were always holding hands. They were young and attractive and gifted; they even wrote a few books together. And then we discovered how weak our powers of observation were, or conversely how hidden were the private lives of our friends. Louise accused Michael of having abused her daughters. Then it was revealed that Michael wasn't an Indian at all but an Anglo posing as one. His supposed tribe had no record of him. And then the news came that he'd checked into a motel and killed himself.

Once MC and I had dinner after a reading with John Hawkes and his wife. Hawkes had just won a French literary prize for one of his recently translated novels, and I remember that MC and Hawkes were both gobbling their antipsychotic pills at the table. When I described the whole scene over the phone to her a while later, my mother said sagely, "If you're looking for normal people, there are millions and millions of them out there."

"Jack" Hawkes was a jolly, passionate man who approved of the extremes of desire in all its forms. He might have agreed with William Blake, who wrote, "Better to kill a baby in its crib than nurse an unacted desire." Hawkes was one of the few novelists who actively *admired* me for writing about sex. He was a truly passionate zealot, like John Brown, say, but his zeal was for experimental fiction and the world of the senses. Although he was a true New Englander—born in Connecticut, educated at Harvard, a professor at Brown for thirty years—he was an anti-Puritan, though he brought the same glittering-eyed fanaticism to his radicalism. He told us that he seldom read but that once a year his wife would read out loud a masterpiece such as *Moby-Dick* and then he'd write his own version. (I loved his strange, twisted novels and wondered what classic had triggered my favorite, *The Blood Oranges*.) He arranged for me to replace him as a professor of creative writing at Brown.

I would stop by MC's apartment late in the afternoon and she'd be in her bedroom. The big bed where she slept at night became her office by day. The bed was covered with a Chinese spread. The shelves along one wall were groaning under books, most of them old and in French, classics one might want to refer to. On the big desk and on the floor all around, under the desk, were piles of new books—the proofs she was reading and evaluating as a literary scout. MC would be propped up in the bed, smoking and drinking smoky Lapsang souchong tea.

This room, like the adjoining salon, was papered in gold squares that had dulled attractively and acquired a faintly green patina. Anne would be watering the dozens of plants; because she was obsessive-compulsive, she had to kneel beside the plants to make sure the moisture was seeping through, just as when she closed the front door, she had to stand and look at it for several minutes to make sure it was really closed.

Anne came once to pick up Marie-Claude from a party where most of the guests were arty lesbians, French and American, and they all swooned over Anne, whom they'd never seen before. It's true that she was a handsome person, with a somber charm, lightened from time to time by a deadpan humor that could easily be missed. Older people, her mother's age, who'd known her forever, were very fond of her; perhaps to them there was something eternal about the "young lady" of the house.

MC did all the shopping in lightning-fast visits to the open-air market over in the Place Maubert. I never went with her (I would have only slowed her down!) but I knew she had her speedy methods—she'd whisper to each merchant how much she wanted of each thing and then swoop back in five minutes to collect it and pay for it, unless she'd been allowed to a run a tab.

When I sat beside her in the afternoon sipping tea, I would often be privy to her phone conversations, which were as slow and thorough and repetitious as her shopping was swift. My own telephone style was brisk and terse when I couldn't avoid talking on the phone altogether (I was really meant for instant messaging, though my fingers are too clumsy). I was amazed that MC immediately assumed that other people would be so interested in the details of her triumphs and defeats, which they were. She ended a conversation most often with the Italian words *"Avanti, popolo!"* ("Onward, people!"—the opening words of a Communist song, "La Bandiera Rossa").

When her Scottish friend Suzy was going through a messy divorce, MC was capable of listening to the details for hours. Without espousing the language of feminism for a moment, she at least subscribed in silent practice to the idea that sisterhood is powerful. Her friends confided in her and were, in turn, treated to her confidences. I would have feared boring people with the minutiae of my life, although I knew as a novelist that a story becomes involving only once it takes on flesh. I recognized that in all the most exciting prose there was a constant pressure to describe, narrate, recount, and that the syntax was always buckling under the weight of squirming details.

MC's sister, Thérèse, lived on the rue de la Grande Chaumière just off the boulevard du Montparnasse in an artist's studio. Thérèse's husband was a sculptor whose art consisted of stacking green squares of glass one upon another. Occasionally he had a show, and occasionally his dealer sold a piece. The government had bought a large piece for a rest stop on the autoroute not far from Paris. Thérèse had a daughter who taught yoga and a son who was a photographer, so MC worried about all of them. The husband was terribly melancholy about his lackluster career. As a journalist, I'd known many rich, famous artists. I understood, however, that most working artists in every country were poor and unrecognized, even in France.

MC's mother was an amateur artist painting modest realistic scenes. MC owned one from their Mexican years, and I wondered if MC supported every family member to some extent. Until the death of her mother's sister, both of the old women had lived on the aptly named rue de Paradis, seldom going out. MC's mother shopped and cooked and waited on her sister, who was bedridden. MC could never specify what was wrong with her, who she said was *"très, très malade."* Like MC, the two older women lived on homeopathic medicines, mysterious sugar pills that melted under their tongues, which specialist "physicians" administered. And although almost everything about the French health system was admirable—so many Italians headed for the great cancer hospital at Villejuif that the operators answered in Italian—there were a few things about it and the French public's attitude toward disease that were maddening. It used to be, for example, that doctors and patients alike seldom pronounced the word "cancer."

Chapter 7

Ned Rorem, the American composer, came to Paris. I had known Ned for ten years in New York and, like many gay men of my generation, had read his *Paris Diary*. After the war and well into the 1950s Ned had lived in Paris, kept by Marie-Laure, the Vicomtesse de Noailles. She'd died in 1970, long before I arrived in Paris, but among old gay Parisian men Marie-Laure was still famous for her wealth and taste and eccentricities. In fact, these same men constantly discussed "Marie-Laure" and "Marie-Hélène" (de Rothschild). Marie-Hélène de Rothschild was still alive then, but she'd moved to New York, whereas to her dying day Marie-Laure had lived off the Champs-Élysées in a huge modern house on the place des États-Unis. The house was known for its splendor, its cuisine, its Goyas, and its salons designed by Jean-Michel Frank, the walls lined with squares of white fawn leather and the little side tables covered with split straws under clear lacquer. Her husband, the vicomte, turned out to be gay. Marie-Laure was most certainly the most celebrated "fag hag" of high culture and seemed to have been enamored of the beautiful young Ned, whom she dubbed "Miss Sly." Her lover was a sexy but heavy-drinking Spanish painter who did Picasso rip-offs. She had herself buried beside him, not her husband.

Everyone in Paris now talked about Marie-Laure as if she were still alive—her amusingly cruel sallies at dinner, her patronage of truly great artists including Buñuel, Cocteau, Dalí. Marie-Laure had begged Ned not to tell in writing that they'd never slept together, but in the first of his diaries, *The Paris Diary*—a bit of a cad—he reported that very detail. Ned's legendary beauty had been idolized by everyone, including the eminent composer Francis Poulenc; Ned had always claimed that he didn't "get it"—since, as he wrote, "I'm not my own type."

Having left Paris for New York and Nantucket summers (both settings for his later diaries) a long time ago, Ned would return to Paris every ten years in order to declare once again that Paris was *finished*— the way an angler might say of a lake that it was fished out. In the same way, his old acquaintance James Lord (who'd returned to Paris after trying America, again, for a few years) would announce that Venice and Rome were finished. Maybe in Paris mythic figures such as Picasso, Corbusier, Matisse, Giacometti, Gide, Genet, and Poulenc had all passed on, but there were still world-renowned filmmakers around, like André Téchiné, Alain Resnais, and Éric Rohmer; the architects Jean Nouvel and Christian de Portzamparc; the brilliant writers Emmanuel Carrère, Jean Echenoz, and René de Ceccatty; and celebrated couturiers such as Azzedine Alaïa, Hubert de Givenchy, and Yves Saint Laurent. Because Paris was no longer a world capital—due to a loss of financial and military might—its artists were no longer universally esteemed. Surely it was no accident that the all-powerful Louis XIV had been able to consecrate "his" playwrights Molière and Racine—or his architect Mansard or his gardener Le Nôtre. Fame in the arts accompanies world domination: America at its postwar height had even been able to sell such an intrinsically unappealing school of painting as Abstract Expressionism and make it a worldwide movement.

Yet even now Ned talked and wrote about Marie-Laure constantly (his memoir *Lies*, for which I wrote the introduction, has the best portrait of her in words). James Lord also wrote about her in less intimate, more acerbic terms in one of his many personal remembrances, *Six Exceptional Women*. There he told a story, one he recounted numerous times to friends as well, about how back in the fifties an American general had brought his wife from Kansas to Paris, where they had been invited to one of Marie-Laure's dinners. The general had befriended Marie-Laure after the liberation in 1944. At the table, the wife apparently said they were on their way to Italy with stopovers in Rome, Florence, and Venice; everything had been arranged by American Express. "What!" Marie-Laure exclaimed, grabbing a silver serving spoon. "And not Bologna? You must go to Bologna, where they teach you how to give the best blow jobs. You must lick it all over like this," and she proceeded to fellate the spoon. The couple grew darkly silent and took their leave early. Bernard Minoret, an extremely cultured Parisian who'd been James Lord's lover in the forties, intended to write Marie-Laure's biography, but somehow he was blocked as a writer. Bernard's portrait, to my mind, would have been the best one, since Bernard was disabused but compassionate and had two great writerly gifts—curiosity and memory.

At a party Bernard gave for Ned, Bernard introduced me to James Lord and many of the younger gay or bisexual writers and intellectuals who gathered around the older ones, and I instantly felt that this would be one of my circles of close friends in Paris.

In his day Bernard had known everyone and was still the paragon of kindness, generosity, and continual mental brilliance. He took me to meet the actress Arletty, and on the way a Romanian beggar, his barefoot daughter on his shoulder, handed us a plea for help written in bad French (perhaps someone else wrote it for him). Bernard pulled out a hundred dollars and gave it to him ("There is a chance in a hundred he really is in need," he explained). Arletty, who lived in public housing behind the Maison de la Radio, was entertaining three ancient actresses from the Comédie Française, and they were attended by an adoring fan, whom she called "Figaro." She had been a movie star; her 1945 film *Les Enfants du Paradis* was recently voted best film ever by six hundred French film critics. But she'd had an affair with a German during the war and afterward been convicted of collaboration, though she famously defended herself: "My heart is France's. My ass is my own." When I met her she was blind; years before she'd grabbed the wrong eye drops. We guided her to a neighborhood restaurant, where there was a special table reserved for her, decorated with a copy of her memoirs and a rose in a vase.

Because he was blocked as a writer, even at his great age Bernard was seeing a shrink, hoping to overcome his inhibition. His problem, he complained, was that he couldn't bear a writer's solitude. Still, he'd written a successful play about the salons of the past with a young collaborator, Claude Arnaud (who later became a formidable Cocteau biographer), two books of pastiche with Philippe Jullian, and screenplays with his friend Jacques Fieschi.

Marie-Laure would have been a difficult subject for a biography, one that perhaps only Bernard could have breathed life into—because she fought no wars, signed no treaties, and left nothing of personal material interest behind. The most elusive biographies are of people who've done nothing but shape a whole era as patrons or tastemakers merely through the power of their personalities and sensibilities—people like Misia Sert, the great patron of the Ballets Russes. With his total recall and his vivid apprehension of the nuances of social reality, Bernard could have recreated, for instance, Marie-Laure's style of dinner conversation in all its wickedness and erudition without making her sound like a complete monster.

Physically, Bernard was tall and bald and had a comical rubber mask of a face. When he went out he was always beautifully, tastefully, and conservatively dressed.

Bernard was the last of his line and an only child. He had inherited extensive forests that he'd since sold off and a considerable fortune he'd dissipated, or "dilapidated," as the French put it. I used to say that every time you went to his apartment, he'd sold another Hubert Robert painting so that for another six months he could invite his likable band of layabouts out to dinner for another month. As a true old-fashioned Parisian, Bernard would never go Dutch. He was always the host.

When Bernard died in 1983, his obituary by the writer Benôit Duteatre said, "He had made of his residence in the seventh arrondissement of Paris the last of those salons where several generations of artists met . . ." The article was titled "Bernard Minoret, writer and dandy."

Of course, Bernard knew many of the older rich women of his generation. One of them, learning that he was being booted out of the impressive duplex where he'd been living for years, gave him a six-room apartment in a building she owned. Another lady, a Rothschild, famous for her vast knowledge, "invited" him, in the French sense (all expenses paid), to accompany her and other titled ladies to Saint Petersburg. Typical of him, Bernard read thirty books on the city and convinced a curator he knew at the Musée d'Orsay to arrange a private, guided visit of the Hermitage. They stayed at the best hotel. We were never introduced to these women, though the possibility was sometimes dangled before us. Bernard liked to "compartmentalize," as Americans say—but why? Was he afraid these ladies would be scared off by the overwhelming proof that he wasn't just an eternal bachelor, a perennially unattached escort? Although they were too discreet to mention anything as tacky as homosexuality, one of them, the American-born Ethel de Croisset, broke her silence long enough to phone me for advice when her butler was diagnosed with AIDS. Ethel was such a fascinating woman—she never said anything you could predict. She was a serious archeologist and went on digs. She bought Matisses and Giacomettis right out of the artists' studios. She was always driving herself about Paris in search of culture in her little car and with her badly fitting contacts. She had been born a Woodward; it was her brother who was murdered by his wife. The wife pretended she had thought he was a thief and shot him in self-defense. The dead man's parents backed up her story because they didn't want their grandchildren to have a convicted murderer as a mother. Truman Capote related it all in a chapter of *Answered Prayers*; the day after that chapter came out in *Esquire* Mrs. Woodward committed suicide.

Or did Bernard fear that one of us would replace him as *cavalier servant*? Bernard never regarded women as a bore, the way his friend James Lord did. Usually when I tried to bring James and MC together for dinner, he'd say, "Oh, let's not have a complicated, formal evening. Let's just be *en famille!*"—which to him meant no women. MC was relaxed and homey; she didn't know how to sparkle in society. And though she and Bernard would have been able to talk books, he would never spend a whole evening with her. Which was particularly galling, because Bernard was a close friend of MC's longtime friend, my French editor Ivan Nabokoff's wife Claude.

I did once have a long lunch on James's upper deck on new white-canvas-covered chairs under a fresh white awning before a view of Paris with two women, Lauren Bacall and the fashion goddess Hélène Rochas ("She is *une idole*," as Bernard carefully explained to me). I preferred the silence of Rochas and her good-guy companionability over the strident charms of Bacall. Bacall was, however, the star of one of my favorite films, *Key Largo* (and no Parisian would ever permit himself to be thought ignorant of such a silver-screen masterpiece). When the film first came out, my chemical-equipment-broker father had parked me the entire day in a theater in Charleston, West Virginia, while he went around on his business appointments. My father's business day was long, and I sat through the movie four times before he came to retrieve me. Now, I kept trying to recover Bacall's iconic slender body and huge eyes beneath the loud, opinionated harridan in front of me.

I suspected that James thought MC was too dowdy and unimportant to occupy such a large part of my affections, which naturally I resented.

Bernard took me to meet Amyn Aga Khan, who seemed like a nice, regular, tall Harvard grad and businessman. He lived in a lavish *hotel particulier* behind the Musée d'Orsay. Amyn owned a real estate development along the Costa Smeralda, in Sardinia, but he appeared humble and cozily collegial until the servant took our drinks order and said, "And Your Majesty?" Then I remembered that Amyn's older brother was worshipped by millions of Ismaili Muslims. He was Rita Hayworth's stepson.

I had met the king and queen of Sweden when I interviewed them at the Drottningholm Palace. I didn't have to bow, but I did have to present my questions in advance. Everything was regulated by a female protocol officer—even the hotel I had to stay in. The king looked out at the dying trees in the park and said he couldn't replace them because he was the poorest monarch in Europe. He said he was a feminist and had decided that his firstborn child would inherit the throne regardless of gender. The firstborn was a girl and is the princess royal, though he has a younger son. (Later I discovered it was parliament, not the king, that had ultimately determined the succession.)

The queen showed me the charming opera theater she said had been "benignly" forgotten for a century. They still had the original lighting—candles were stacked on cylinders that could be turned to raise or dim the illumination—and original sets by the Bibiena brothers. That night they were doing Salieri's *Don Giovanni*, as opposed to Mozart's more famous version.

When we left the private quarters for the public museum, Queen Silvia (who'd originally come from Heidelberg and worked variously as an Olympic educational hostess, flight attendant, and language interpreter—she spoke six different languages, including sign language), said, "Here we go, it's show-business time!" I thought no royal born and bred would have said something so playful.

Bernard, who never had the catalog of aristocratic European lineages (the *Almanach de Gotha*) far from his reach, liked women. But his women were kept, as I suggested before, in a separate compartment— just as his sex life was. Once I dropped by in the afternoon to deliver a book I'd promised him and discovered a handsome Moroccan ironing Bernard's shorts. If I got it right, the young man was the same sort of youth who, in Parisian lore, made love to monsieur and at the same time was a trusted family retainer who prepared little at-home meals— *un homme à tout faire.*

Bernard devoured books the way other people ate croissants—one or two daily. There were stacks of books on every surface. Did he read in the afternoon, or late at night, after everyone had gone home? He read everything about the Mitfords—in fact, one of the women I met at his house was Charlotte Mosley, who was married to the son of the English fascist Diana Mosley, herself a Mitford sister; Charlotte was the editor of a collection of letters between Nancy Mitford and Evelyn Waugh.

He knew everything about the seventeenth-century salons and gave expert advice to Benedetta Craveri, the granddaughter of the philosopher Benedetto Croce and the wife of the French ambassador to Prague—and the author of a good study of conversation. Bernard is acknowledged in her book as well as in many others, including my biography of Genet. Bernard was also an expert about Napoleon and he'd read all the memoirs relating to that period, but then again what did he not know? Whenever a subject came up—Japanese prints, Robert Wilson's plays, or the poetry of "Edgar Poe," as the French called Edgar Allan Poe—Bernard had the last word on all due to his sixty-one years of uninterrupted reading. He was always prepared to deliver a dictum. He said, for instance, that Poe was no good except as translated by Baudelaire. Japanese prints had been good until spoiled by aniline dyes. Robert Wilson was a great opera director, but his own plays were tedious.

Bernard twisted coquettishly in his chair and wondered aloud how I might portray him. Like many, he ascribed superhuman powers of observation to novelists, not to mention a vicious misanthropy. He assumed that I was always taking notes, but in fact I was far too lazy to start scribbling when I got home at midnight. Bernard was the one who was observant and generous. When you said something mildly clever, he held a hand up and called out, "Did you hear the witty thing that Edmund just said?" Then he'd repeat it—as Madame du Deffand might have repeated something Horace Walpole had said. Bernard was a bit like Charlus in Proust, a complex, bristly, adorable character.

Who were the members of Bernard's salon? One was Jacques Fieschi, a successful writer of film scenarios who was also an amateur boxer (he had the smashed-in nose to prove it). Jacques had been Bernard's lover for many years, then fell for Claude Arnaud. Rather than losing Jacques in a fit of jealousy, Bernard decided to "take the couple" and so he moved Claude in. In that way he was like Cocteau, who, learning that his longtime lover—the much younger movie star Jean Marais—had fallen for a lifeguard, Paul Morihen, set his rival up in business as the proprietor of a bookstore downstairs from his apartment in the Palais-Royal, thereby extending his family by one member rather than diminishing it to zero.

Claude was a lean, gangly young man who sprawled like an American rather than sitting up, all limbs neatly tucked in, like a Frenchman. The American way of sprawling (which is caricatured in the first woodblocks of Commodore Perry's sailors in mid-nineteenth-century Japan) is, I suppose, more suited to America's wide-open plains than Europe's crowded, pinched salons. I remember asking two French friends what had most struck them most after their first hours in New York and they said, "How floppy everyone is in this city. The careless, reckless way they career down the sidewalk—they'd be considered crazy in France, or arrested. They're not *contained*."

Claude wasn't crazy, but his legs were too long and his clothes too tight. And he didn't mind slumping down in his chair, even when he was holding up a finger in objection. His body language suggested he was sure of himself. Though he wasn't conventionally handsome, he was lean and sexy, and because he was such a human pretzel his body was always in the forefront of our minds. Which reminds me of the pronouncement Bernard made about my lover Michael in his presence: *"Tu n'es pas beau, mais très sexe."* Needless to say, it didn't flatter Michael being told that he was sexy but not handsome. That sort of "objectification" of someone in front of you was something Americans instinctively avoided, though it was an impertinence privileged Europeans indulged in. I remember a celebrated woman painter and her movie star husband once discussing in front of me whether I was intelligent or not (they couldn't make up their minds about that conundrum).

Another regular in Bernard's salon was Arnaud Deschamps, an elegant young aristocrat who was always impeccably dressed, seldom spoke, and whenever addressed smiled shyly. He made a meager living dealing in antiques while anticipating a giant settlement in his favor, one that was delayed year after year. He'd had an aunt in the south of France who'd willed him her Murillo, a Spanish masterpiece. But she'd taken as a lover a very tough younger woman and she changed her will in her favor. Once the aunt had died, the younger woman sold the Murillo to the Louvre in a reputedly prearranged deal, and Arnaud had little chance of winning.

In France the institutions always won out. Decades before, a woman had been accused of murdering her first husband, an art dealer, Paul Guillaume, then later her second husband, Jean Walter, an architect. It was Jean Walter's son, frightened for his own life, who lodged the accusations, but Madame went to André Malraux, the minister of culture, and ironed out a deal. If all charges were dropped, she would leave her entire collection of paintings to the state, upwards of a billion dollars' worth of canvases: ten Cézannes, twenty-three Renoirs, twelve Picassos, ten Matisses, twenty-two Soutines, twenty-seven Derains. She drove a hard bargain and was allowed to retain ownership of the paintings until her own death in 1977, at the age of seventy-nine. By then the

Soutines and Derains had fallen out of fashion, but that still left a number of undeniably great works, and her collection now hangs in the Orangerie.

Our typical evenings chez Bernard started with my arrival at eight thirty; being American I was always on time, and for nearly an hour I would enjoy an entertaining, exclusive audience with Bernard. The others, being French, would drift in at nine or even nine thirty. Coming to one of my evenings, MC obeyed French time, which made me furious if I was cooking. I usually planned on a half hour for drinks before going to the table. She eventually reformed, or at least was always sure to have a good excuse. (No wonder so many French hosts warm up meals, often picked up from the downstairs caterers, at the last moment in their microwave ovens.) More and more she was putting in long hours up in her studio assembling her boxes. "I was working!" she would say importantly. Then, wide-eyed, she would assure everyone who'd been waiting on her that they had no idea how exhausted she was.

When we were all at Bernard's and the others were well watered with champagne, we'd go out to a neighborhood restaurant for green salad followed by a duck confit, a single perfect vegetable, and a chocolate marquise, the whole thing accompanied by generous pours of red wine at Bernard's expense.

The French seldom drank after the wine was cleared away with the meal—wine is a food, not a conversation enabler to be poured hours after the dinner. Since I didn't drink at all, I found American-style drunks like James Lord annoying, with their precarious walk and their repetitious remarks, a terrible bore, to use the word he himself hurled at his own pet peeves as the evening wore on and he became more and more inebriated.

After dinner and lively conversation, often about Bernard's reading or something Claude or Jacques was writing, we'd saunter back to Bernard's salon, which was decorated with family antiques and 1830 portraits of two brothers, his ancestors. Claude had already begun his biography of Cocteau, whom Bernard and James had known personally. Bernard retained a strong sense of the period and alliances back then and could indicate the exact emphasis Claude should give to

Cocteau's so-called "collaboration" with the Nazis or his long, troubled friendship with Picasso. I was very surprised and touched when Claude dedicated his Cocteau biography to me. I took the dedication seriously and longed to "protect" the book. I arranged for Yale University Press to publish it in English and coedited an anthology of Cocteau's English-language writing to come out at the same time. In a similar way, Bernard helped me with the nuances of Parisian gay life in the 1940s for my biography of Genet, which I was working on from 1986 to 1992.

Or Jacques Flesch: would tell us about his sexual adventures (*histoires de cul*, "ass stories") or his latest dealings with the world of film. Jacques worked regularly with the actress and director Nicole Garcia, who invited me to a large buffet dinner with the English actress Kristin Scott Thomas—who, living in Paris full time, was perfectly bilingual and married at that time to a French gynecologist. Nicole Garcia was a glamorous, middle-aged woman living in an apartment in a cul-de-sac in the seventh arrondissement, near the Italian embassy. Though the apartment wasn't large, it felt big because of its many windows, through which we could watch Kristin Scott Thomas bicycling home. Women liked Jacques because he was so masculine—at once unavailable and courtly, though courtly not like a major-domo but like a baron. What always struck me about this thick man with the dark chest hair sprouting above his shirt and the Mediterranean good looks—the sort of man who'd probably smell if he didn't take two showers a day—were his refinement and intelligence, which had naturally led him to Bernard, who was more intelligent than us all, though considerably older and deemed handsome only by courtesy. I felt that I'd been slow in maturing and launching my career because I'd always been attracted to younger men, whereas Jacques (while sleeping with Claude or younger ethnic guys) had moved in for years with Bernard. From him Jacques had acquired the astonishing "general culture" that was fully evidenced in his very original script *Un Coeur en hiver* (in which, it was said, he dramatized his own emotional frigidity). The hero, played by Daniel Auteuil, encounters a beautiful young woman, played by Emmanuelle Béart, who falls for him and makes him a declaration of love that he rejects—brutally, and improbably.

Had Jacques been transposing his own story into heterosexual terms? I'd heard that he'd rejected Claude after a long affair in just such a cruel and abrupt way. (In fact, the story made it into one of Claude's autobiographical novels.) In all the years I knew him, Jacques—who was so desirable as a sensitive, virile man, rich from his family as well as from his own métier, with brilliant social connections—was almost always alone except for friends like Bernard and the occasional "adventure."

Meanwhile, Claude was bisexual. After Jacques rejected him, he took up for a time with Anne Fontaine, the film director, and later he married Geneviève, a stunning Haitian woman who was obviously *une métisse*, with pale skin, blond highlights, and light eyes (from the Dutch side of her ancestry, she explained). She and Claude had met in Haiti at a dance club and he'd invited her to stay with him the next time she visited Paris. Having perhaps assumed that Claude would be a sexless gay pal, she was astonished to find herself making love with him all night, no doubt believing like many of us that gay meant 100 percent homosexual.

Perhaps such men required very bold women. Was that the Duchess of Windsor's secret?

Chapter 8

I met a young man I'll call "Brice"—one of the most important men in my life—at a party that James Lord gave. Brice is alive and well in Paris and has become one of the leading furniture designers in France, regularly showing his one-of-a-kind pieces at a prestigious gallery. His work is very playful, like him. He'll have a chimney above a fireplace shaped like a giraffe's neck. Or a red and green velvet settee resembling a rose, complete with plush green stems and carefully elaborated red velvet petals. Or a bronze vase that can be turned vase side up for a bouquet, or reversed when you have no bouquet except for the sculpted metal flowers on which it rests when it's ready to receive real flowers.

Brice had been the boyfriend of Gilles Roy-Lord, James Lord's official lover, heir, and adopted son. Their affair was long since over—and I couldn't believe this charming little guy with the light-brown hair the French call "blond," blue eyes, and aristocratic nasal tones was coming on to me. He was at least twenty years younger than I was—a mere twenty-one or twenty-two—and at the time was working a dull insurance job he wanted to quit so he could become an artist.

I realized that I was of secondary interest to him at the party. He was primarily drawn to a tall, lean, balding man with a sepulchral voice who'd once been a model. They fooled around on the stairs leading up to the roof garden. Though his target was obviously turned on, he was inhibited no doubt by the presence of his handsome, talented, long-term lover.

Brice was a small, merry guy. He often looked in the mirror and said, *"Quelle sale gueule!"* ("What a dirty mug!"), which meant not filthy but sallow.

He'd grown up in Lyons, where he'd attended deb parties called *rallyes*. He liked to emphasize how wild they were—how the boys would tear the girls' pretty frocks and everyone ended up drenched and drunk in the pool. Typical preppy hijinks, and one of the highlights of his life. We dated twice and had dinner conversation and I wondered if such a cute guy would ever go to bed with me. But after the second date, in the taxi he said, *"Tu exaggères!"* ("You're going too far!") and invited me in.

Very soon we'd fallen into a routine. We were very verbal. Our sex sessions usually followed a dinner I'd cook, or I'd invite him to a restaurant.

I introduced him to a few young people I'd met, among them Frédéric, a young psychiatrist and novelist who lived with his parents, or rather up in the maid's room that went with their large, luxurious apartment on the boulevard du Montparnasse. Frédéric was a small, perfectly formed young man, and hairless. He professed to be a fan of my first novel, *Forgetting Elena,* but thought that every book I'd brought out since then was an artistic failure. He himself wrote a strange novel that took place in a village in Normandy and involved the ritual murder of a Christ-like man. He dedicated it to me. How difficult it was for people to get published in the States, but in France the publishers put out hundreds of first novels during the *rentrée*—the period of "return" in September from the August vacation—hoping they'd win a prize later in the fall, even though everyone knew that the prizes were rigged by the three major Paris publishing houses. I once told a judge of the Prix Médicis or the Prix Femina that the judges for the Booker Prize in England changed every year, and he nodded and said that that was commendable but excessive.

I liked Frédéric intensely and couldn't have been more stunned when one night at dinner he looked me in the eye and said, "You know, Edmond, you're really very stupid."

I burst into tears, not because I thought what he was saying was either true or false but because I was shocked by his cruelty. I never did figure out why he turned on me.

Christine was a beautiful young blonde I'd met at the gym, an affectionate girl who looked like the actress Sandrine Bonnaire. Christine was friends with an up-and-coming screen actress who'd willed herself into losing weight and carefully adjusted her look in order to become a major beauty. Her transformation from a chubby dumpling into a sleek contender was miraculous; I was used to girls making New Year's resolutions they promptly broke. What was unusual was this iron will to change and the complete transformation it wrought. She was also a funny and excellent mimic.

In those days, sex dates in the gay world were made on telephone party lines. We taught her to call out, *"Bouffeur de cul cherche cul"* ("Ass eater is looking for an ass") over a gay party line and she said it in the voice of a raw teenage boy from the suburbs. Since the rich live mostly in the old center city, the historic part, it turns out the suburbs or *banlieux* are where the poor live in projects or HLM (*habitations loyers modéré,* or "average-rent residences"). Soon she had an ass that wanted to be rimmed on the line and she whispered to us she didn't know how to get off the call. We said she should say "his" parents had just walked in downstairs and he had to hang up.

And yet I don't think she approved of our jesting and loose morals. She seemed very straitlaced to me. Christine, by contrast, was game for anything. She lived on the rue de Caire in Paris's garment district with Douglas Freeman, a gay Ohioan who was a personal trainer and masseur (the two professions most commonly open to undocumented Americans). Once Christine was flirting with a cute boy who lived opposite beside a building decorated with sphinxes. She was coyly standing in her window and wiggling her fingers at him when Douglas (we pronounced his name "Doo-gloss" *à la française*) held up a dildo, pink and as long as his arm, behind her and above her head and pointed down at her as if she were its owner. The boy hastily drew his shades.

Christine had a father but otherwise everyone in her family was female: her mother and two sisters and many cousins and nieces and eventually her daughter. She was from Tours, the home of reputedly the best French accent. Because her parents were both retired teachers, she spoke with a clarity dear to every foreigner's heart.

And although she was a head-turning beauty herself—blonde, blue-eyed, fairly tall, and slender, with a beautiful, full bosom and a sweet smile—she was indifferent to the way men looked, or rather she could overlook ugliness if it was offset by charm or intelligence or talent. Her first love when she was seventeen had been a much older screen actor renowned for his ugliness. Later she lived with a man for many years who was exceedingly plain and blunt, even obtuse, and known for his bad manners. But he was an esteemed director and was the first to adapt a novel by Michel Houellebecq, who became his friend; the two men were similarly difficult socially.

After this director left her, I introduced Christine to a handsome young aristocrat I knew in Geneva, Vladimir de Marsano, who had a Serbian mother and an Italian father but who "lived" in French. I'd first met Vladimir years before while he was having an affair with a beautiful older woman, a titled divorcée who headed the Save Venice Committee (her office was the throne room of Napoleon's appointed king of Venice). Because of Vladimir's affair with Maria Theresa Ruben, I assumed he was heterosexual and I felt confident about introducing Christine to him. Admittedly, Vladimir was vague about his personal life. But with his glowing green eyes and slender body, a slight scar from a harelip repaired at birth, his seductive baritone voice, and his unwavering smile, Vladimir was irresistible, and soon Christine was sufficiently under his spell.

But then, as we were sitting with Vladimir and "Doo-gloss" at an outdoor café in Geneva, Douglas's sexy Spanish lover came gliding by on his bicycle. Vladimir looked intensely embarrassed and a minute later excused himself for the evening. The lover, Javier, later told us that Vladimir had often hired him to pee into his mouth. I refused to believe the story and Christine was furious with me: "So that's your idea of a genuine heterosexual!"

My little Brice was an antic soul, so funny and cute. He liked to give theme parties. When he repainted the toilet he gave a *soirée chiottes* (a "crapper evening") where we ate chocolate pudding and used toilet paper for napkins. He liked bad European pop music, the songs sung by Princess Stéphanie and Dalida and Claude François, and once had a dance evening, a *soirée ringarde* (a "tacky evening"). One of our crew was a boy named Hubert, whose patron saint Hubert was the saint of the hunt, so on his saint's day (November 3) I gave a venison dinner party with little ceramic stags on the table and hired someone to blow the hunting horn in full costume (I'd spotted him busking on a nearby bridge). The horn busker slipped in unnoticed and emerged from the bedroom in full regalia, tooting away his deafening, lugubrious tones.

Brice worked, as I mentioned, for an insurance company, which probably pleased his conservative parents. He had a buttoned-down brother whom he called "Old Cock" whereas his brother called him "Big Cock," but when I dared to use one of these nicknames in private it rubbed him the wrong way. Brice had a strong if weird sense of propriety. When I would give dinner parties to amuse him he would always have to leave with the other guests, then come back a half hour later. Was he afraid to be considered gay? My boyfriend?

He knew that I hadn't had a drink since 1982 (only four years then), and this prohibition infuriated (or maybe tempted) him. One night he decided to be my "master" and to order me around (I was very cooperative and excited). Among other things, he ordered me to drink a half bottle of red wine. I did. No alcoholic consequences.

While he was still working for the insurance company, he did large gloomy paintings that I praised excessively. Before long he decided to take advantage of one of the many government perks that existed under Mitterrand. If an office worker went back to school to learn new skills, the state paid him a stipend and full tuition for two years. Brice went to a furniture school and learned how to design and craft furniture.

We went to Syria with my translator Marc Cholodenko and his mistress, Annabelle d'Huart, who was the wife of Ricardo Bofill, the Catalan architect. Annabelle spoke like a ten-year-old girl, in an absurdly high baby-doll voice. She was a designer of household objects and hated it when magazines linked her name to Bofill, as if her creations couldn't stand on their own (I'd made that mistake in an article I'd written just to please her). She'd studied art in Florence, photography in New York, and design in Barcelona with Bofill. She worked as a photographer, a jewelry and office furniture designer, and a model—and even at an advanced age she was on the runway for Yohji Yamamoto, the same year another model was sent home for gaining five pounds. She eventually wrote two books, one on harems and one on Bofill's atelier— yes, despite her irritation at being identified with him.

I was delegated to go to the Syrian embassy in Paris to secure visas for all four of us. Filling out official forms always intimidated me, all the more so in French. All of us were so apolitical and we so seldom read the newspaper that we had no idea that Syria (already, in the eighties) was a trouble spot. When I was filling out my own visa form, I modestly gave as my profession "journalist" instead of "novelist." I was immediately sent to the ambassador himself, who asked, "Don't you know what we do to Western journalists? We're already holding several of them hostage."

I asked him what I should fill in and he replied, *"Cadre"*—an ambiguous designation for a general employee.

We were clueless as to why the Air France flight to Damascus was half empty and, upon our arrival, the Meridian Hotel was completely empty. In the hotel restaurant, we could order a kilo of Caspian caviar for a few dollars.

In the covered market I bought a heavy ankle-length wool overcoat, blue on the outside and gold within, the whole closed with a big leather belt. I had seen grizzled peasants wearing it riding their motorbikes and admired it. We went to the nearby Umayyad Mosque, on the site of a former Christian church, where the head of John the Baptist was supposedly buried.

On our way out of the mosque a handsome sheik, with a handlebar mustache and a posse of thugs, grabbed Brice's hand and made to abduct him, undoubtedly spirit him off to his harem where he'd tranquilize him on drugged sherbets. To Brice's regret, I tugged on his other hand, trying to keep my pretty boyfriend. The sheik was soon laughing at the situation and melted into the crowd instantly. Annabelle, considered a great beauty in Paris, was miffed to be passed over in favor of Brice. The fact was that she was too skinny, what the French call "too dry" (*seche*), to appeal to Levantine tastes.

We visited the ancient hammam beside a still more ancient fortress. In the hammam all the fixtures and walls were of veined marble. We also walked through the Azem Palace, now a museum but once the governor of Damascus's elegant mansion.

In our rented car, we drove to Homs, lately the site of so much bloodshed. Even then the people looked frightened and cowed. Although older Syrians could speak French (Syria had been a French possession between the wars), they all seemed reluctant to talk to us, as if they might be tortured afterward. We visited a water mill, but there were few other points of touristic interest. Homs had recently been repressed by the first Assad, whose photographic portrait hung from every lamppost. The only thing up to international standards was the highways, no doubt to facilitate the transport of troops. Most working-men were in uniform, and I remembered Genet's pleasant experiences in the thirties in Syria with boys. He'd had an affair with a boy hair-dresser, his first ever that was accompanied by any affection. All the old men playing games in cafés had teased them. Now the cabdrivers in Damascus knew just enough English to ask you if you were married, and if you said no, they turned toward you from the steering wheel indicating their erections.

A young professor of French was sent to accompany us as we went through the Grand Bazaar at Aleppo. He was our guide all day and into the evening. He invited us to his apartment to drink tea and buy carpets. My French friends all said no, they didn't want rugs, but I felt sorry for him and bought a small carpet woven by "Christians in the desert—see the crosses!"

In Aleppo, Annabelle decided we should stay in Shepherd's Hotel because Lawrence of Arabia used to frequent it. The man at the front desk had waxed the long hairs growing from his ears. They stood out in sharp points six inches on either side. We were bitten alive by bedbugs and the next night stayed in a new, deserted, expensive hotel called the Pullman.

We went to the Krak des Chevaliers, a castle built by the Crusaders.

We took another trip to Palmyra, in those days an almost perfectly intact ruin from ancient times. Then, although we had rented our car in Paris for both Syria and Jordan, we were told that we had to abandon it in Damascus. When I became angry about the unexpected change the Hertz man said cheerfully over the phone, "You will always be welcome in Syria." I sputtered, and he repeated, "You will always be welcome in Syria." It reminded me of the matronly volunteer guides at Monticello in Virginia herding along dull, uninterested school kids and obese laggardly tourists by saying, "Thank you. *Thank you.*"

And then it turned out we had to take an expensive taxi to the Jordanian border, wait three hours to pass through immigration, and hire another taxi to Amman—where we rented a new car for Petra. Annabelle was game, but usually French tourists are spoilsports who puff out their cheeks, ever bothered by the weather, and exclaim, "*Ouf! Il fait chaud!*" ("It's hot!") Or, conversely, "*Il fait froid.*" ("It's cold.") Or they'll change their restaurant table five times to avoid the dreaded draft, *un courant d'air*. And you can count on them, like Americans, but unlike the English, to comment on every hardship or inconvenience along the way. Spicy or sweet food they detest. They'll even pay extra for a special insurance that will reimburse them for a vacation spoiled by unseasonable or inclement weather. Brice didn't seem to understand that Americans admire stoicism and sportsmanlike behavior in others—even if we can't always rise to the occasion. On the other hand, when it comes to dying no one is better equipped or less whiny than the French. It's a role they've been rehearsing their whole lives. I'm sorry if that sounds cynical; it's meant to be admiring.

In Syria, Brice and I had lots of sex, but he was always worried we'd be detected by the chambermaids, or by Marc and Annabelle. His sense of discretion—a quality much admired in France—seemed excessive to me. But this was a minor quibble, and Petra astonished us all.

And then one day, back in Paris, Brice announced he was leaving me for a rich man, a famous interior decorator who owned a historic castle near Giverny and decorated apartments for rich Arabs on the place Vendôme (in the bathrooms, rubies for the hot water tap, sapphires for the cold). It really was very Balzacian, Brice's move up in the world.

Soon he was vacationing in Udaipur and was the proud possessor of Bonnard's studio (in a walled community next to the Montmartre cemetery), where he set about fulfilling his dream of designing original furniture. He came back from one trip to India with the bust of a Sikh notable; I asked him to make a plaster copy of it for my Knopf editor, Sonny Mehta (himself a Sikh).

I was inconsolable until I met Brice for "lunch" and we went immediately to bed.

"Bravo!" MC said. "Now you'll be the mistress and not the cuckolded husband."

MC often took a fervent, amoral interest in my affairs. She liked to think of us as the scandalous couple in *Les liaisons dangereuses*—calling herself Madame de Merteuil and me Valmont. I think in her day she'd had a lot of "gallant" affairs and now she was living vicariously through me. I censored most of what I did (I'm much bolder as a writer than as a conversationalist) since I never wanted our friendship to slip below a certain point of "elegance" (her word), but she knew that Brice's defection had wounded me and she exulted in my new status as "the other woman." The funny thing is that just before he'd left me I'd been ready to break up with him; our similar feelings of satiety didn't keep me from feeling bereaved (as Proust observed). I guess in the battle of love the vanquished is whoever gets dumped first. The natural enmity between leaver and left is like the absolute, immediate, but always shifting hostility between driver and pedestrian.

Right on schedule Brice's furniture-making career took off. Soon he had two assistants. Half of Bonnard's old studio was for making things and half for living. He'd designed busts of the pharaohs for a hotel in Cannes; his own bedroom housed plaster replicas of them. In the surrounding "village" of artists' studios, the ateliers were linked by gravel walkways, planted with old trees and entirely surrounded by walls. In the entranceway to his house there were old-fashioned vitrines filled with gleaming insects. Beside his flower-petal couches were side tables of glass posed on metal daisies. Just as a writer must find a "voice" that reproduces his own conversation, so Brice had had to discover the visual equivalent of his own playfulness. The tables were much more expressive than his big, gloomy paintings—but even they, with their superimposed layers of painted glass, couldn't hide his originality.

Fortunately he'd also discovered a patron—a woman who was kept by a Saudi prince in a hundred-room chateau in Provence, every room of which had to be furnished with Brice's unique, fanciful pieces in bronze and rare inlaid woods. That assignment kept him going for a decade. Fortunately his considerable social charms and sex appeal worked on women as well as on men; usually women don't see the attraction of a *gamin*. He was careful to maintain his slender body; whenever he put on a few pounds he'd make a giant pot of soup and eat it for a week. He had glittering blue eyes, an elegant litheness, a shock of straight, sandy hair, the laugh of a kid, and the swagger of a sexually powerful predator. He wore baggy khakis and loose old button-down blue shirts, usually unironed.

He never heard me speak English except once in London, in a roomy, old-fashioned taxi when I shouted directions to the Cockney driver. Brice told me that whereas I had a charming little accent in French, in English I sounded like a rustic braying for more "white wine." He thought every American was shouting "white wine" all the time.

He found a young, beautiful, successful lover. I suppose that's the end of the Balzac story about a young man who comes to Paris from the provinces. He may sleep and work his way up the social ladder, but once he's arrived he can afford a young beauty of his own.

Chapter 9

James Lord and I had instantly taken to each other. A generation older than me (back during the war he was just getting out of prep school and going into the army before I was even in grade school), James had the years and the background—the more formal, heavier-drinking world of American industrial wealth and serious cultural pursuits—to become a second father figure to me when I was convinced that I'd never want another. But now here I was in Paris in my forties, suddenly and passionately, if chastely, involved with yet another mentor. I always felt that special, privileged sense I experienced when as a boy I was (rarely) the object of my father's interest.

James had written a biography of Alberto Giacometti, which remains the standard one. In his apartment, which was all white like a Hollywood starlet's, he greeted guests while sitting on a white love seat beneath a Giacometti portrait of himself. Probably his most admired book was the short *A Giacometti Portrait*, about the eighteen sessions during which he'd posed for this very painting in Giacometti's grim studio devoid of heat and hot water. Few people before James had given a detailed account of an artist's process. Giacometti did endless revisions of every work—painting or sculpture—and James was nearly unique in recording every stage, day after day. Facing him in his apartment on the wall opposite was another portrait of himself, as a young man, by Picasso. James knew that Picasso liked to draw sleeping women, and on one of his first visits to Picasso he pretended to fall asleep in the antechamber and was pleased when Picasso, perhaps catching the hint, went ahead and drew him. Then James, who recounted the episode in his memoir

Picasso and Dora, pretended that he'd lost the sketch—so Picasso drew him another one. Now James had two.

At one of James's cocktail parties I met Claude Picasso, the son, who said to me, "But don't you remember meeting me in the early seventies when you hired me to photograph artists and their collections? Like Andy Warhol and his Aunt Jemima cookie jars? Or Walter Darby Bannard and his scrimshaw?" I have a highly selective memory, but I surprised even myself by forgetting having met a Picasso. At another party I introduced Claude Picasso to Rachel Stella, the artist Frank Stella's daughter. In a stage whisper I called out to him, "Her father is a famous artist!"

So many people in Paris seemed to be the relatives or ex-wives of famous people. I met Paloma Picasso many places, once at a charity party given in Venice by Mrs. Fanfani, the wife of the prime minister of Italy. Paloma was with Karl Lagerfeld, and together they decided our table had the best position in the room and they wanted it. We all had to move, but not before they decided not to stay after all, though it seemed a pretty A-list mix to me, with Prince Albert of Monaco and the singer Dalida (a gay icon in Europe); when these two were introduced, the paparazzi went crazy.

From that I had a bad impression of Paloma, but later I came to like her. I had a secretary from California for a few weeks. I took her to a party, introduced her to Paloma, and cringed to hear her tell Paloma, "You're much nicer, more approachable, than your reputation."

Paloma replied, "I'm so short, people take advantage of me if I'm nice from the start. So I start off cold and intimidating, and then I become more pleasant, and this makes people take me more seriously."

A candor that made her *sympathique* to me.

In those days Paloma was often seen with her small Argentine husband and another man. The trio were called Paloma and the Palomettes. They've since divorced.

James wrote several memoirs near the end of his life; in my vanity I wondered if my own trilogy of autobiographical novels had encouraged him. James certainly read me faithfully, and he did claim to admire my extreme candor about my sexuality. His posthumous book, *My Queer War,* was about his coming out during World War II.

For seven of the years that I knew James, I was working on my biography of Jean Genet. Both he and Bernard had known Genet slightly and they were well acquainted with several of the people who'd played important roles in Genet's life, if only fitfully. Cocteau was the most crucial figure, since he'd discovered Genet. Later, Genet avoided Cocteau, as did Picasso, both treating Cocteau as a clever—too clever—entertainer. What they failed to see was that Cocteau wrote two good novels, two or three excellent plays, what amounted to a slim volume of great poetry, and several original auto-biographies. Cocteau was the perfect impresario who promoted the careers of the talented young men around him. He also wrote—and drew!—homosexually, especially in his remarkable images of priapic sailors. And he directed one great movie, *The Beauty and the Beast*, and wrote and narrated another, *Les Enfants Terrible*. James knew how much I admired Cocteau and twice gave me letters that Cocteau had sent him, not framed or kept in glycine envelopes but just folded and placed between the leaves of a book. For his part, James was impressed with Picasso and Giacometti and almost no one else in the twentieth century, and he was especially full of contempt for his contemporaries.

When I told him I was writing an article on Cy Twombly, James looked livid and he half levered himself out of his chair.

"You *what*? But, my dear, he's a fraud! Are you going to treat seriously those wretched daubs he's managed to fob off on the public?"

I told him that a Twombly recently went for a million dollars and James said wearily, "He gave me one, but I put it out in the trash."

"No! Why on earth did you do that?"

"Because that's where it belongs!"

If he was rude about so many people, he was as polite as a potentate with me. I had to avoid admiring the tie he was wearing or else he'd take it off and hand it to me. James liked to imagine we were exactly alike—the same age and possessed of the same wealth—and he'd often refer to influential friends of his, like the American ambassador to

France, Pamela Harriman, as if I must know her. I was quick to disabuse him, but he'd merely shrug it off.

James lived on the rue des Beaux-Arts, a block-long street lined with art galleries leading to the gates of the Académie des Beaux-Arts. He'd put together several maid's rooms at the very top of his building to create his large apartment—the big living room, the modern eat-in kitchen, a dining room with a table for ten, and James' own bedroom. There, as he put it, he slept in his own well of Narcissus, surrounded by paintings of himself by Lucian Freud, Cocteau, John Craxton, Picasso, Dora Maar, Balthus, Cartier-Bresson—and nothing by Twombly.

James had lived for a while with Dora Maar in a big house Picasso had given her in the town of Menerbes in the Luberon, a hilly lavender-growing region in the south of France. The experience became the basis for his book *Picasso and Dora*. He hadn't been back there since the late 1940s. One day my partner Michael and I drove him to Menerbes, about an hour's ride from where we were staying in Saint-Rémy-de-Provence. The house sat atop one of the highest points in Menerbes and was huge and impressive and commanded the valley—and when we arrived it was full of workmen. They explained that a Texan had bought it, along with the mayor's house at the top of the road.

James, who was very sentimental, was tearful as we toured the shell of the old place. Then we walked up the road to the mayor's house. A willowy young Texan working for the lady of the house was just returning with a whole pack of little dogs he was reproaching for dawdling. I'd lived in Dallas as a child and I put on my best Texas accent and accosted him. He invited us in for a second, where much of the furniture was designed by Alberto Giacometti—not his brother Diego, who usually fashioned the chairs and tables with their little birds and animals—which of course delighted James, the biographer of Giacometti. He was delighted to see the furniture, as was I to see a large Caio Fonseca, a New York friend and the brother of Isabel Fonseca, the wife of Martin Amis.

When we began to point out the treasures one by one and exclaim over their importance, the young man seemed completely unaware of their provenance and said, "Okay, that's neat. But it was really the decorator who chose them."

James shrugged airily, though I wondered if the lack of general culture he encountered in young people—what he'd spent his own youth acquiring—wounded and deeply irritated him.

The hundreds of evenings I spent with James Lord over the next two decades followed a ritual. As with every Paris apartment building, there was a regularly changing code to be punched in to open the solid, heavy, ornamented door from the street. In the inner courtyard, there was an intercom that James's butler answered. Then the slow-creaking elevator that had been created a century earlier to fit into the stairwell took you up, up, up.

The "correct" and traditionally liveried and white-gloved butler, a good-looking man in his forties, friendly but formal, took your coat and drink order. Michel was a butch gay man with closely cropped hair (a fashionably forbidding gay style the French call a *para*, since it was how French paratroopers kept their hair), and I joked with him once when I ran into him at a gay bar in the Marais. Even then Michel insisted on calling me "Monsieur White."

Michel took care of Monsieur Lord's clothes on a daily basis and helped with the heavy housecleaning. He served drinks and James's favorite pretzels and (on rarer and rarer occasions) dinner. For a while there was a cook, whom I never met—a man who prepared three-star meals but was frustrated because Monsieur Lord so seldom entertained at home. James liked to invite his friends to rue des Beaux-Arts for drinks and pretzels, then take them to the Voltaire, on the quai Voltaire—a small jewel box of a wood-paneled restaurant so exclusive it did not welcome evaluations from the listings magazines or the Michelin or Gault-Millau guides, and where it was nearly impossible to make a reservation unless one was already a habitué. Looking up from your plate you suddenly realized that sitting at the next table was the deeply tanned designer Valentino with a retinue of beautifully dressed, unboisterous friends. There were just a handful of booths and tables in the main room, though in the summertime there was a sidewalk café looking out on the Louvre, across the Seine. James had been coming to the Voltaire for such a long time that on the menu there was a starter named Oeuf James Lord, a hard-boiled egg in mayonnaise priced at a few francs. It had not always been called Oeuf James Lord. One day after the hard-boiled egg in mayonnaise had disappeared from the menu, James had complained so vociferously to the owner and management that the dish was reinstated and named for him.

Once I had what might be called a Proustian moment at the Voltaire. When I was a kid I'd seen an opera at Chicago's Lyric Opera, *Lord Byron's Love Letter*, by Raffaello de Banfield. It was based on a libretto by Tennessee Williams, who was inspired by Henry James's *The Aspern Papers,* except that Williams had set the opera not in Venice but in New Orleans. At age fifteen I was very moved by the music, which I now realize was sort of sub-Puccini. That evening at the Voltaire, James saluted a man his age eating alone, then when we were alone together at our table said, not too softly, which was never his style, "There's that old fraud, Raffaello Banfield."

"What! He's one of my favorite composers."

"Don't stare or he'll come over and we'll never get rid of him. *Quel raseur!*" ("What a bore!")

"But I love *Lord Byron*. I even had an LP of it."

"Sweetie, I'm sure he hired someone to write it for him."

And yet how happy I would have been to meet one of my teenage idols.

James liked to make a spectacle of himself in restaurants, though seldom at the Voltaire.

Or maybe he couldn't control himself. In the beautiful hillside town of Les Baux-de-Provence, we had dinner many times at the Oustau de Baumanière, and it could have been such a special treat. The pleasantly shaded outdoor restaurant overlooked a gorgeous, irrigated valley sunk between dramatically steep walls of craggy reddish stone—and just beyond, the lowlands that swept down to the Camargue, with its wild white horses and pink flamingos.

Drunk, James became something of a control freak, as bullying with the servants as he was generous with the pours of expensive champagne for his guests. The sun was going down over the colorful lowlands and all James could worry about was keeping the champagne bucket next to his chair, where he could reach it just at the moment he was ready to pour from it himself. After all, he was the host—and in his lapel he wore the red button of the Legion of Honor.

The wine steward, no doubt afraid for his job, refused to relinquish the duty, and there ensued an argument we believed might come to actual blows. The bucket stayed in the steward's territory off away from the table, the steward guarding it haughtily, until James could no longer take it and began shouting in English, "I *said* I want it *here*—and I mean *now!*"

With difficulty, the young man finally did what he was told. Maybe since dinner for six was costing thousands of euros, he was obliged to obey.

For a while James owned a summer house outside of Perpignan, not far from the Spanish border, until he could no longer take what he and his lover perceived as the cheeky service of the couple they'd hired to bring in homemade meals the wife had prepared each day. In fact, James would always complain about hired help, confiding, not too softly, that they were ripping him off and that it was better to cancel such arrangements and repair to a restaurant for the major meals.

Once in one of these restaurants, the rather grand young neophyte headwaiter arrived, as was the old custom, to the table with a number of other waiters each bearing a single silver dome concealing each guest's main course. As always, the domes were lifted at the same moment, and then the headwaiter proceeded to announce in detail each of our selections in an officious whisper-shout: "Monsieur has ordered the baked baby lamb in its coulis of charred artichokes and Roman honey, served with three purées of carrots, cauliflower, and spring peas."

At once James cut him short and said, "You can skip it, sweetie."

Dumbfounded, the headwaiter stood by steadfastly, unblinking.

In French, James assured him once again that the traditional ceremony wasn't necessary.

"And do you know why?" he went on, grinning. "It's because, and I'm going to astonish you [*je vous étonne*]—we ordered it!"

I laughed, but then I caught a waiter's gaze and rolled my eyes derisively, but he just stared through me: I was with the enemy. Yet I'd always been conscious of the burdens of waiters and tried to anticipate and eliminate their problems. I overtipped and always had, ever since I was a child eating alone in the dining room of a hotel where I lived with my mother and my sister after my parents' divorce. I'd sign the bill, adding 20 or 25 percent to it.

In France in the provinces there was always the exhausted but handsome young waiter who'd be there until one or two in the morning, and who dreamed of only one thing: "mounting" to Paris one day and working in a still more temple-like restaurant.

Certainly there seemed something potentially sexual in the relations between diner and waiter in France. When my lover Hubert Sorin was dying of AIDS he was always trying to fix me up—posthumously, as it were—with the cute busboy at the hotel, whispering, "There's one for you."

Proportionately, fewer servers in America were men. If they existed they were old, and if they were young, they'd soon move on to a better, or at least less obviously servile, job. In France they were boys from the provinces in search of a position in a fine restaurant. After that, with some luck and help, they might someday start their own restaurant—or, failing that, a newsstand and tobacco store–cum–bar with a few tables. The luck they were counting on might flow from an older client.

"It's all like a Balzac novel," Edgardo Cozarinsky once observed to me, making me think of my own Brice.

Although Edgardo was a Polish Jew who'd been born and brought up in Buenos Aires, he had lived in Paris for decades, working as a writer and filmmaker, and he took at least one meal a day at the Café Select on the boulevard du Montparnasse. One day when we were eating there, he pointed out a slender waiter with thick, curly hair and a disturbingly pale face. Edgardo had an unfailing sense of Paris life, and he set about, rather like Balzac, delineating the waiter's story.

"Now that boy, for instance, grew up on a farm in the Auvergne. His mother looked at him one day and decided he was too slight to make a farmer. She sent him off to her brother in Lyon, a coiffeur. The uncle, in turn, had a friend in Paris, at the Select, who was looking for a busboy. Now, two years later, Jean-Pierre has a protector, a 'Monsieur *très bien,*' and he's been installed in a cozy little studio apartment in the fifteenth arrondissement. He and his monsieur take little holidays during the year and spend the whole month of August in Cassis. No, it's just like a nineteenth-century novel," Edgardo added.

And the fact that Edgardo looked exactly like the middle-aged Henry James (bald, portly, distinguished) only lent greater authority to his words. Recently he himself switched from boys to girls.

James Lord himself had an adopted "son," a former hairdresser who took the Lord family name. I seldom saw Gilles Roy-Lord, who seemed ashamed of his sketchy English and didn't have much in common with James's friends. Gilles owned an apartment downstairs from James. James's cook would prepare Gilles's dinner in the kitchen in James's apartment and leave it on the kitchen table for him. We rarely ever saw Gilles.

He had a painting studio where he turned out pastiches of Matisse and Van Gogh. James, who condemned almost everything artistic his eyes landed on, nonetheless remained loyal to Gilles's daubs. James's Paris friends would keep up with the latest books and read the classics and knew everything about serious music and the history of cinema; Gilles was more like the stereotypical contemporary gay guy—addicted to Madonna and Grace Jones, fashion, interior decoration, and *The Golden Girls*. Gilles eventually turned James against his butler and his chef and the woman cook who replaced him and got them all fired. Gradually Gilles, I knew, was isolating James.

The concierge in our building often referred to my new partner Michael as my son (*"Votre fiston est déjà sorti"*); older gay men called their companions their "nephews." One time I was with Bernard when he ran into a *tante* (queen) who said, "Do you know my nephew?"

"Yes," Bernard replied, "he was my nephew last year."

Bernard loved making cheeky *répliques*. When an older society woman said she didn't like fags (*"Je n'aime pas les pédés"*), Bernard replied, *"Quel dommage, Madame. C'est votre avenir!"* ("Too bad, Madame. It's your future")—only queens hung out with older women as their "capons" or "walkers."

I would see Gilles and James drinking an aperitif together at a café on the boulevard Saint-Germain and they wouldn't be talking; they'd look terminally bored. When James wasn't bored, he'd be jovially drunk or gleefully playing at being wicked. I recall dinner once at Tan Dinh, a Vietnamese restaurant on the rue de Verneuil. Seated next to us was a chic-looking family—the dishy teenage son, handsome father, and heavily face-lifted mother (*tres liftée,* in Parisian slang).

"Isn't it nice," James said loudly, "to see *three* generations of the same family together out for dinner?"

Gilles wasn't cutting. He was close to evil, and like many Parisians he adored feuds. He hired Brice, an ex-lover of his, to redecorate his apartment, and then fought with him over the bill.

Brice said to me, "Every windowsill had to be custom-cut to nonstandard dimensions. Of course that cost more. The fabrics were dyed just for him. I had a dozen craftsmen from India creating the mirrored shelfs. And of course, all that adds up."

Slowly I was learning that Paris had invented *le luxe*. Europeans, unlike Americans, were not content to hang valuable paintings over store-bought furniture or leave the interior of a closet unfinished: few Americans would spend forty thousand dollars on the detailing of a closet, which no one would ever see and within a decade would be condemned as démodé and replaced.

Although James was imperious and rude, he could also be exquisitely tender with his friends. He was my link to the Paris of Giacometti, Picasso, and Gertrude Stein. He was a very serious writer who worked every day, no matter how hungover. My own finances were always precarious, and though I never touched him for money, it was a comfort knowing that in an emergency I always could. He's dead now, but I can still hear his ridiculous American accent; he told me that when he met Gertrude Stein after World War II he was shocked she had such a terrible accent in spite of living in France for nearly thirty-five years; now, he admitted, he'd been there even longer and spoke just as badly.

Every year he wanted to lose the pound or two he'd gained in the last twelve months. He'd go to a spa in Quiberon, where he was put on a gourmet low-calorie diet, sprayed with salt water (*thalassotherapie*), and forced to exercise. He never befriended anyone new but stayed by himself reading a late novel by Henry James.

Although his various memoirs were precise and factual, his many novels (only one or two published) were absurdly romantic and sentimental. Like many hard-bitten cynics, he cried easily and was always falling into fluttery love with his type, clean-cut Yalies. We were really opposites: outside I was as gushy as my Texas mother and inside cold and calculating.

Chapter 10

James, like every *salonnier*, continued to have his "faithful." Jean-Luc Champion, a Gallimard editor, was a handsome ex-model who spoke in a low voice. His lover, a museum curator, had worked for Jack Lang when Lang was mayor of Blois. Lang, who'd previously been the minister of culture for France, was as tyrannical and frustrated as Napoleon on Elba. In France, the cause of culture was as furiously planned out and budgeted as a military campaign, which was why not only French people loved France. France had set the tone and led the way. And at James's cocktail parties, there were always art historians who were visiting from America, like Gary Tinterow from New York's Metropolitan Museum of Art.

Through James I met Phyllis Rose, an American writer, critic, and literature professor at Wesleyan University. Phyllis was renting the boulevard Saint-Germain apartment of Harlan Lane, another American academic and a leading expert on the deaf community. Harlan and his boyfriend, Frank, had become close friends of mine. Whenever I needed to get out of Paris to work on Genet, Harlan and Frank lent me their farmhouse near Vendôme.

Did I introduce Phyllis to Marie-Claude? I still ask myself. It would be logical that Phyllis would have sought out MC, since Phyllis was up-and-coming, less academic than a mainstream writer. She'd already published a well-reviewed study of five Victorian marriages called *Parallel Lives*. Now she was researching a biography of Josephine Baker, to be called *Jazz Cleopatra*. It would be a study of comparative racial attitudes. Phyllis was strictly a feminist: her first book had been about Virginia Woolf. The whole project—about racism and feminism—was greeted less than enthusiastically by the French.

Phyllis looked like a younger, more innocent, more *American* version of MC: also Jewish with light corkscrew curls, large, curious eyes that quickly empathized with any gaiety or suffering in her vicinity, and a flirtatiousness that could veer off into maternal concern. MC was genuinely interested in her friends, as I've said, could listen for hours to their woes or whims, and spent half her life on the phone. But Phyllis was always so close to losing the thread of someone else's chatter that she frowned and nodded the whole time—as if she were courting a migraine or about to fall asleep. She had to concentrate hard in order to listen, perhaps because she was a scholar.

I didn't discover the details until later and then never in great depth. MC had noticed her husband Laurent's fascination with Phyllis right away and encouraged it, knowing Laurent was bored with his life, that he wanted to change his habits completely (as had his brother the monk), that he found MC's salon stuffy, that he'd lost his inspiration as an artist, or feared he had. MC, in other words, I feel, *wanted* him to have an affair—a light little restorative affair with a sweet, intelligent American woman. What MC had forgotten was that American women play for keeps; American women don't understand the rules of an affair in the same way the French do. Phyllis would say that MC was neglecting Laurent and didn't want him interfering with her high-flying literary life.

Phyllis was certainly ready for an adventure. She'd lost ten pounds and dyed her hair blonde before coming to Paris. Though I was a new acquaintance, Phyllis told me she wanted me to invite her to dinner with an eligible unmarried *straight* man.

I said, "But what planet are you living on? Are there any unmarried straight men in their forties *anywhere*—unless they were widowed ten minutes ago?"

She said that in the town where she taught, Middletown, Connecticut, most of the men in her age range were blue-collar workers or married or gay academics. She'd had a brief liaison years earlier that had produced a son, thank God. He was her joy. But if she hoped to find a single eligible man in Paris, I thought, she was fooling herself. Then again, maybe she'd already figured that out on her own and had decided to make a play for a married man.

I never suspected that Phyllis and Laurent had found each other until I gave a dinner for a few friends at a good restaurant that no longer exists, Dodin Bouffant. I'd invited my French editor, Ivan Nabokoff, a relative of the writer, and his wife, Claude. I'd asked MC to join us but she'd refused, which was out of character for her. Phyllis and Laurent came. The whole dinner was for Bill Whitehead, my New York editor, and his current boyfriend.

Normally nearly extinct at social gatherings, tonight Laurent was excited as a flea. I'd seated him for no particular reason on the opposite side of a round table from Phyllis. He kept bouncing around in his chair and waving just his fingertips and cooing, "Hello, Phyllis! Hello!"

She smiled radiantly.

Oh dear, I suddenly thought.

By the time the dessert was served, he had taken the chair next to Phyllis and, I suspect, was holding hands with her under the table.

The whole process took a few months, but by the following autumn Laurent had left Paris and moved to Middletown, Connecticut.

Marie-Claude had spent the summer partly with Laurent on the Île de Ré in the charming fisherman's cottage they'd bought together years ago, with a garden, huge fig tree, and high stone privacy walls. For me the sequence of events was like a bad print of an old film in which entire scenes were missing and the celluloid burned or skipped frequently. In August I got a call from MC in Ré, in which she said, "He's leaving. I've lost. I've lost everything. Oh, Edmund!"

And then she hung up sobbing.

Back in Paris in September, MC seemed to be going crazy. She had a frantic, galvanized energy that kept her from sleeping. Her sister Thérèse called me and said she was afraid that MC might harm herself. "Maybe you could do something, *Edmond . . .*"

By then MC wasn't too keen on seeing me or any of her usual friends. She wasn't eating or sleeping. She was dashing about, explaining her life, her wonderful, calm, magical life, to the bus driver or strangers in the marketplace. Her telephone answering machine, she told them, had become a center where people from all over the world could store and exchange information and be instructed as to what they should do next in their lives. She could not linger or explain. But if people would trust her, all would come clear—everything was going to be all right.

When finally she agreed to see me, I tried to calm her. I held both her hands and attempted to talk some sense into her, but her hands squirmed like mice. She was bathed in sweat and her lips were so dry they stuck together for a second when she tried to speak. Her eyes, like those of an autistic child, would avoid direct contact with mine. She couldn't bear to sit for a long time or stay indoors; she was constantly out on the street accosting strangers—those people who wouldn't contradict her or scorn her excesses, maybe because she frightened them.

Then her sister called to say MC was locked up in a clinic.

"Did she try to hurt herself?" I asked.

"Yes," Thérèse whispered over the line. "Years ago when Laurent threatened to leave her for another woman, she also tried suicide, and he backed down. But this time he is determined to leave, he's already left. Anne called him to say what MC had done."

The next thing I knew I was on the train out to the Clinique Médicale de Ville d'Avray, on the rue Picadier in the suburb of Ville-d'Avray. The clinic was old and didn't seem altogether clean. It smelled horrible. I was shown up to the top floor. The door was unlocked for me, I was ushered in, and then the prison-barred door was locked behind me.

MC was dressed in one of her bright red Japanese robes of crisp silk, and she had on a turban that made her face look like that of a man, a starving man.

I felt sorry for her, and I wondered if she'd ever regain her sanity. I had witnessed something similar with my mother after she'd stopped drinking and was going through the DTs. My mother had had her ecstatic two weeks and then plunged into despair. I'd hospitalized her in a psych ward, but she checked herself out the next morning and hired a car and drove off to a remote hotel in Wisconsin where she stayed for weeks, frantically writing her memoirs, which I promised to publish in a limited edition: *Delilah: A Life in Progress.* I thought writing would save her life, as I felt it had mine. She followed through and so did I, and she was able to peddle the book to the ladies at her church, although it must have shocked them with its frank accounts of my father's promiscuity and bouts with gonorrhea. It turned out room service was the best cure for craziness; a handsome young waiter would bring food at your bidding and you could dismiss him whenever you chose. Complete control.

And yet my mother had been a capable woman for decades, administering a clinic for the mentally retarded and brain-damaged at Cook County Hospital in Chicago. Then she'd retired, undergone surgery for breast cancer, and lost her lover of many years (she'd lied about her age and he'd chanced upon her passport). Of course, it had been a shock to see her fall apart, just as now it was devastating to see MC in a lockup cell at a clinic. My mother came for her annual visit and told MC, "Now, Marie-Claude, we'll see what you're made of. Will you be strong enough to recover? We'll see . . ." MC was offended by her lack of sympathy, but this challenge, or the galvanizing indignity of it, possibly helped mobilize her forces of recovery.

I paid repeated visits to the clinic, with its inmates gabbling to themselves in the day room or sitting in a drug-induced stupor. After a while MC was doing well enough that she was put in an ordinary room with another woman. Eventually she was judged able to go on long walks with me through the Parc de Saint-Cloud. Here there had once been a royal chateau that was destroyed by the Communards in 1870, although the grounds were left intact. Around 1904, Eugène Atget, the great photographer of Paris, had taken dreamy, misty pictures of the grounds and its sculptures. It was that Saint-Cloud we were visiting, MC and I. Steadily, arm in arm, we strolled along the parterres, down two steps, up three, flanked by white marble goddesses and nymphs, everything damp and pearl gray.

I thought of us as the two eighteenth-century ghosts in Verlaine's "Colloque Sentimentale":

> In the old park, solitary and icy,
> Two forms just went by.
> Their eyes are dead and their lips slack
> And you can scarcely hear their words.
> In the old park, solitary and icy,
> Two specters have summoned up the past.

One of the ghosts asks his companion if she still sees his soul when she dreams and she replies, "No." When he tries to remind her that in the beautiful days of the past they joined their lips, she says merely, "It's possible."

It wasn't that I thought MC and I were glued together despite our extinct passion for one another. It was just the idea of two people no longer young tottering arm in arm through an icy old park that struck me. It occurred to me that Europe in general and Paris in particular had been painted and written about so thoroughly that every experience has its correlative in art—whereas American life still goes unmapped. That's why it sometimes feels so raw. And so challenging to a novelist.

In her suffering MC began to cling to me, literally, sometimes, and I'd come back to the Île Saint-Louis still feeling her iron claws digging into my arm. But she must have seen how I was afraid of her neediness. I wasn't going to be her new husband, though I was happy to be her new escort and her friend—her brother, possibly, but not her new mate.

Not immediately but very quickly she reset her dials. She found that perfect combination of elements to enable our friendship, the combination other straight women I'd known had failed to adopt. Some heterosexual women acted patronizing to their gays, their "capons," as we said in America. They'd perk up for a real man, a heterosexual contender, no matter how played out he was. Or they'd want to have "girl talk" with a gay guy about how to trap a man or save a broken nail. Or late at night, after three drinks or ten, they'd become amorous—their kisses opening up full mouth and lingering too long. They'd press their bodies against their poor gay companion's.

MC avoided all these embarrassments. She'd let me pick up the restaurant check, but she invited me to dinner frequently at her house.

She relied on my judgment and even my physical strength for certain jobs around the house in Ré, but she eschewed all hubby-wifey role playing. She was very feminine around me, wanted my approval of her new shoes, and took my arm, but she never presented me with a sexual invitation, or even hint. It was seduction without the sex, intimacy without the boner. I suppose seduction *à la française* works well because the fiction is that it's open-ended. No one can say where it will all end— and yet this vagueness about what the future holds is never alarming. I liked going in public with such a stylish woman.

Eventually MC got better. Our walks through the gardens of Saint-Cloud went on longer and longer; the rains never let up, but they were gentle mists, really, as if the landscape were sprayed with an old-fashioned gold-mesh atomizer attached to a cut-glass perfume flask the color of amethyst. As if we were living inside a pearl.

MC's will—or was it her recklessness?—remained strong. One day she was out of the clinic. She blinked a lot and looked newly hatched, like an aviator who'd been severely burned and only now was freed from her bandages. She looked freshly *unwrapped*.

Her sister and daughter were on hand to welcome her home. After returning home, MC became more extravagantly feminine, with her Japanese beige scarves lined in black silk and printed with delicate paulownia flowers, her heady honeysuckle perfume, her immaculate red shoes with the black soles and spool heels, her full skirts, and her layered blouses. I thought of those ancient Japanese court women who attracted approval uniquely by the colors of their layered kimono sleeves left to trail from the windows of their litters. While MC became more feminine and espaliered, her female helpers became more male, both clad in dark blue trousers and military shirts, their hair bobbed and their faces scrubbed clean. If MC was their queen bee, they were her drones, patient, attentive, entirely focused on Marie-Claude in all her operatic splendor.

I gave Phyllis Rose, MC's villain, her sobriquet of La Belle Dame sans Merci, which soon enough was shortened to "La Dame." Nor did anyone in this household want to hear Babar referred to as anything but the Pachyderm. Laurent became the Pater—in the best Victorian Latinate manner. I caught sight of Phyllis every January in Key West, but MC wouldn't permit me to socialize with her—very awkward, since Key West is such a small community and Phyllis was at the center of things, and a very nice woman. Eventually, after several years, MC relented.

I thought that what had most wounded MC was losing her status as Madame de Brunhoff. She regretted this more than losing Laurent, though I'm sure she'd loved him. Now she began to see that she was still just as magical to people as she'd been in the past. People appreciated MC because of her kindness and her creativity, not her name. She became even kinder and more generous to her friends and even strangers. She said she was imitating my example—kindness, she said, was an American trait.

Laurent came back to Paris on business and MC encouraged me to invite him to lunch, possibly to sound him out. He evidently didn't like my three-course hot lunch and told me that in America people ate just a sandwich at noon. I was too embarrassed to ask him questions about his "intentions," but it was obvious that he had none. He was merely passing through town. He was in love with Phyllis.

MC now became practical and bellicose. She felt she had to secure her own rights and protect those of "the children," Anne and her always strangely absent son, whom I was never permitted to meet—not once in the twenty years of my friendship with MC. I did see him once in the distance, tall and limping in the Bois de Boulogne, but we weren't introduced. Antoine had had a childhood cancer of the knee, which, when treated with radiation, left the tissue soft and weak. He was married to an older Polish woman and they had an adopted son, Victor. Antoine had trouble earning a living and would do Babar-related odd jobs designing elephant carpets or bedspreads. But his fees were unrealistically high and he was often outbid.

MC's illness had brought us closer together. I was no longer "the house author," the way Georges Perec and Julio Cortázar had been before my time (they were dead by the time I came along), but an intimate, a member of the family.

I remembered the memoirs of Virgil Thomson, in which Virgil had been so proud of his friendship with a normal, middle-class French woman—more proud of this than of his artistic collaboration with Gertrude Stein. I suppose it was at this point that I learned that unlike Americans—who claim everyone they know as a friend—the French were quite sparing of who deserved to be called *un ami*. The French had an entire taxonomy for friendships. There were acquaintances (*connaissances*) and then buddies (*potes*) and companions (*copains*). An acquaintance was addressed as *vous* except among Communists and among the collegial young or at a gymnasium, where everyone became *tu*, even if one didn't know his or her name. A *pote* would almost certainly be called *tu*. There was an anti-racist slogan in those years in Paris: *Touche-pas à mon pote!* ("Keep your hands off my buddy!").

Among the older bourgeoisie, a *copain* and even certain *amis* would be addressed as *vous,* even as Monsieur or Madame. And only a handful of people at any given moment were ever considered *amis*—an honorific that carried with it certain duties and privileges.

A true friend could be called on at any time, day or night. He would never bad-mouth his friend—or brag about their link if the friend was well known. Friends could borrow large sums from each other without question. I suppose I learned about French attitudes toward friendship when I wanted to mix members of the press with a few famous friends I'd acquired in Paris at a party for the launching of a book, and Ivan Nabokoff, my editor then as now, let me know that in France you might have a party for your real friends and another for the press but you wouldn't try to mix the two. Of course, this discretion was foreign to everything I'd learned in New York, where you had to guarantee two or three celebrities to reporters if you expected them to attend your event.

Chapter *11*

The party for the translation of my novel *A Boy's Own Story* (*Un jeune Americain*) was being held at Azzedine Alaïa's new showrooms across from the BHV department store on the rue de la Verrerie, a venue that was already an automatic cause for excitement.

I'd written an article for Vanity Fair about Azzedine and become rather close to him. It was my good luck that I'd been assigned to write about such a genuine artist. He lived with a tall, aristocratic German above the store. His dream was that many of his "girls," the models he worked with, would live there with him. Azzedine was a tiny Tunisian who told endless stories about the great ladies he'd known. One was the writer Louise de Vilmorin, who'd treated Azzedine as her confidant and court jester. When she was reunited with her American grandson (her first husband had been an American real estate tycoon and they'd lived together in Las Vegas), Louise had asked Azzedine's advice about which side of her face she should show the boy and what she should be wearing? Where should she be seated?

Greta Garbo was another client. Cecilia Rothschild, who was Garbo's companion at that time, before the deal was done had said to Azzedine, "I have a very special client for you but you mustn't make any sort of fuss over her." Azzedine promised he wouldn't.

As it turned out, he and his boyfriend had seen *Queen Christina* at the cinema the night before their encounter with Garbo, so they recognized that sublime face right away. Garbo wanted Azzedine, who at that time was dressmaker for just a few ladies, to make her a military greatcoat. She already had the fabric. He draped it over her and pinned it up. All night long, he experimented with the coat; his German lover, who was tall and thin like Garbo, modeled the coat in their tiny rue de Bellechasse apartment. Then he returned with the perfected coat. Garbo gave him suggestions after each fitting. Azzedine claimed that Garbo's suggestions had helped purify his taste. "Human taste," he told me, "was at an all-time low in 1970, when orange and black were the popular colors!"

By the time I knew him, Azzedine Alaïa was working through the night with the young, very young, Naomi Campbell—who he said was like a daughter to him. She would stand on a raised model's dais as he wrapped and draped her, occasionally sticking her with a straight pin, which would elicit a yelp. There was a full-time chef on hand, who'd cook at midnight a lamb roast with honey and mint leaves sealed in aluminum foil. Or Azzedine would invite everyone to the terrace of the Voltaire, where we'd eat looking out at the ghostly outlines of the Louvre.

He was exactly my age but he seemed full of experience and wisdom. He wanted me to write his biography but was unwilling to pay me the price of even one of his dresses.

He did have wonderful stories. When he was a boy, his grandfather would send him to a local café in Tunisia to reserve a seat for him next to the radio, the only one in the village. When it came time for Umm Kulthum to sing (a performance that was broadcast across the Arab world from Cairo), Azzedine's grandfather would sit in his reserved chair, place a jasmine sprig behind his ear, and weep at the beautiful words and music. Umm Kulthum was the Maria Callas of the Arab world, and one of the few popular things America ever did for the Arabs occurred when a doctor in Boston operated successfully on a node on her vocal cords. Once in Jordan, as I rode in a taxi all night through the snow from Petra to Assam to catch a plane for England the next morning, the flirty driver and I listened to his tape of her haunting voice while he told me about his unhappy marriage to a Texan whose parents insisted he must be a Mexican since he had a funny accent and was tan.

Azzedine could never manage to show at the same time as the other couturiers, so the big buyers from America would have to make a second trip back to Paris to see his collection.

What were his influences? Aside from Garbo, he was very impressed by Arletty, who in her 1938 film *Hotel du Nord* had worn a dress that had a zipper on the bias from top to bottom. This dress fascinated him, and years later he was designing similar things. Another influence was Madame Madeleine Vionnet (1876–1975). The Musée de la Mode didn't know what to do with the boxes of cloth panels it received from the House of Vionnet; it was Azzedine who sorted them out and draped them over the wicker mannequins the museum had decided to use.

Like Vionnet, Azzedine was known as an "architect of the body." She had used such unusual materials as gabardine panels that clung to each other. In his work, he was called the King of Cling; she had cut her fabrics on the bias so the dresses would move with the body rather than try to mold it or hold it in a predestined shape. She had been influenced by Isadora Duncan and by our modern ideas of ancient Greek clothes— all floating panels of cloth moving with the body. People always said that Azzedine's clients (Grace Slick, Tina Turner, Madonna) already had great bodies, slim and athletic, which only needed to be revealed rather than suppressed and contained. Madame Vionnet's dresses moved with a similar fluidity, with the body's natural curves freed of corsets.

Azzedine told me about his visit to the archives of the Fashion Institute of Technology in Manhattan, where the European designers were on the opposite side of the room from the Americans. Azzedine came upon a dress marked as American and said, "You've put this on the wrong side." It was by Charles James, the British couturier who lived in New York and who, like Azzedine, did not bother to keep pace with the seasons. He had designed a dress like Arletty's with a spiral zipper, but his dresses, unlike Vionnet's, were very heavy and obviously structured.

Azzedine was interested in a certain mill in Italy that made a synthetic fabric that would stretch in one direction but not in another. He worked with this mill for years, perfecting his specifications in order to get the exact textile properties he wanted.

Everyone in Paris seemed obsessed with fashion, especially women. Some older ladies were content to appear merely neat and clean, but younger women, especially those in daily contact with the public, invested a large part of their yearly income in a single outfit, which they wore every day for a year and which would testify to their status and chic taste. Unlike Americans, who would have a closet stuffed with cheap, ill-fitting dresses, a French woman would have just one or two every season—perfect and way beyond her means. Some went to a cheap fabric market, like the Marché Saint-Pierre below the Sacré-Coeur, bought five-meter bolts, and cut and sewed their own garments that were rip-offs of the latest designs.

People in Europe liked to talk about American "puritanism," by which they meant not only prudishness, but also distaste for luxury. The French liked clothes and interior decoration for their own sake, not as status symbols alone but also for the comfort and pleasure of contact with fine things. Americans, especially ones who fancied themselves intellectual like me, found it hard to believe in this obsession. A typical compliment, if one were nicely dressed with some care, was "*Comme tu est chic!*"—which always embarrassed an American. We wanted to look presentable, not *coquet*. We hoped to look respectable, not *séduisant*. We imagined our personalities consisted of our thoughts and words, not our looks, yet we paid a lot of attention to working out at the gym so we could gain bulk and definition, which would be apparent when we were undressed. Frenchmen wanted to look slender, since that made them ideal mannequins for hanging beautiful clothes on.

Working out was a form of discipline and virtue, changing our bodies or ourselves, but to the French staying slim was an art of civilization, a mere look rather than a fundamental identity. One was a way of adding muscled weight to the self, the other a way of subtracting weight and weakening the body. Whereas we Americans thought we were offstage in the wings as we walked the streets, entering onstage only as we stepped across the threshold into an office or a friend's apartment, a French man or woman was onstage the minute he or she left home. A woman would never wear gym shoes on the street, then step into her high heels the instant she went into her office, as women did in New York; a French woman had to look her best anywhere in public.

Nor did any of the Americans I knew like to follow the latest or most extravagant fashions. You'd often hear one American woman say to another, "No one would wear that—it's ridiculous." Younger French women *wanted* to cause comment, even court ridicule. I remember that in *The Autobiography of Alice B. Toklas*, Alice is pleased the workmen are hooting at her small hat and Picasso's mistress's larger one: "Here come the sun and the moon!" the men joked. Alice saw the comments as proof their hats were a success. In my day older French women had figured out what showed them to advantage, and they stuck with that. Americans made the mistake of imagining that the outfit made the woman and that anyone wearing something beautiful would look good. French women knew how to suppress and benefit from their bodily peculiarities—how to deemphasize a fat ass or disguise a flat chest or thick waist. All things being equal, a French woman would like to look stylish, but not if the new styles emphasized her weak points.

The Sunday magazine of the *Times* in London asked me to write a piece about Yves Saint Laurent. In those pre-Google, pre-Wikipedia days it was more difficult to research someone, even someone as celebrated as YSL. I was given an appointment (or *rendezvous*, as the French say routinely, not knowing that the word in English always suggests a romantic meeting) at his avenue Montaigne headquarters. I was shown into the study of the great man. He seemed to be heavily doped, probably high on the tranquilizers to which he was said to be addicted.

YSL had been discovered by Michel de Brunhoff, editor of French *Vogue* and a relative of Laurent's. Brunhoff had introduced the young YSL to Christian Dior, because the young man had done designs resembling those of the master and Brunhoff had seen the newest designs of both men the same day and there was no way YSL could have copied Dior's. At first the young man was a huge success, becoming head designer for the Dior company when the master died, but then he had a bad year: he was conscripted into the army, Dior fired him, and he had a breakdown and was administered electroshock and tranquilizers—which began his addiction. His lover Pierre Bergé sued Dior for breach of contract and won. With the settlement they opened their own couture house and it was an immediate success.

He continued to put out great collections season after season—both haute couture and ready-to-wear, fall and spring—but he began to appear so bewildered during the *defilés* that the models sometimes had to lead him off the catwalk.

YSL was known for his fresh and shocking color sense and for his "world" fashions—drawing on every ethnic tradition. He was the first designer to use black or Asian models. He was the first to popularize women in tuxes (a tux in French is called *un smoking*).

Here he was in front of me. Being interviewed was obviously a torture for him—*une supplice*. He didn't exactly answer long questions with a "yes" or "no," but I felt he wanted to. He of course was beautifully dressed. I was tired of reading interviews in which the interviewer never mentioned his own problems, so I brought up my own past alcoholism (and spoke of it in my article), but my candor was not rewarded. I wondered how long he could go on, and I wasn't surprised when he retired in 1990.

Later I was asked to write an article about his Russian-style dacha, on the grounds of his large house near Deauville, the Château Gabriel. The dacha was full of bric-a-brac, designer-bought mementos (photos, icons, furniture) from someone else's past, not his; nor was YSL present.

After his death, everything from his Paris apartment and the Château Gabriel would be auctioned off in a spectacular sale. His lover and business partner, Pierre Bergé, was impatient with Saint Laurent when I interviewed him—"I complained he never read anything and so, guess what, he reread *Proust!*" he said with great exasperation—but after his death Bergé wrote a beautiful homage to him, *Letter to Yves*, which he sent me and asked me to translate, though I turned him down (I don't know how to translate). Yet years later when I asked him to help subsidize the translation of Claude Arnaud's biography of Cocteau (Bergé was the head of the Cocteau society), he immediately agreed. During his years with YSL, Bergé had made no secret of having outside affairs, and he was the owner of the trendy gay magazine *Tetû*. After an early affair with the kitschy painter Bernard Buffet (who'd left him for a woman), he had shared his life with a great force of nature, and he never forgot that privilege, exasperating as YSL could be.

Christian Lacroix was the last couturier *Vanity Fair* sent me to interview. An editor, Marie-Paule Pélé, drove me to Arles, where Lacroix was renting a villa, perhaps in order to lend credibility to his first collection, which derived its motifs from bright Arlesienne patterns. I was skeptical about his reputation as a heterosexual (at last, a couturier who loved women—as if the others didn't), and I was curious to meet him. As it turned out he was a soft-spoken art historian born in Arles who'd married his wife, Françoise, in 1974. In the walled garden of their villa they were attended by two young brothers from Champagne who were kept in the nude. Not that I mentioned that.

My article swooned over his heterosexuality and his courage in launching the first major Parisian house of couture in years. (His business is now closed, having never turned a profit. He turned to costume design; the theater had been his first love.) I remember seeing various ladies around Paris wearing that first collection with its loud colors and embarrassingly short, bouncy skirts that made it difficult for a woman to get into a car.

When Gaby Van Zuylen, an American and the sister-in-law of the Baron Guy de Rothschild, came out of her luxurious building on the avenue Foch, a *poule de luxe* (high-priced prostitute) huddling in the doorway timidly asked her where she'd bought her dress.

Gaby proudly said, "It's a Christian Lacroix original."

The next day the woman was wearing one of her own.

(I once asked a taxi driver how much it cost to buy a *poule de luxe*. He said he was much too handsome to need to pay—"Nor would you, with your charming accent," he said. "Anyway, you can seduce a woman seventy percent of the time if you can make her laugh. You must make women laugh.")

On our way to Arles in a jeep Marie-Paule had rented, we stopped to see some interesting Americans she'd been told about. We rang the bell at the gate and were greeted by a handsome, distinguished man who spoke French and English falteringly. We were kept waiting a moment then were led into the courtyard where the amplified strains of the *Don Giovanni* overture were playing. At last a chubby woman tightly laced into eighteenth-century robes slowly descended the outside stairs, wrapped like a package in yellow silk ribbon. Her husband, outfitted with silk stockings and a silver cane, simultaneously issued forth from the salon doors—and soon enough we'd learned their story. The couple were antique dealers from San Francisco who liked living in a make-believe century. They gave us a tour of the estate, where life-size nineteenth-century dolls with porcelain heads dressed in nineteenth-century clothes sat on every available chair, dozens of them.

The same distinguished man who'd answered the door then served us tea, with his wife assisting. We asked our hosts who these elegant servants were. The chubby wife, clawing at her silk ribbon, said impatiently, her words in character for a period novel, "All our visitors ask us about them. If you must know, they're a penniless Spanish duke and duchess; they wait on us the two weeks a year we're here and then they have the run of the place the rest of the year. The neighbors have told us they entertain heavily."

Chapter 12

Each time I left Bernard Minoret's on the rue de Beaune, I'd walk home. I'd go past my favorite building, the Académie Française, with its Italianate cupola (to join the academy is "to be received under the cupola"). The only part of the academy I had ever visited was the library, an astonishing seventeenth-century interior built by Mazarin.

I'd known two or three members of the academy. Through Bernard I'd met Jean-Louis Curtis, a postwar novelist who adopted an American-sounding pen name and also became the pet academician of the American millionaire Seward Johnson, the sculptor, and his novelist wife, Cecilia. A more colorful academician, who was a friend of Diane Johnson, was Jean Dutourd, the author of *The Horrors of Love*. Diane had met his scatterbrained, nearly demented wife one day when she, Diane, was apartment hunting. The empty apartment and theirs were on the same landing. Diane could see that Madame Dutourd was very lonely and she felt sorry for her. When Diane discovered her husband was an academician and a fine novelist (whose reputation was on the wane because he was a right winger), she invited them to dinner. The wife made screwball comments and the husband would growl. He had published more than thirty books—including *The Horrors of Love*, which I'd read in America because a friend of mine wanted to make a movie out of it. It was a very long novel about two worldly men strolling through Paris one afternoon talking about love.

I asked Dutourd over dinner what the academicians actually did besides wearing their pretty historical uniforms and swords at

ceremonies, and he replied that they worked constantly on their dictionary. They were up to the letter C.

"What will happen when you finish it?"

"We'll print it and start all over again."

"How many copies do you sell?"

"About five thousand."

"Would you say your dictionary is descriptive or prescriptive? That
is, do you describe how people actually talk or do you tell them how
they should talk?"

"Of course we tell them how they should talk. We set the rules."

"What if they don't do what you tell them?"

"We fine them. In fact we monitor all broadcasts and publications
for irregular usages or foreign words or inadmissible back formations,
and then we fine the culprits."

"What else do you do?"

"We elect new immortals and give literary prizes."

(Members of the academy are called immortals.)

"Do you have any special perks?"

"The right to put on a title page that the author is an academician.
They have several nice apartments in their gift, and of course there is
the use of the Bibliothèque Mazarine."

I wanted to see the main assembly hall with its cupola. I knew that
one day a year, all the locked doors in Paris were thrown open so
that one could visit every secret place or exclusive establishment. One
winter day Raymond Carver, wearing a leather jacket, and I had our
picture taken in front of the Academy, knowing that we would never
get any closer during his stay.

Once I met the young heir to Arthus-Bertrand, the jeweler on the
square in front of the church of Saint-Germain-des-Prés and next door
to the café Les Deux Magots. He told me that all the future academicians had to choose their swords, but if they selected diamonds and
their friends, who sponsored their ceremonial regalia, were cheap, it
was his duty to steer them diplomatically toward the zircons. Sometimes
an academician was especially well loved. When oceanographer Jacques
Cousteau, for instance, was invited to "pass under the cupola," his

admirers all over the world put together a coffer to pay for his custom-made sword of glass waves in crystal. When Pierre Nora, the historian and companion of Gaby van Zuylan, became an academician he named his sword "Gabrielle" in her honor.

My translator Marc Cholodenko said that the academy had decided once to induct a writer of real talent, but it hadn't worked out and they never tried that again. They went back to the usual art historians, auctioneers, scientists, bankers and so on—cronies. Every businessman and lawyer in France has written a book and wants to be considered a writer, which means that in theory at least every businessman and lawyer and politician who deigns to pick up a pen and call himself a writer is eligible to join the academy.

Of course, the French are masters at lighting their own monuments—lights that not only illuminate the mass of imposing buildings but also excavate and articulate their ornamentations. On my walks home from Bernard's, I was conscious that this was a "miracle mile" of beautiful buildings reeling against usually stormy skies filled with big, shifting clouds. I walked across the wood-planked pedestrian bridge, the pont des Arts, which connected the Academie Française in the Palais de l'Institut with the Louvre—specifically its oldest part, the ravishing Cour Carrée. Then I'd saunter down the Right Bank, past the church of Saint-Gervais across from the Île de la Cité, with its lit statue of Henri IV, and the medieval-turreted Conciergerie, where Marie Antoinette was imprisoned just before she was beheaded.

I passed the Théâtre du Châtelet—where Diaghilev's Ballets Russes had danced—and the Théâtre de Ville, which the Nazis renamed; before, it was called the Théâtre de Sarah Bernhardt, after the Jewish actress. I always thought it should go back to its original name. Finally, the Hôtel de Ville, a reconstructed Renaissance building that the Communards had burned down in 1870.

At last I crossed the pont Louis-Philippe to the Île Saint-Louis where I lived for eight years. It was often wrapped in fog and was five degrees cooler than the mainland.

This sumptuous route home was the most beautiful I'd known, with its historic buildings displayed like diamonds on the black velvet of the sky—nearly soundless except for the whir of passing cars and the lapping waves caused by Bateaux Mouches with their lights engulfing the façades they passed and the running commentary in English, French, Italian, and German.

There were almost no people on my route except the guitar-playing, pot-smoking young tourists sitting cross-legged with their mangy dogs on the pont des Arts. Everywhere the light emanating or reflected from the buildings was refracted by the river, which itself was divided by the two islands in the Seine. The night was haunted by the smooth sound of an alto saxophone with its oddly human sound under the bridge.

Chapter 13

This is confusing, but I had a lover named Hubert, whom I was with for five years and whom I wrote about under the name of Brice in *The Farewell Symphony* and Julien in *The Married Man*. He was sick the last four years I knew him.

I met him at the gym above the Pontoise public swimming pool. He started to let some weights he was pushing collapse on his chest when I rushed over to help him. He was very young, in his late twenties, dark, with a permanent five-o'clock or rather seven o'clock stubble, and had the rather sepulchral voice that certain Latin men have trained to be deep (as opposed to the boyish piping of so many educated American males), a sound that comes off as Boris Karloff creepy when they laugh. He was slender, a bit of a poseur, and very hairy, as I quickly discovered in the locker room. I also learned that his wife was swimming downstairs.

He was intrigued by my accent. I don't think he'd known many Americans, but in his traditional French way he thought of us as breezy, modern, on the right side of history.

When he told me his name was Hubert Sorin and handed me his business card (but not his home phone number), I said, "I had a lover who was called Hubert," lest there be any mistake as to my orientation. I also recognized that as a married man he needed to be discreet.

It turned out he was the very definition of discretion. I never found out much about his past amorous or sexual history, not from him directly at least, and his family history was a tissue of lies. The French have a relatively benign word, *mythomane,* which suggests someone who is a spinner of myths, which aren't necessarily self-serving or designed to conceal the truth but are spun for the pure pleasure of spinning. Some friends of his told me they thought he was overwhelmed by my "fame" and that's why he invented so many glamorous facts about himself.

Hubert came to dinner alone and we ended up in bed. He seemed delighted by my apartment on the Île Saint-Louis, its casement windows giving onto the church of Saint-Louis-en-l'Île, with its huge stone volute, slate tiles, and somber, apparently uninhabited adjoining nunnery. Up under the eaves of the church lived a blue-haired pot-smoking youngster and his girlfriend, maybe the sexton's son. They would wave feebly at us; perhaps they weren't quite sure whether we were swingers or squares.

I was used to buying clothes for Brice; now I bought a few suits and jackets Hubert selected. He had strange taste; he was hell-bent on acquiring a double-breasted green linen jacket with gilt tin buttons, two rows of them.

He was very slim, with a full head of hair he wore long and carefully brushed. He must have once had very bad acne; like many oily-skinned Mediterraneans he had some interesting facial scars and the odd boil on his back. He was a poor young architect without a personal fortune, but it was clear he would have been a dandy if he could have afforded it. I bought him some Church's shoes he practically enshrined in his closet in protective bags and engorged with shoehorns. He had a blue silk scarf covered with a pattern of gold trumpets he wore as a foulard, although it was too thick and long to fold neatly at the neck. He had found it in an Egyptian's shop full of sun-faded goods in Addis Ababa, an item that had been in the fly-blown window since the 1930s and probably was a bolt of fabric meant to be sewn into a formal blouse.

He showed me photos of himself in Nantes, where he went to architecture school—in them he was even thinner and his hair (which had a will and a density of its own) was even longer. He wore white cambric pirate shirts loosely laced at the neck, with mutton-sleeves, the whole stuffed into wide-wale corduroy trousers, the sort Rodolfo might wear in Act I of *La Bohème*—bohemian and elegant, an amusing variation on a worker's costume. He also had black-and-white snapshots of a reedy naked young woman toiling in a fisherman's net on the parquet.

In some of the same pictures he was striding through nearly empty rooms in highly polished hip-high black boots. His shabby student apartment had been the piano nobile of an eighteenth-century town house, he explained, on the Île Feydeau in Nantes, complete with the stone masks of slaves under the windows who'd been transported and temporarily housed on the island until the French Revolution ended the slave trade. Nor is the island an island anymore; the rivers around it were filled in after World War II. But Hubert had loved the aristo-cratic history of the town house, even though he lived there without heat or even electricity.

All that was before I met him, as were his years in Addis Ababa. He went there in a sort of Peace Corps alternative to military service; he was teaching architecture to Ethiopians in French.

"Do they know French?"

"No, but they think they do. Knowing French is part of their cultural heritage."

"Did they learn anything?"

"No, I just threw their finals out the window without reading them." He laughed his deep, unconvincing laugh.

"Could you speak any of their languages?"

"That's how you could tell the spies: they spoke Amharic. The rest of us spoke English or French or both. My wife speaks five Ethiopian languages—she's not a spy, she grew up there." He explained that her father was an expert on deserts, and they'd lived many places where deserts were encroaching on the land.

He had peculiar relics of those days, which now belong to me: a tiny gold lion, the emperor's symbol; a painting of Communist soldiers holding red flags, all looking the same way; a giant ostrich foot with a lethal spur; a postcard of the famous underground churches carved into the living rock. No guest ever guesses the painting of the soldiers is Ethiopian. Most people think it's Haitian. It was done by Haile Selassie's court painter, who went Communist when the emperor (whom Hubert called "the Negus") was deposed. Hubert used to have a double-exposed snapshot of the painter, as skinny in his robes as an ebony stick mummi-fied in cloth. The double image made him look somewhat ghostly. In his opinion the Ethiopian women were beautiful, whereas the men were balding and either pudgy or starving.

He claimed he was from the *petite noblesse* (I suppose he thought the lie was more plausible if it was modest). He said that his mother had been a promising concert pianist but his evil father had forced her to give up her career. He said that his ancestors had built the medieval church in Nantes; when the tower had tilted the architect had committed suicide. He said that his father's infidelities had driven his mother to suicide. He said that he attended a reunion of the Knights of Malta in the Opéra-Comique and that six of your eight great-grandparents had to be aristocrats in order to belong. He spoke fondly of some impoverished blue-blooded friends in the sixteenth arrondissement who lived without hot water in a vast noble apartment with an open water basin flowing in the kitchen.

I asked Hubert why he never sought out these friends and he said he preferred to visit them in his thoughts. He was a very poetic young man, a sort of Hamlet-Byron-Tristan. He would never tolerate a mean word said of my few titled friends. He always insisted in a seemingly innocent but actually tendentious way on Marie-Claude's Jewishness; once he asked, "Elle est juive d'ou?" (She's a Jew from where?). I became angry and said, "She's French, just like you!" He was very proud of the fact that of the fifty or so architects who worked for his *boîte,* he was the only one who had all four grandparents born in France. And yet he suspected his own father was a Jew. He was circumcised and his grandfather's name was Isaiah; had the family converted for safety reasons?

He loved to talk negatively about his wife, and when a real fatso would waddle past, he'd say, "There goes Fabienne in five years." And yet he insisted we meet her for lunch. She had unruly dyed red hair and wore black leather; the combination seemed to me more German than French. She'd been the girlfriend of an English punk rocker, apparently a famous one. She made a living screening African political refugees. She regaled us with imitations of their bad French and tall horror stories contrived to win sympathy, usually implausible and absurd; it reminded me of my Texas grandfather's "nigger jokes," full of dialect and instances of "the cute things they say." She didn't seem nearly beautiful or refined enough to be Hubert's wife, but since I was neither beautiful nor refined I thought he merely had odd taste. He divorced her within months of our meeting. They were already separated and had been for about a month. They lived apart.

He loved me, and since my ego had taken a bruising from Brice and I already thought I was impossibly old for gay life, I felt grateful and happy. Gratitude is my chief erotic emotion. We had very hot sex, but I figured out he wanted to be dominated (only in bed), which wasn't my natural role, though I hoped to bind him to me by playing it. For me a current lover has always been like whatever current book I'm writing—an obsessive project orienting all my thoughts. I have such a geisha temperament that I long to please men; I always assume that in a marital squabble my friend, whether male or female, is at fault in failing to please The Man. I'm not talking about sex roles, much less dominance in real life. I'm talking about the submission I feel and project onto my friends.

Hubert was so mysterious. If I'd ask him a direct question about his sexual experiences in the past with other men or women, he'd just grow silent. He wouldn't say anything. I felt I was being a nosy American. He was always tired and losing weight, though he was already skeletal. Then he developed a chancre on his penis that wouldn't go away. I made him go to my gay doctor, who told him he must have the test for HIV. Hubert was indignant. How impertinent!

Maybe we wouldn't have stayed together if he'd been negative. He loved me, but we weren't really compatible. I was liberal, he was a royalist. I had a nearly automatic American respect for minorities; he was scornful of difference. I was compulsively social; he was a one-man dog who hated to share me. But then I believed maybe he really was an inexperienced straight man whom I'd infected, though we used condoms and practiced "safe sex," whatever that was.

No one I knew could give a straight answer to the question of what was safe. Was oral sex safe? Was kissing? Was pre-come dangerous? Were we both going to die? The doctor said his T-cell count was so low, below a hundred, that he'd obviously been positive for many years, longer than me. And yet, since I knew nothing of his past, there was always the possibility I'd slipped up and handed him a death sentence. It may have served his purposes to keep me in his thrall through ignorance about his past and guilt. He was a strategist in love, whereas I, like most Americans of my generation, was always eager to blab the truth in the name of honesty.

I got a job as a full (if underpaid) professor of creative writing at Brown. Hubert wanted to accompany me and live in America. We'd been together only a year. I was touched that he was willing to leave his job, his language, his family—all for me. He had already divorced his wife. Of course he and I both thought we had only two or three years to live.

Hubert wanted to work as an architect in America. Little did we know that the American Northeast was going through a severe recession that had hit particularly hard the building industry. In order to get him a professional visa to work, we had to find an architect in Boston to say he was indispensable. I convinced two Boston-based South American architects I had profiled for *House & Garden* to say they needed his expertise in order to enter big international architectural competitions. Then they backed down, saying they were afraid their own visas might come under scrutiny. After a brief panic I located an American architect friend of James Lord's, a handsome, kind millionaire who didn't actually practice architecture but signed the voucher out of amiability.

My stupid American lawyer in Paris didn't know that an alien couldn't enter America on a tourist visa if he was waiting for a work visa. Hubert was turned back at the Boston airport and held under armed guard for eight hours until he was sent back to Paris at his own expense. After anxious hours spent in vain in the airport, I remember the lonely taxi ride to Providence through the winter snows with a Sikh taxi driver. To ask directions we pulled up to an aluminum-sheathed snack trailer, the only thing open in downtown Providence. Steam was rolling off the trailer's windows and it was surrounded by drunks, who began to pound on the top of the car and shout, "Go home, towelhead." I cried and cried. I'd rented the big, dowdy house of another writer professor on sabbatical. I'd also bought his VW Sirocco. I had to drive through the sleet to the supermarket to buy provisions. There the canned music was scratchy and the aisles were fluorescent lit and empty.

The gum-chewing checkout clerk looked in her teens but was coiffed with an enormous helmet of teased hair; her fingernails were painted with swirly colors and had zircons somehow implanted in them, one jewel per nail. I wept as I ate a whole carton of cottage cheese, which you can't find in France. I'd also bought a Sara Lee carrot cake, which didn't exist in Paris either.

I called Si Newhouse, who owned all the various periodicals I wrote for, and asked him if anything could be done for Hubert. "That will backfire in the States," he said. "This isn't a banana republic like France where you can use pull or bribe officials. Just wait for the normal procedures to work." I was astonished that Si, one of the richest Americans, couldn't influence someone; everybody in the countries I knew, France, Italy, or Spain (the "Garlic Belt"), could be bought. If I wore my French honor (Officer of Arts and Letters) I could get a seat on a full Air France flight; Paris was the capital of the Garlic Belt. *Egalité* and *fraternité* were fictions.

Hubert could get into Canada, and to be with him I flew to Montréal for a weekend. It was January. January in Canada (at least before global warming) was a trial. I'd found him a B and B in the gay part of town, which he detested. He was snooty about Canadian French (*un ami* became *un chum* in Canada, *une voiture* became *un char* because it sounds like "a car," although in French the word means "chariot" or "tank"). He seemed to hate queens of any sort, the peroxided workers in the B and B who talked about cock size and getting drunk and who smoked Kools and filed their nails all day long. To break the monotony on my second visit I rented a car and drove him through a blizzard to Québec City, the only walled town in the Americas. The snow was so blinding that I couldn't see the edge of the road. He had to walk ahead, feeling for the edge with his boot, and I had to follow him at a snail's pace. It must have been the beginning of February, because our arrival coincided with the Winter Carnival; everyone was blowing toy trumpets and drinking potent Caribous and visiting the huge ice sculptures from various Nordic countries and even China. Finally we found a room in a modern tower on the outskirts of town.

Hubert was happy. The city was old, the eighty or so ice sculptures were unique, everyone was merry and slipping and sliding up the cobblestone streets, and the trumpets were echoing off the stone walls. We had great sex as always. I felt guilty that my lawyer had misadvised us.

Finally his work visa came through. Though he got into the States at last, he was angry at the whole country and bitter. "No one wants to come here anymore, at least not from the first or second world. France is superior to America."

My nephew's heart had been broken by his wife in Tokyo. He flew to Providence and joined us. Hubert couldn't bear him. Keith would get drunk and scream at his wife, Tomoko, in Japan over the phone round about two in the morning. The worst was that they communicated in pidgin English: "Me no wanty come back Japan!" he would shout. Neither he nor Hubert had any respect for our landlord's house or furniture. "It's all store-bought furniture, new, it's worth nothing," Hubert declared.

"Americans spend a lot of money on store-bought furniture," I said. "They're very proud of it." In one of the bedrooms there was a spooky, life-size doll of a grandmother, reminiscent of Mrs. Bates in *Psycho*. My nephew hauled it down to the basement, where it became filthy. I could see an invisible adding machine touting up vast sums I would owe the landlord for the damages. Eventually the sum came to ten thousand dollars. The parquet floor was thin and easily scarred. Hubert didn't like the placement of the dining room table and shoved it to a new place, leaving behind deep grooves in the floor. We bought a basset puppy who gnawed holes in the upholstery. The balloon ceiling in the entrance hall filled with overflow water from the bathtub above, although our landlord had warned us of that possibility.

Finally Hubert threw my nephew out of the house after he said patronizing things about the Italians, as if they were all stupid day laborers. My nephew had never traveled to Italy, but his self-esteem was so low he needed to feel superior to someone. Was it Stendhal who said the French were Italians in a bad mood? Certainly the bond between the Italians and the French is a very tight one, ever since Catherine de Médici arrived in Paris with her pastry chefs, or perhaps since Petrarch fell in love with his Laura (who may have been an ancestor of the Marquis de Sade), or even since Caesar conquered Gaul.

But Hubert was sort of compassionate. He introduced my nephew to a Finnish weaver twenty-five years older than Keith, a woman who he realized would take care of Keith, as she did for the next twenty years. They became lovers.

I'd met a woman in Paris named Christine, a teacher in a *maternelle* (kindergarten), and invited her to accompany me to Providence, all expenses paid, so she could develop her talent as an illustrator while I started my teaching job at Brown. I thought she'd be good company for Hubert, who until recently had had a wife. And after all, both Hubert and Christine wanted to be illustrators. As a woman, she'd take the curse off an all-male household. It was an experiment that resulted in Christine becoming an important, in-demand children's book artist (she ended up doing children's books with Julie Andrews and her daughter), but was otherwise something of a disaster.

In fact, Hubert didn't like her—either this or he wanted me all to himself.

Christine was constantly irritating Hubert, though she did her best to soothe him. She was always desperately in love, and there was no reasoning with her if she was in hot pursuit of a man. She'd met an Israeli, a grad student at Brown, and, in spite of Hubert's specific prohibition against inviting anyone to the small house we'd rented in Key West for the month of January, she secretly asked him down for a weekend. When it turned out she'd ignored Hubert's will, he became furious and disappeared, riding his bike across the island for twenty-four hours. I was terribly anxious and sensed that somehow he thought this was all my fault.

In turn, Christine was hurt that what Hubert called her nymphomania so vexed him. As a man used to flirting with women and sleeping with them, he wasn't afraid of them or on distant, polite terms with them as I was. He talked openly and crudely with women about their pussies and their "insatiable" needs. Which never struck me as funny, though he laughed a lot with a big, hollow laugh.

Because Christine was so nakedly needy, she seemed to me like another gay man—like me whenever I was infatuated. Both she and Hubert, so young and so good looking, were frustrated because no one in Providence cruised them. I explained that in America it was considered rude (or gay) to look fixedly at someone. It seemed symptomatic of the national differences to me that the word "cruise" in English applied only to gays, whereas the French equivalent, *draguer*, applied to heterosexuals as well.

"But have we lost our looks?" Christine asked.

In some ways very sophisticated, she could also be naïve and credulous. When she'd first moved to Paris, a chubby, middle-aged Turk offering to "audition" her had made her parade around for him in a sheer dress, then a bikini, then nude—explaining that he wanted to make her a "top model" (the two English words are always said together by French speakers, as if they constitute a necessarily bound form). When it got late and Christine could see he was agitating something in his lap, she started to cry, wailing, "I don't want to be a *topmodel!*"

She'd gathered up her clothes and fled. The man lived in the place des Victoires, which was deserted at midnight, and she looked back over her shoulder to see if he was pursuing her.

The least French-seeming thing about Christine was her love of telling tales that exposed her own naïveté, which she mocked and gloried in. Hubert and I teased her about the Israeli grad student, who was portly, trying to hide from her behind a tree.

"The pregnant tree," Hubert said, and in the air he drew a tree with a stomach.

Christine's drawings were of childhood innocence and would often show children with their grandmothers or would illustrate idyllic memories of her grandfather's estate beside the Loire and long summers playing there with her girl cousins.

Hubert's drawings were satirical of grown-ups saying pretentious or fatuous things. It was as if, since he was obliged to say farewell to this world, he must first denigrate it. As a favor to me, Linda Spalding and Michael Ondaatje printed some of Hubert's drawings in their magazine *Brick,* but several readers found them so offensive they canceled their subscriptions. I thought it was heroic that Hubert still cared enough about the world to satirize it.

Chapter 14

John Purcell, who'd been living in my old apartment in New York, had become ill with AIDS. I took him and Hubert both on a trip to the Yucatán where they squabbled the whole time. I had promised John I would take care of him if he ever became ill, but Hubert forbade him to visit our house in Providence. In the Yucatán John wanted to open the window of our rented VW Bug but Hubert, with his French fear of drafts, insisted he close it. Then Hubert was constantly saying, "Pardon, pardon," whenever he entered a door first, and John exploded that he mustn't keep saying that. Hubert wailed that John was trying to denude him of his exquisite manners. I was ready to tear my hair out.

I had to fly to Mexico City to interview the ageing movie diva María Félix. She kept me waiting for a day while she washed her hair. I couldn't contact John and Hubert, who were clawing at each other in Mérida, to say I'd be delayed. I couldn't find the hotel phone number. I contemplated jumping from my hotel's thirteenth-story balcony. I'd been in Mexico City with my father in 1953, when it was a beautiful Art Nouveau city of a million. Now it was a polluted slum of twenty million with some of the world's richest people living behind barbed wire protected by guard dogs and swarms of the poor clamoring to sell lottery tickets at every traffic light. It wasn't so much that I *wanted* to jump as that I felt drawn against my will to the balcony. I had to lock the glass doors and pull the curtains.

I'd been chosen to interview María Félix because she spoke French but not English. *Vanity Fair* was looking for a sad *Sunset Boulevard* portrait. They'd sent Helmut Newton to shoot her, but he was so old he couldn't brave the capital's thin air; María Félix had to descend to her villa in Cuernavaca so that he could shoot a hostile photograph of her ropy hands around the neck of her young Polish lover (no face-lifting for the hands). The problem was: I liked María Félix. Sartre had written a film for her. When Carlos Fuentes wrote a bitchy novel about her, she asked to play the part in the movie version. When I asked her how she could walk through the Bois de Boulogne at night and risk being attacked by huge, fierce Brazilian transvestite whores, she replied, "Oh, Monsieur White, I admire them so. We are just biological women; they are artistic, *constructed* women. They are the real women."

When I returned to Mérida, we drove to a primitive little town on the north of the peninsula and saw pink flamingoes at dawn; Hubert had seen bigger flocks in Ethiopia. We went to the pyramids in Chichen Itza; both men seemed attracted to the idea of human sacrifice. In Cobá we stayed in a former Club Med, the Villas Arqueologicas, where bougainvillea blossoms floated on infinity pools and Mayan ruins punctuated the jungle nearby. I rented us a modern house between Playa del Carmen and Tulum. John found a bar with congenial drunks nearby; Hubert went on poetic walks alone along the beach in white pedal pushers. Europeans could never master the casual American beach look.

I was so happy to get back to freezing, dreary Providence. Hubert had been so hateful to John that I wondered how I could take my revenge on Hubert without leaving him. I couldn't leave him; he depended on me completely. I remembered Gide's wife had punished him for running off with a teenage boy by burning the hundreds of letters he'd sent her over the years—his best writing, he claimed. I decided to stop sleeping with Hubert. I'm sure he thought I had a real distaste for him now that he was ill. My "solution" was as pointlessly cruel as Madeleine Gide's. Soon enough he really was too ill to have sex.

A few months later I told John I would take him any place he wanted. India? France? He chose Disney World in Orlando. I thought it might be a hoot, but I found it intolerably boring and tacky. At Epcot, we went to some horrid replica of the Eiffel Tower when we'd lived in the real Paris for years. After standing for hours in queues, we went on a fun-house ride past leering dolls popping out of the wall, singing "It's a Small World" in chipmunk voices. The only authentic pavilion was the Morrocan restaurant, where we ate couscous, spoke French to the waiters, and made dates with them. John was happy because he seduced a black preppy father pushing a pram.

Then Christine phoned me that Hubert was hospitalized in Boston. I rushed to his side on the next plane. John was furious, as if Hubert had staged this illness to spite him. In those days Brown did not have domestic partner health coverage, so the doctor very kindly had risked charges of fraud by registering Hubert under my name. It was a very curious thing having to address Hubert as "Edmund." He had had to invent a whole story of a lost GI father in order to explain why he was called Edmund White but could barely speak English.

We knew we had to go back to France, for the great, inexpensive medical care, if nothing else. Diane Johnson let us stay in her charming Paris apartment, a block away from Marie-Claude's. MC had come to visit us once in Key West, but she was always worried she'd run into her ex-husband and his new wife. Laurent and Phyllis had a beautiful house there and were very popular, but for a decade MC forbade me to see them, which was silly. At last she relented. I'd always liked Phyllis, who was bright and inquisitive and who'd turned herself into a talented photographer; Laurent, of course, was an old friend.

John Purcell returned to the Catholic church. His mother had found a kindly priest to play his spiritual guide, Father Mike, whose brother had died from AIDS. John moved back to his parents' home in Concord. I saw him twice more—in Venice, where we spent a week alone and where he cried because I bought him expensive new clothes ("That shows, Petes, that you think I'll go on living"), and in Key West, another vacation I ruined by bringing along a twenty-two-year-old English soccer star who was terribly jealous of John—though he was helpless and bedridden—and shockingly rude to him. Oh, and once I took John to a French island in the Caribbean, Marie-Galante, but in those days it didn't have the luxurious accomodations an invalid needed. John's only regret was that he'd been in love with the ulti-mate black preppy in New York, and that man had dropped him ("I wanted just one affair to work out before I died"). John's high voice, boyish body, and youthful way of dressing—the very thing that attracted many older gay men, the guys who bought him drinks at Julius'—put off straight women and many educated gay men. I tried to get him a job with a top New York decorator, but there was no work. My friend Nathalie was going to hire him to represent a line of furniture she wanted to launch in New York, but she was spooked by his "young girl's voice" over the phone. Hubert despised him as "a cretin." I was shocked that these guys didn't have compassion for each other, since they were dying of the same disease.

Hubert was shutting down. One day, in a state of curiosity rather than panic, he noticed he couldn't write French words any more. Nor numbers. I rushed him to the hospital and they discovered he'd been attacked by toxoplasmosis, a parasite in the brain. It was reversible, thanks to a drug they'd just discovered (an old drug, though this new application had just been verified). He became thinner and thinner. He could no longer work as an architect; he turned himself into an illustrator. I wrote the text and he did the drawings for a little book called *Our Paris*. We contacted Claude Picasso's mother, Françoise Gilot, who now was married to Jonas Salk, the inventor of the polio vaccine. He put us in touch with a Paris researcher who was replacing the plasma of long-term AIDS patients with transfusions from newly infected patients. The idea was that the long-term patients would be helped by the high T-cell counts of the newly ill. It was a good theory, but it didn't work. We traveled to Marrakesh, which he loved for its warmth. I tried to rent a riyadh, a mansion in the heart of the old city, but when the caretaker saw Hubert's skinny frame he invented an implausible prior claim on the house. Perhaps he was afraid Hubert would die on his property.

We returned to gray, rainy Paris; Hubert longed for the heat of the desert. Our beloved basset hound, Fred, became too big and strong for him. Hubert was afraid of him and gave him to his gay brother, Julien, and the brother's lover, François, who was my age. They lived in Nice in a house with a garden; there was a puppy belonging to the upstairs neighbors for Fred to play with. Hubert's brother and his lover doted on the dog.

John's mother called and said he'd died kissing the Cross; they'd inscribed a public bench in Concord with his name. I hosted a big dinner in his honor at Da Silvano in New York, where everyone toasted him. It seemed appropriate.

Hubert and I went back to Morocco, this time to Agadir, where we hired a car. MC said she thought Hubert was too ill to travel, but I imagined riding around as a passenger in a car would be effortless. It turns out it's exhausting for someone who's weak and suffering. Hubert was vomiting all the time, due to pancreatitis. He couldn't hold down any food. The seams in his blue jeans hurt him. so he switched to long Arab robes. His skin became weirdly dark in the sun. Between his robes, skin color, and thinness, everyone assumed he was an Arab, a poor, beat-up, fleshless one; I caught two gold-toothed Moroccan boys nudging each other behind his back and laughing at him.

He slept all the time. He was too weak to climb into and out of the bath; I had to hold his body in my arms to help him. Naked, he looked like an Auschwitz victim. He wouldn't turn back, but like the dying Kit in *The Sheltering Sky* kept urging me to go deeper and deeper into the desert. Finally we reached Zagora, on the Algerian border. He became incontinent—he pissed all over himself. The desk clerk didn't want to give us a room, though the hotel was empty. I was writing something; Hubert had always listened to my latest pages, but now he was too weak to pay attention. He just smiled at me.

Because I insisted, we started driving back toward civilization, but it was the end of Ramadan and crowds were making merry in the nearly impassible roads. We were about as cheerful as a hearse as we waded through all these laughing, smiling people in their best clothes. When we got to Ouarzazate, Hubert collapsed on the way into the hotel. He kept saying he was finished, and when I insisted he get up he told me he detested me; those were his last words to me. A passerby called an ambulance, which meant Hubert was taken to a filthy Arab hospital where even the food for the patients was brought by family members. I'd been struggling against all odds to keep him alive; now I completely lost it. My act of will had come to nought. Moroccans gathered around his body lying in the grass like characters in a painting by Giotto, eager to drink in, to *witness*, this calamity; they were allegories of observation. I was extremely frank with the three attending physicians, but I'm not sure they knew what AIDS was. They kept assuring me he was on the mend; they seemed determined to be optimistic.

We'd taken out emergency health insurance. I called the agent and he arranged for an ambulance to drive us through the freezing Atlas Mountains to the dirty Clinique du Sud in Marrakesh. On the way through the cold night he moaned and complained about something stabbing him in the back. The driver stopped and turned him over but couldn't find anything. I assured Hubert there was nothing wrong, which made him hate me all the more (maybe he was feeling pain in the pancreas). The Moroccan nurses at the clinic almost laughed at Hubert's pitiful state. A male intern hurt him in inserting a saline drip in his arm. I was allowed to sleep in the same room. When I woke up in the morning in the gay sunlight, the saline bag was no longer bubbling; he was dead.

The very severe and unsmiling insurance agent showed up and told me I couldn't take Hubert's body back with me. Many papers had to be filled out. Nor did they believe, the Muslims, in embalming. I convinced them to seal him in a lead coffin, though I knew he'd quickly turn to bouillabaisse in the heat.

MC brought her nightgown and toothbrush and spent the night with me when I got back to Paris. I noticed that my hair had turned white, I'd put on fifty pounds, and all my clothes needed dry cleaning. Hubert's brother Julien and his lover flew up to Paris. They went through all the formalities with me and arranged for Hubert's coffin to be repatriated. Only the Père Lachaise cemetery had ovens strong enough to blast through the lead coffin to cremate him. Looking at the smoke coming out of the tall chimney, again I thought of the German death camps.

Julien told me that Hubert had lied to me. Their mother had been a hairdresser and had played the accordion, not the concert piano. His grandmother came from Nantes for the cremation. She was a little, fat peasant woman, always joking. She was no aristocrat but lived in a two-room house with a mud floor; she was a simple, kind woman and

I was sorry that Hubert's lies had kept me from knowing her. Julien told me that Hubert had had sex before meeting me with dozens of men over the years in the woods covering Montburon, behind their house. Even though I'm an atheist, for a long time I lit candles in every church I visited.

Chapter 15

In the years that I was living in Paris I paid hundreds of visits to London, sometimes on book tour, but usually just for pleasure. The English could be far more spontaneously social than the French. For one thing, they got drunker more often than the French. The French were constantly tippling wine but were seldom visibly drunk, even if they did have a high percentage of deaths from cirrhosis of the liver. In England, people drank to get drunk, and it was not uncommon to see someone's mother, a duchess or an important editor, fall down in public.

My English friends could give a drinks party with just a day's advance notice, and in spite of the vastness of London were willing to travel on the tube many miles. In New York it took me two weeks and in Paris one week to assemble friends for a full-blown dinner party. In London I could start calling and inviting a day or two before.

The English were witty and irreverently gossipy. My agent, Deborah Rogers, always said, "Let's get together for a good chin wag," or "Let's put our knees up," when I was coming to town. The French, being human, enjoyed gossip but officially were opposed to it. If someone served too much "dish" he ran the risk of being told he was no better than a concierge (who are stereotypically regarded as spies and snitches). The French had such active sex lives and inhabited apartments in such close proximity that they lived in mortal fear of being found out. The English seemed to me more moderate in their sexual exploits and lived in greater isolation—very often in detached houses in vast neighborhoods that were scattered across enormous London. Plus, their press, which was scandal driven, had bred in them a taste and a tolerance for outrage.

In France, by contrast, a law called *l'atteinte de la vie privée* meant nothing spicy could be written about public figures. In order to learn about sex scandals among the powerful French players, everyone had to consult the numerous Spanish or English magazines trafficking in loose innuendo and salacious he-said, she-said. In France, even if a reporter came armed with loads of evidence and testimony, the accused could bring an immediate lawsuit against the publishers and a fine could swiftly be imposed—a system that helped guard against poorly substantiated, career-killing hearsay, but that also defused investigative reporting. In many ways the invasion-of-privacy law kept French life unpolluted, but it also tranquilized press vigilance, which meant that there was a weak opposition press in France.

One of my dearest friends in England was Neil Bartlett. While he was still at Oxford, he asked if he could stage parts of my novel, *A Boy's Own Story*, and I was quick to say yes.

When we met to discuss his ideas, I was still a young-looking and presentable forty-three, used to sleeping with, or attempting to seduce, every gay man I met. After all, we'd just emerged from the seventies, the "golden age of promiscuity" (as Brad Gooch later put it in the title of one of his excellent novels). And even though AIDS had since intervened, I imagined that being in Europe constituted an AIDS holiday, a recess from the emergencies of the disease.

I slept with Neil, who was twenty years younger than I and vulpine but strangely courtly, a bit of a dandy with a touch of the thug. He was attracted to drag and he even wore a dress in a book of photos called *Men in Frocks*. And yet he was "the man" when we made love.

Right after Oxford he lived in a council flat that was in the East End and a stone's throw from Lime House. I would stay with him and his adorable roommate, the terribly appealing straight director of the Theatre de Complicité, Simon McBurney, with his childlike face and rubbery, hairless body. In England, more than elsewhere, I met many straight men who were *sympathique*. I had the good luck to observe both men rise in the theater world. The Theatre de Complicité toured outside of England and in England was hosted by the National Theatre on the South Bank. Simon became a recognized screen actor, and Neil went on to take over the direction of the Lyric Hammersmith. Once he presented Benjamin Britten's *Michelangelo Sonnets*, and for the program notes he asked me to translate Britten's choice of the sonnets into English from the original Italian.

Neil also became one of England's finest writers. He wrote a landmark book, *Who Was That Man?*, about Oscar Wilde and fin de siècle gay London. His novels *Ready to Catch Him Should He Fall*, *Mr. Clive and Mr. Page,* and *Skin Lane* all had their historical dimensions. He might have dedicated himself just to fiction, but he was also attracted to directing theater pieces of an extravagant, stylized, somewhat campy variety, such as Balzac's *Sarrasine*, Racine's *Bérenice* and Neil's own adaptation of *Camille*. *A Vision of Love Revealed* was based on Simeon Solomon's 1871 prose poem, and Neil himself performed it in the nude in a warehouse. He did adaptations and translations of plays by Molière and Racine and farces by Labiche, as well as the English-language premiere of Genet's posthumous gangster play, *Splendid's*, which I had told him about during my research for Genet.

Neil found a lover, James Gardiner, a collector of vintage postcards who produced a book of letters and photographs called *A Class Apart* that documented an Edwardian affair between an amateur gentleman photographer and his well-hung "butler" who was willing to indulge his employer's taste for uniforms; the butler wrote touching, misspelled love letters to him when he went off to fight in the First World War. Neil and James bought a bijou residence in Brighton where they entertained me more than once.

When Neil got hepatitis, he had a liver transplant, but at first the new liver refused to kick in. Neil never succumbed to convalescence completely, and even when he seemed close to death kept busy and artistically active—until miraculously, at seemingly the last possible minute, the liver began to function. I've often thought of Neil's courage in facing these travails during my own health scares and emergencies.

Once Neil, when he was still in his twenties, came to visit me in Paris. Because his plane was delayed (this was before the Eurostar Chunnel train running under the English Channel), I told him to take a taxi directly from the airport to MC's. She had also invited to dinner Yannick Guillou, an elegant, uptight (or *guindé*, as the French say in reference to spats) Gallimard editor, who played the harpsichord for half an hour each morning before going to work, and who owned a castle in Normandy.

Neil arrived in a black leather biker jacket and jeans with the whole seat torn out and no underwear. Yannick was astonished by this vestimentary oddity but charmed by Neil's Oxford accent, education, and exquisite manners. Neil's personality was both outrageous and decorous.

Equally odd were the clothes of the gay English writer and critic Adam Mars-Jones, who wore striped military pants and an officer's tunic. Because in France there was no youth culture, these costumes looked particularly strange to Parisians. But Adam also spoke beautiful French, was tall and slim, wonderfully polite and *sortable* (meaning you could take him anywhere). He met some of my ladies, such as Didi d'Anglejan, an American who'd married an aristocrat and gained a title. I'd told my ladies that Adam's father was a judge and a lord—that worked wonders. Nor did it hurt that he'd attended Westminster and Cambridge.

On one of his visits to Paris, I prepared him lunch and said that unfortunately I'd been in a rush and that the only thing I'd had time to prepare was rabbit and mustard sauce. My wonderful butcher on the Île Saint-Louis kept a stone vat by the front door of rabbit parts marinating in Dijon mustard. The trick was to bring this mixture home and sauté it with white wine, then at the last moment stir in crème fraîche. It took ten minutes to do and was served with rice and a vegetable.

Adam exclaimed, "You've been too long in France. Imagine, apologizing for rabbit!"

He was still young, but already Adam was a blocked writer, making him a severe critic of film and other people's fiction. When I'd first come to England for the very successful launch of *A Boy's Own Story*, which eventually sold a hundred thousand copies there, Adam wrote a negative review, but I invited him all the same to my launch party and after that we became friends. He stayed with me in Paris that one time and I stayed with him in Islington rather often. Once, I introduced him to Amy Gross, then the features editor of American *Vogue*. I wanted Adam to become the film critic for *Vogue*—he was strapped for cash since he'd fathered his daughter Holly. Amy told me, "His prose is beautiful, his argumentation is brilliant. But I never ever agree with him about a single movie." She hadn't hired him, out of that very personal whimsicality characteristic of all the best editors; she then went on to work for *Mirabella* before helping launch *O, The Oprah Magazine* as editor in chief.

MC was intrigued by Adam's daughter, and I feel that Holly humanized him. Sometimes he seemed nothing more than an overgrown, precocious lad, a sort of Eagle Scout of the intellect, master of some intricate sophistry du jour that he served up to everyone. MC bought Holly a pretty Parisian frock, which made Adam bluster, and then he became a latter-day Colonel Blimp.

Adam had provided his very high-grade seed to a lesbian who'd selected him to fertilize her. I remember being shocked when Adam took Holly to Gay Pride while she was still a little girl; children make us conservative, or at least in my experience they usually do. We subject them to conventions we ourselves have paradoxically been fleeing all our lives. Adam also presented Holly to his various lovers, usually men who weren't as smart and attractive as her father. I'd known people who've always taken inferior lovers in order to point up their own superiority. I remember once trying to make conversation with one of Adam's Scottish lovers with whom I didn't have a lot in common. Knowing a little about his background, I finally decided to ask him how tweed was made. He came to life describing how everyone in his family would pitch in and stretch the tweed they'd woven while singing a traditional tweed ballad. He sang and demonically stretched the imaginary tweed, making his knuckles so sore and red that Adam had to bandage them.

I thought I'd make an ideal partner for Adam, but he apparently thought otherwise. We did, however, collaborate on a collection of short stories called *The Darker Proof*, published in the UK by Faber. I came up with the title and he came up with the idea. Adam thought that the AIDS epidemic had produced nothing but doctors' warnings and no dramatic accounts of or by the people directly concerned. Gays, who'd been the province of experts for a century, were in danger of being "re-medicalized." He'd written three stories and I two long ones, which if presented together made a nice-sized volume; publishing it as a paperback original made it more affordable for readers and got it into print sooner. Each of us kept writing more of the stories and years later collected them in separate volumes. Mine was called *Skinned Alive*, after the late Titian of Apollo cutting off the flesh of the satyr Marsyas following Apollo's victory in a musical contest. I remember vividly lying on a mattress in Adam's front parlor, looking up at a poster of Morrissey on the wall. That Adam should have Morrissey as his favorite singer in common with my nephew was unexpected. I also remember visiting Adam's parents' huge flat in the Inns of Court, where he prepared me once a breakfast of fish: "sprats," every bit as exotic to me as rabbit.

In the years that he was "blocked" as a writer, not only did Adam write the stories in our book (which later were included in his own second collection, *Monopolies of Loss*), but he also wrote one of a series of "broadsides" published by Chatto & Windus, edited by Carmen Callil—polemics that could be read in a single sitting on a contemporary subject. Adam's was called *Venus Envy* and it opened with the idea that male authors like Martin Amis—being envious of female writers and their feminist apologists, and searching for other important-sounding topics they might themselves credibly address as straight men and fathers—took on the utterly uncontroversial and unobjectionable cause of ridding the world of nuclear weapons and defending the environment in order to regain their "rightful" moral high ground. Adam also wrote a novella, called *The Waters of Thirst,* that portrayed an AIDS caregiver as a sort of emotional saprophyte feeding off his patients. It seemed typically perverse of Adam to be critical of the very professionals who were so scarce and in need of encouragement in the early years of the plague. I suppose I learned from Adam, and the English in general, that the spirit of criticism should be unrelenting and never put off for a more "appropriate" time.

The two most intelligent people I knew in London were Adam and Marina Warner. I was happy to bring them together for an evening; although they were cordial, they never sought each other out independently of me. That's perhaps always the case when two people are *semblables*. (I don't know how many times well-meaning friends have wanted to introduce me to a potential suitor, usually another elderly professor.)

Marina, a novelist and mythographer, trailed a reputation of having been one of the great beauties of her day, going back to Oxford. She became a chat-show staple in the seventies, and the English band Dire Straits even recorded a song about her: "Lady writer on the TV. / Talk about the Virgin Mary . . ." The singer is thinking about his girlfriend while the lady writer on his screen is discussing her new book (Marina's groundbreaking *Alone of All Her Sex*). One of my wicked friends once sped up a video of Marina; her head constantly tick-tocked from side to side in her usual display of little-girl winsomeness. She combined all the arts of an experienced beauty with the fierceness of an omniscient intellectual and a militant feminist.

Unlike some feminists, Marina was very womanly. Her house in North London was delightful, with a small garden out back, a large, comfortable eat-in kitchen, and a double salon. There were many, many books, some of them sent to her for review; curious bibelots and pictures that she'd come across in her mythographic researches; some decorative reminders that her mother was Italian and her grandfather, Sir Pelham Warner, was a celebrated cricketer. Marina sounded very posh, a bit like the queen. She'd grown up all around the world, including Cairo and Brussels, had studied Italian and French at Lady Margaret Hall at Oxford and on the Continent, and could read several other languages. Marina wrote novels, but she was best known for her exhaustive nonfiction compendia on subjects ranging from religious symbols to supernatural phenomena like ghosts and fairies and ectoplasm.

I think I liked Marina more than she liked me. I chose her as my best friend in an English newspaper feature, and we were photographed together in a London square under her parasol, but when I swapped flats, my Paris apartment for a lovely house on Gloucester Crescent, and lived near her for two months, I never saw her (to be fair, she was going through a period of bad health and a nasty breakup). Although she'd been married to the writer William Shawcross and had a son, the talented artist Conrad Shawcross, since her divorce she'd been for many years with Johnny Dewe Mathews, a painter and an eternal boy, handsome and scatterbrained, a wonderful comrade to her Conrad. Johnny was a talented watercolorist whose style was unfashionably traditional and realistic. Marina, like me, was friendly with Bice Curriger and Jacqueline Burckhardt, the Swiss directors of the avant-garde art magazine *Parkett*. Marina was always trying to get them to write something about Johnny, whose work must have looked trivial and *rétardataire* to them. Later, she had an affair with a longhaired, younger academic who looked like a seedy rock musician and was writing his thesis on literary hoaxes. Finally she ended up with a much more appropriate man, an Oxford don of mathematics. She was hired as a professor by the University of East Anglia, which freed her from endless scrambling after freelance assignments. For years Marina had worked so hard to keep afloat with her house and her son. Conrad turned out to be a trendy sculptor in the tradition of Jean Tinguely, by which I mean he made pieces that destroyed themselves. Once I was with Marina in Paris, where everyone was impressed with her convent-bred French and vast erudition, beautiful manners—and enduring beauty.

I think Marina wasn't really comfortable with homosexuality. She and I first met in Manhattan at a luncheon talk she gave to the members of the New York Institute for the Humanities. I can't remember her subject, but in the question-and-answer period, I brought up what I thought was a relevant example about gay male pornography. She often mentioned my comment in the years to follow as a bit of cheekiness at the moment of our meeting. And once when I took over her house while she was away, Marina left as her only instruction, "Don't let the char catch you boys naked." Every part of that sentence alarmed me, since in America we said "cleaning lady" and in France *technicienne de surface*. "Char" sounded Dickensian to my ears, and why should we be running around naked, especially my superconservative Brice? All we did in her house was invite twenty of my English friends to dinner and serve them the duck breasts I'd brought over from France.

If I mismatched the two brains, Marina and Adam, I made a similar mistake with Julian Barnes. He came to Paris with his wife, the literary agent Pat Kavanagh, and I took them to L'Ami Louis, one of the "in" restaurants then—a place that looked like a simple, neighborhood restaurant, decidedly plain, where the cheerful waiters threw the customers' coats up onto a ledge above the booths and where the cuisine was Lucullan, with slabs of fois gras and big chickens or lamb legs roasted on the spit, the opposite of the (to many) mingy nouvelle cuisine then so popular.

Since Julian was the most Francophile of Englishmen, I mistakenly thought he'd like to meet his opposite number, my translator Marc Cholodenko, a novelist who'd won the Prix Goncourt but more relevantly was the most Anglophile of French writers. Later, I realized neither man was interested in the other country except as a way of criticizing their compatriots through counterexamples. That evening, the conversation was stiff and had frequent silences until Marc drifted off and chatted with a pretty woman in a neighboring booth who was with an older man.

Marc returned to us with a thoroughly French tale. The woman was a call girl and was on a paid date with an Israeli industrialist. Marc knew her because years before his best friend, a timid young duke of seventeen, had been taken by his father to Madame Arthur's bordello where he'd lost his virginity to this very woman—then considerably younger and more beautiful. Unexpectedly he fell in love with the woman and wanted to marry her and make her his duchess. He fought for days with his outraged parents, who were at last worn down and conceded. But then the call girl refused. She liked her work—and here she was, years later, middle-aged though still pursuing her profession.

Julian was suitably impressed. When he went to the toilet, Pat (who was notorious in London literary circles for her affair with Jeanette Winterson), looked around and said, "What's annoying about Paris is that every woman looks like a lesbian but none is."

Pat was one of my favorite people. I used to say it was because I liked cold women, but that was just one of the provocative things I liked to say. Pat adored Julian and was, in fact, very ardent—a slender, beautiful redhead with high cheekbones who was originally from South Africa and had an Irish family. She'd been an actress, appearing in the film version of Dylan Thomas's *Under Milk Wood*, but was now one of the best agents in London, representing James Fenton, Andrew Motion, Ruth Rendell, William Trevor, Adam Mars-Jones, Hermione Lee— and Martin Amis, until he left her after twenty-three years for Andrew Wiley, the notorious poacher. Pat died of a brain tumor in 2008 at age sixty-eight, and Julian was and still is, I think, inconsolable.

People used to say the great love marriages were always childless. Certainly Julian and Pat seemed very much in love and inseparable. Children would have spoiled their complicity. Their idea of a good vacation was to go hiking together through Provence.

While they were in Paris on this same trip, I invited them to see an Azzedine Alaïa fashion show, which Julian thought was preposterous ("You've been thoroughly corrupted"), but once he was there, I made sure he was seated next to Tina Turner, who told him that he was one of her favorite authors. Despite his low esteem for something as frivolous as fashion, he could see that Alaïa's dresses were perfectly molded to bodies that were unusually fit.

Once, a few years later, Pat and Julian invited me to a meat restaurant in London and said, "Edmund, you've been gossiping about us," and I said, "Of course. You're the only subject of conversation in London, and if I didn't gossip about you, I'd have nothing to say. I'll tell you exactly what I said. That Pat is a lesbian and she's in love with you, Julian, and you're in love with her." They nodded and said, "Essentially that's true."

Julian had written a negative review of my 1985 novel *Caracole,* but then again almost no one had liked it. I thought it wouldn't be very sportsmanlike to hold that against him. He said, for one thing, that it was under-aerated with dialogue. I had been influenced by Nabokov's observation that if he wanted to see whether a novel was a crappy bestseller, he'd just flip through it and if he saw too much dialogue, he knew it wasn't for him. He reasoned that since dialogue always sounds alike, the writer couldn't establish his own special tone if he handed the book over to his characters and their banal yammering.

Julian and I quickly established a truce of not reading each other's books, which was a relief, though on the sly I've read half a dozen of his novels and admired them.

He and Pat did everything perfectly. They took turns cooking—he did the salad and she the main course and the pudding. They had me and my partner, Michael, to dinner with the painter Howard Hodgkin and his very camp partner, the music writer Antony Peattie. Howard said that he regretted that England's culture was more literary than visual, though he has collaborated with at least two writers, Julian and Susan Sontag. A late bloomer, Howard was an abstractionist whose canvases, at least to his mind, often commemorated specific encounters with friends.

Like Philip Roth, Julian has very intense friendships with women, notably Hermione Lee, who was one of his first readers, Judith Thurman, and Lorrie Moore. Like me, he's attracted to brainy, ardent women, people like Dorothea in *Middlemarch,* though not so gullible.

He also had a laddish side. He has an immense snooker table that fills one whole room of his North London house. But Julian is not a natural wit like Martin Amis, nor does he share Martin's fascination with low life. Julian is a headmaster's son and has that gooseflesh, underloved, boarding-school look, complete with the horsey face and long, blue nose. He's the most British man I know, and I always felt my highly colored American ways were somehow cheap and glaring in his eyes.

I liked the English and I think they liked me. I was better known in Britain as a writer than anywhere else, and of course that was agreeable. And yet I wasn't a caustic éminence grise like Gore Vidal but rather a pudgy, easygoing but witty guy like millions of others. It was always very exhilarating for me in England. They had so many newspapers and I was always being asked to do a column about "My Hero" (James Merrill), my five favorite books about New York, or some other ephemeral subject. I was on lots of book-chat shows on the radio, where I tried to keep up with the fleet-footed English talkers and eschew American ponderousness. Three times I was on the hourlong TV arts program *The South Bank Show*. When I was in England it was thrilling to be able to speak my own language, or some version of it. When I spoke French I felt I was a rat in a maze, guided by a single point of light in the right direction but constantly going down blind alleys and having to retrace my steps (*rebrousser le chemin*), whereas in English I could just babble and occasionally astonish even myself with what came out of my mouth.

Nigella Lawson has become such a symbol of glamour, the domestic goddess of television, that it feels presumptuous to claim friendship with her. When I met her, she worked as an editor for the *Spectator*. I was enough older than her and her friends that I played the role of an eccentric uncle. Nigella was very extravagant. I always stayed in Durrants Hotel behind the Wallace Collection off Marylebone High Street, and Nigella (who was named after her father, Nigel Lawson, Mrs. Thatcher's chancellor of the exchequer) once filled my room at Durrants with a giant bouquet of blue nigellas, a flower sometimes called "love in a mist."

Later she was the deputy literary editor of the *Sunday Times*. I remember writing a review for her comparing Joe Orton to Oscar Wilde, both of them living out their homosexuality in North Africa. Of course I recognized there were differences—Orton was working class and Wilde, I said, was upper class. Nigella called me in Paris and asked if I'd change upper class to upper middle class. I'd forgotten that these nuances meant so much to Brits.

Her mother, a famous beauty, divorced her father and married the philosopher A. J. Ayer, the popular author of *Language, Truth and Logic*. He had been married previously to a woman called Dee Wells, someone I met once at a dinner party given by Natasha Spender, shortly after Stephen Spender's death. After the early death from cancer of Nigella's mother, Ayer remarried Dee Wells.

Nigella has sold hundreds of thousands of cookbooks, which contain her airy, lighthearted remarks. She has always rejected the term "professional cook." She's had her share of tragedy. Her mother died in her forties, her sister, Thomasina, died in her thirties of breast cancer, and her husband, John Diamond, a journalist, died of throat cancer. I can remember eating with them in Nobu in New York. His meal had to be ground into a liquid he could ingest through his tracheotomy. Nigella said that given the amount of cancer in her family, she was virtually placing a curse on her two children. Once John, who was reduced to writing everything he wanted to say in conversation, heard a maddening voice chattering away on the radio—and he realized it was his own voice in a rebroadcast of an old program. Now he said he regretted the years of what he called wasting his words. Nigella once invited my partner Michael and me over for a lamb roast in her kitchen, where the star guests were Stephen Fry and Salman Rushdie. Before publishing his second novel, *Midnight's Children*, Salman had worked in advertising at Ogilvy & Mather as a copywriter and he told us that his great triumph at the firm had been a slogan for a cream cake: "Naughty but Nice."

Fry wasted no time in rejoindering, "You could launch a slimming product: 'Cut-wah Out-wah the Fatwa.'"

We all looked around to see if Salman would laugh at this impudence—and he did.

It was especially dramatic since Salman was still in hiding.

I was spending a lot of time going back and forth between Paris and London in 1989, the year I was a judge for the Booker Prize—when we crowned Kazuo Ishiguro's *The Remains of the Day*. Nigella was my date for the dinner, and her father had resigned from Thatcher's Tory government that very day. Nigella had earlier created a scandal by revealing she voted Socialist. The Anglo-French journalist and literary biographer Olivier Todd was seated next to Nigella and he grilled her for a quote about her father for *L'Express*.

To keep Todd from harassing her, I said, "We have much bigger news—we're getting married." I was happy that night because not only did Ishiguro win but Sybille Bedford, the only gay writer in the competition (and the author of the sterling *A Legacy*, a much earlier book), was on the Booker shortlist for her latest, *Jigsaw*—and I got to meet her. She was already seventy-eight and had her arm in a sling.

A decade and a half later, when my book *My Lives* came out in London, Nigella attended the launch party and created a giant stir. By that time John Diamond was dead; she had moved in with Charles Saatchi nine months after John died, and eventually married him.

Though she was criticized for her "haste," I defended her. I'd taken up with someone new a year after the death of my French lover, Hubert Sorin. In each case, Nigella and I had been a caregiver during a long illness. We'd had plenty of time to say our farewells during an illness that was inevitably fatal. And I, at least, was lonely and terrified and in need of affection.

Alan Jenkins, an agile poet who wrote beautiful verses about unhappy loves and about his nautical father, was the deputy editor of the *Times Literary Supplement* and a dear friend. MC adored him for his good humor and excellent French. He was always a star at my dinner parties. And he visited me more than once in Paris. I was always careful to have a bottle of J&B Scotch around, which did not go untouched, but Alan was the kind of drinker who blossomed conversationally and became a lot of fun, like so many of the English. When I'd been a drinker, I was an alcoholic.

Alan was just a bit of a drunk, which seemed appropriate for a poet. I felt that his poetry was underrecognized, partly because he was a powerful editor—a fate shared by Howard Moss, the poetry editor of the *New Yorker*, whose work was also neglected because people were afraid of looking as though they were currying favor.

I stayed with Alan more than once in London. People were always speculating about which lovely, intelligent girl he'd marry, but he kept hesitating and then, exhausted, the various girls would move on—which would provoke a new storm of his lovelorn poetry. When I broke up with the younger writer Christopher Cox, the composer Virgil Thomson (his friend and boss), told him that I'd always be restless and unhappy in love. It's what I wrote about. Was Alan also a perennial bachelor because he wrote about love?

Alan had a winning Harry Potter schoolboy look, his eyeglasses smudged and crooked, his longish curls confused into a great mop, his preppy clothes rumpled. The one thing that didn't go with this nerdy collegiate image was his beautiful tenor speaking voice, a poet's arresting tones as persuasive as a good cello. Where one might have expected a high squeak or sudden adolescent crack, one got instead this lyrical instrument, ideal for reading his kind of verse, which was at once social and deeply felt—a lesser version of James Merrill's poetry and voice without Merrill's sham mysticism.

And although he was often genuinely unhappy in love (it wasn't a pose), Alan was always gallant and plucky. Some days, it seemed, he'd turn sour with disappointment and grief, all the more striking in such a resolutely cheerful man. He was quick to express his agreement, nodding furiously at anything one said. An utterance felt delightfully collaborative with Alan. His years of working at the *TLS* had given him a familiarity with every domain of intellectual endeavor, but he was never professorial, possessing an urbanity usually missing among American intellectuals and artists. I remember an elegant luncheon in Paris that the *TLS* gave in the late 1990s to celebrate its French connection at Drouant (where the Goncourt jury holds its annual luncheon)—hallowed ground for literary people. There I met the very suave and elegant essayist Marc Fumaroli, the author of *Trois Institutions Littéraires* and a star of the Academie Française.

One evening in London, Alan invited Michael and me to dinner with Marie Colvin, the well-respected war reporter and Alan's best friend and confidante. She wore a black patch over the eye she'd lost in Sri Lanka. Marie worked for the *Sunday Times* of London, but was an American from Long Island. She and Michael talked about Yemen, where he'd been stationed in the Peace Corps. He'd been a teacher there and although he'd enjoyed his year there, it was dull, basically bureaucratic stuff. Marie had once slipped into Yemen, as she told us, by dhow (a small sailing vessel) across the Red Sea from the Horn of Africa. In the next moment she was talking about Proust, training her cool good eye on each of us. And indeed her memory was Proustian, full of adventures and assignments in many exotic locales, and held together by a network of rich associations. Nor did she for one moment seem cynical. She hadn't happened onto her career, according to any of the flood of obituaries and accounts in the press by her colleagues and admirers following her death—she'd chosen it, and though she'd seen terrible things and reported on them soberly, she laughed and had the kind of optimism that I suppose all journalists witnessing daily horrors need to keep going. She was credited with saving the lives of fifteen hundred women and children in a compound in East Timor. Later, after the start of the events known collectively as the Arab Spring, she was killed in the crossfire when the Syrian government began pushing back against its rebels.

Alan's friend and former *TLS* colleague Alan Hollinghurst was another person who'd once negatively reviewed my work before we met, which didn't keep me from reviewing his first novel, *The Swimming Pool Library*, in the *Sunday Times*, calling it the best gay book yet written by an Englishman.

When I finally met Alan, he struck me as someone rather dignified, but with a slyly frivolous side. Alan's favorite writer was and is Ronald Firbank, a taste we share. Alan had written his Oxford thesis on Firbank.

Alan knows everything about architecture, one of his specialties at the *TLS*, and he's one of the few people I know who thinks London is more beautiful than Paris—it certainly has more varied extant architecture from more different periods. It's true that what gives Paris its unity—the uniform look of Haussmann's apartment buildings, the orientation of streets radiating out from monuments like the Arc de Triomphe, and the repetition of its street furniture and Wallace fountains—can make it dull to the historical connoisseur. As anyone who's read his novels knows, Alan has a Proustian fascination with titles and stately homes, although, like Proust, he is also critical of snobbism. I envy him his flat in Hampstead; everything in it peaceful, beautiful, and neatly organized. Now the definition of the professional novelist (especially since he won the Booker Prize for *The Line of Beauty*), he's arranged his life so that he has to do nothing but write his next perfectly phrased and carefully considered narrative—usually over the course of five or six years. Perhaps he's the most consistently polished writer in the UK today. Unsurprisingly, he doesn't travel much.

And yet like so many Englishmen, he's intrigued by France and its literary classics. He's translated several of Racine's plays.

Although most educated French people say they prefer "English" to "American English," they can rarely understand Brits, who gargle and swallow their words and let their sentences trail off. Alan is a great mumbler and quietly and drily camp (there's no reliable French equivalent to "camp"). One time Alan and I gave a reading together in Brighton. He was hoarse and said, "I'm terribly sorry, but I seem to have done something facetious to my uvula."

No French person would understand why that was funny.

Once I was invited to give a talk for Amnesty International at the Sheldonian Theatre. I was so nervous about speaking at Oxford that I asked to be accompanied by my English editor at the time, Jonathan Burnham, the same Jonathan who couldn't bear overly disciplined French gardens and who was my handsome, clever, well-dressed, and ambitious sometime boyfriend. The man who was supposed to introduce me was an Oxford don of French language who years before had been Jonathan's "moral tutor" at Oriel College. Because Jonathan kept sobbing over boys, he'd been sent down for a year by this moral tutor—who was flanked in his office by portraits of his wife and daughters.

Now the don greeted us in a sleeveless, low-necked, black leather T-shirt with gold bars through his nipples; in the intervening years, he'd come out.

Oxford continued to intimidate me. When I was asked years later to give the prestigious Clarendon lectures, I backed out at the last moment. Every general idea I had seemed either wrong or banal. I pled to the organizers, "I knew Calvino, and he worried so much over the lectures he was supposed to give at Harvard, it killed him. He had a stroke. I'm not going to die over *this* assignment." They said I was the first person to back out in a hundred years. A lecture, where there's no given topic, is torture for me.

Isabel Fonseca and her husband Martin Amis became great friends. Just by coincidence, the evening Tony Blair was elected they gave me a book party for the last volume in my trilogy, *The Farewell Symphony,* in their new house in Primrose Gardens. The atmosphere everywhere in London was festive, and I was reminded of the night a decade and half before when Mitterrand had been elected and Paris lit up.

People made the rounds from party to party. Everyone from literary London was at mine, including Ian McEwan, A. S. Byatt, Hermione

Lee, Will Self, and Salman Rushdie. In France writers were so lavishly hosted by "society" that they seldom clustered in one another's company except in small bunches of two or three friends. But in England the aristocrats were interested only in other aristocrats. It was one of the great differences between the British landed gentry and the French aristocracy of the court, where wit and culture had always played an important part and writers were treasured. After all, in France Rousseau and Voltaire had brought down the monarchy.

Isabel was a true beauty, with olive skin and long lustrous black hair. On her father's side she was Uruguayan (he was a sculptor, just as two of her brothers and her American mother were painters). Brought up in America but an Oxford graduate who'd worked for a time at the *TLS,* Isabel was intelligent and terribly funny and warm; she wrote fiction and an excellent study of the gypsies called *Bury Me Standing,* which had required her to live for weeks on end among her impoverished subjects in Romania. She'd lived in a single room with twenty other people to get her story, learning the language and observing her subjects with great determination. Later she and Martin and their two little daughters moved to Uruguay because she was hoping to write about her father's extremely large family. Martin was happy there and according to Isabel every morning would go out of the house, stretch, and gaze at the beautiful scenery, exclaiming, "The northern hemisphere is fucked!" Now they've moved and are raising their girls in Brooklyn to be closer to Isabel's mother, though he is not so sure he approves of New York's "transectional" society.

I'd known both Isabel and Martin before they ever met and married. I'd lent my apartment to Isabel once when she was having an affair with a handsome young poet. Martin visited me in Paris with his first wife, who was rather haughty. Perhaps no serious English writer has been as maligned and scrutinized and dragged through the mud by the press as Martin, from his divorces to his book advances to his expensive American dental work—all of it shocking to me, since novelists in America are almost never mentioned in the media. Of course, we are much less famous but also less often hounded. Martin's every move was (often erroneously) reported on the front page, as were his feuds. In

America the only writers making the news were those who, like Norman Mailer, had stabbed their wives. Nor did anyone in America know or care what any writers looked like. In Britain, "literary" writers were treated like stars.

Of course Martin was aware that he was part of a great dynasty. He once showed me all of his father's books on the shelf of a Waterstones bookstore, pointed to his own, and indicated where his son's books would go.

Although famously heterosexual, Martin always treated me with a certain gentleness bred out of respect for my age, perhaps, or my friendship with Isabel, as if he were a polite schoolboy. His dearest friend, Christopher Hitchens, also treated me that way. I would have preferred to be more of a buddy to Martin, but I didn't know him that well and anyway I always felt insufficiently well read to have a really exhilarating conversation with him about literature—a subject he could discuss with a leaping jester's wit and a scholar's ability to recite at will. He knew that my first novel, *Forgetting Elena*, had been singled out by Vladimir Nabokov as his favorite American work of fiction by a contemporary author—and Nabokov was one of his major enthusiasms.

Martin was compelling with his smoker-drinker's chuckle, boyish curiosity, and disabused world-weariness—a fascinating combination. He seemed remote, as if entirely self-sufficient, a bit like a friendly emissary from another planet. And yet, all these years later, with only the East River separating us in New York, after I had my first stroke, Isabel made me about a dozen meals from scratch and froze them, and she and Martin were the first to visit me when I came out of the hospital. We sat at the dining table eating Isabel's food and opening wine while one of their girls sat on the sofa in her PJs across the room from us amusing herself with her laptop.

Martin has always been a good, concerned family man, and prolific (with two sons from an earlier marriage and the two adorable daughters with Isabel, as well as an illegitimate daughter, the fruit of a brief youthful adventure whom Martin welcomed warmly into his domestic circle)—but in a way, he seemed more like a wise, retiring grandfather, benign but always slightly disengaged.

In the country, on Isabel's mother's Long Island property, Martin and Isabel knew how to entertain like Victorian gentry—they left you alone all day to read and write and take long walks and got together with you in the evening for drinks and dinner, a perfect rhythm for writers. You were given your own little house with a refrigerator Isabel had stocked herself and a library. But Martin, no matter how many people were around him, seemed a bit isolated, like that Hungarian queen who was also a saint and went through all the court ceremonies but moved about inside an invisible nun's cell that traveled with her everywhere.

He also had his impish side and became fascinated by the detritus of twenty-first-century American and English life—and he was laddish enough to relish certain aspects of it. During the run-up to the 2012 presidential elections, for instance, he'd mastered his impersonation of Texas governor Rick Perry—whom one could count on to flub his lines hilariously at the debates.

"Now Rick's my boy," he said, sliding into a twang; "don't you say nothin' about Rick."

Some of his finest writings are profiles of American figures from the eighties collected in his first book of essays, *The Moronic Inferno*. Observant and perspicacious but never completely arch or mean-spirited, he gave us subtly gimlet-eyed views of the Reverend Jerry Falwell, Gore Vidal, and Ronald Reagan—Martin is uncannily at home with born-agains, Cold Warriors, and their equally flawed critics. In person, Martin could make a perhaps rehearsed observation sound off-the-cuff and fresh in his plummy Oxford rasp. He'd hoard a few gems from the common junk pile of the news and then spring them on you. He'd obviously been rubbing his hands over these gleaming observations knowing they'd delight just the right connoisseur. He had a faintly satirical view of gay life, but no more than his hero Nabokov does in his funniest novel, *Pale Fire*.

I accompanied Martin when we were each invited to a big party for the queen's golden jubilee at the Royal Academy of Art. Mrs. Thatcher was there, already half gaga, dressed in a shocking cyclamen-colored suit. Martin was in the inner circle and was presented to the queen. He reminded her that she'd knighted his father, and she said, "I have no memory of that." I was in the bigger group of those who wouldn't be presented, but at least I got a chance to talk to the stork-skinny tenor Ian Bostridge, who came with his young son, and tell him that his music had meant more to me than that of any other singer's.

When I was a Booker judge the year of *London Fields*, I tried to get this masterpiece of Martin's on the short list because I was sure it was the one recently published novel that people would be talking about fifty years later. The two women on the jury, while admitting the book's superiority, threatened to resign if the novel was nominated because of its supposedly politically incorrect view of women. David Lodge, our chairman, caved. I tried to no avail to argue that the violently misused heroine was an allegory for Mother Earth, who was being ravaged—and that it was an ecological parable.

At the same time, I wasn't abreast of the rising volleys in political correctness in English-speaking and particularly American culture. I'd been in France too long. When I was asked to speak on the air about this "amusing" new fad of political correctness at the Maison de la Radio in Paris, I had to admit I was completely out of touch. So much so that when I edited *The Faber Book of Gay Short Fiction*, I was criticized in the United States for just including the stories I liked and only one by a minority, James Baldwin. Not in England. There I was criticized for being too sex-obsessed. Still, I had to admire the frankness of English reviewers; one English woman critic wrote, "I've always wondered what gay men said and did when alone. And now I know and it's completely boring." No one would have dared to write that in PC America.

Lucretia Stewart was another friend who managed to endear herself to me by attacking me in print. I met her in the London house of my publisher Sonny Mehta, who gave me a memorable drinks party for *A Boy's Own Story*. This was 1983. The waiters were all sniffing cocaine and trying to keep a straight face with whitened nostrils; a beautiful Weimaraner was dashing about wearing a pearl necklace. Sonny's wife, Gita, wearing a sari, showed up late. She'd just parachuted out of an airplane with Princess Margaret's son, David Linley (a furniture maker, and the only talented one of the royals), to celebrate her fortieth birthday, and pled breezily, "I wanted to do something I'd never done."

Those were such heady days. I'd never had a successful novel before and I was forty-two. Nor had *A Boy's Own Story* had an easy time of it finding a home in print in England. The publisher of my previous books there, André Deutsch, had turned it down, saying it wasn't up to my first two experimental novels. Now in the confusion and unexpected glare, I hadn't noticed that Lucretia's article about me—a Page Six–type column—had ended by addressing me personally ("Well, Mr. White . . ."), saying that though I said I was so pleased to be in England, I might be a bit less welcome when everyone turned against American gays for spreading AIDS. And here I'd thought Lucretia and I had had a very nice moment chatting together before Sonny's party. She telephoned me the day of the publication of her article and told me in tears that her editor had added that sentence and that she would never have said anything so gratuitously cruel. But already I was catching on that all Brits in the public eye came in for their drubbings in their naughty but nice press, and all of them seemed to take it on the chin. After all, *Harpers & Queen* had paid me the compliment of calling me "the most maligned man in America" for writing gay fiction and for my militancy.

I was being praised enough that it was easy for me to forgive her. Lucretia became one of my best friends, since she, like Marie-Claude, has always had a true gift for friendship. Not only is Lucretia attentive and tender, but she's also *persistent*, which is a crucial trait with someone as socially passive as I am.

When I first knew her she was married. When her husband found out that I knew Italo Calvino and his tiny, spunky Argentine wife, Chichita, he wanted me to invite him to dinner with them. The dinner in Paris was very nearly a disaster, since the husband plied Calvino with lots of annoying questions about his "process." Luckily I had seated Lucretia next to Calvino, who was enamored of her lovely, fair features, as cleanly drawn as those on a freshly minted dime, and her luxuriant blonde hair. Calvino had a childlike side and became intoxicated with her hair, which he kept touching, like a Nepalese seeing his first Swede and mistaking her for an angel.

Lucretia was spiky and full of contempt for my American gaucheness. She was certain I didn't know how to refer to aristocrats or use their correct honorifics: "Oh you saw him, did you, the *Lord* Rock Savage?" She complained bitterly about her mother's cruelty: "She actually said at my father's funeral, 'Do you know why he was ashamed of you? It's because you'd become so horribly fat.'" Lucretia was a natural, graceful writer, was very tender with animals, and at a surprisingly early age claimed that she'd given up sex (she was barely in her fifties). All the more surprising because she'd been known, sometimes in the pages of the London tabloids and broadsheets, for her high-flown affairs. In the settlement for their unusually civil divorce, her husband set her up in a flat in Camden Square.

There she was raped by a marauding stranger. Luckily she wriggled out of her ropes and hit the panic button installed above her bed. The rapist was rooting through her valuables and he immediately dropped her credit cards, then fled. She wrote a shockingly honest article about the whole experience (she said she worried that when the rapist pushed her legs back he'd notice her cellulite), and soon enough she sold her flat and moved to Greece, into a centuries-old house high up in the walled hilltop district of Naxos, the Kastro. Since then, Lucretia had been finding ways to beautify already superbly simple interiors, and whenever I visited she was always leaping up in the midst of one's monologue and shouting at her cats: "Dido! I told you not to run away! Dido, get down from there! Yes, you!"

A diplomat's daughter, Lucretia had been born in Athens when her father was the British ambassador to Greece, and now she was systematically setting about learning the language and becoming a part of not only the alcoholic British expat community but also that of the sober local merchants, clergy, and social luminaries. She'd learned the protocol, and just when she'd become quite fluent knew that it was time to acknowledge their gestures of warm welcome—and began planning a cocktail party with hot hors d'oeuvres, worrying for weeks over the arrangements for her Naxos "debut."

She converted to Roman Catholicism and became pious, but not annoyingly so. Usually I can't keep from sniping at the pious, but never

Lucretia, since she had such a simple, pure faith, so refreshingly free of shrill dogma, so private—just a simple belief, not a *position* she wanted to or could defend. Her religion seemed to mitigate her otherwise foul temper. Although she had no money, with everything tied up in property, she was always ready to help out our truly poor friends. And of course I was grateful to her for her no-strings embrace of Marie-Claude.

I'll only talk about one more English friend, David Gwinnutt. He liked older men when he was young; he fancied "gentlemen," but somehow I cut the mustard. In order to meet real gentlemen, David worked first in an exclusive hat shop, then mucked out stables and rose to be an instructor of dressage. David had a crazy streak and once got drunk and twirled around naked in my Paris apartment, peeing on everything in a broad-reaching lawn-sprinkler spray.

But he was also an accomplished photographer who'd painted his Nikon white and once took an arty picture of just my nose in a mirror, but also snapped an oft-reproduced portrait of me stretched out in a beautiful dressing gown from Lanvin—and one of Neil Bartlett and me seated close together on a staircase. Many artists admired him, including the painter Patrick Procktor.

Once I invited David to go to France with me to a château in Uzès that belonged to a very rich Englishman, Gordon Turner. Someone in his family had patented the brake or something. Gordon's family paid him a very large yearly allowance to stay out of England, being Plymouth Brethren—and he'd refused to get married. He'd gone to Paris in 1945 when he was forty-five and taken up with a small aristocrat: "He was tiny, absolutely bijou." They had bought a fairy-tale castle together in Normandy and improbably combined the avocations of hunting stags, doing needlework, and raising a variety of roses of very special provenance: "The comtesse de Paris, who's the wife of the pretender to the throne, don't you know, gave me the most wonderful roses from her estate in Morocco." This by way of referring to the Bourbons' forced earlier exile for a time from France. Gordon and his little aristocratic lover lived happily together for decades hunting and doing bargello together in front of the fire—until the Frenchman died of old age.

I had been introduced to Gordon by Bruno, one of YSL's top assistants, who was dying of AIDS and who had been given a generous settlement by Pierre Bergé. He'd become Gordon's confidant and convinced him to leave the fairy-tale castle in Normandy with its painful associations and to buy this place in Uzès. There Gordon lived in great state (ten servants in white gloves lined up at the entrance path to greet us). The château was an eighteenth-century extension to a medieval tower, at the top of a small village. Next to our bed in the tower was a biography of the very butch Duchesse d'Uzès, who'd been a pioneering pilot. David gave Gordon spurs from his stable as a gift, and Gordon was delighted with what I thought of as a rather naughty gift.

He lived not only with the dying Frenchman but also with an aging fantastical alcoholic American drag queen named Douglas, who drifted wispily through the salons in scarves and organdy. The only other bright spot was an English society doctor, Patrick Woodcock, who lived nearby and came to dinner one evening. Woodcock was a friend of the English actor Alan Bates and many other celebrities and had been the model of the gay doctor character played by Peter Finch in John Schlesinger's groundbreaking gay film from 1971, *Sunday Bloody Sunday.*

Bruce Chatwin would come through Paris, suffering from a mysterious "wasting" syndrome, though he never named it. He said it was a rare disease you got either from eating whale meat or from being around Chinese peasants in Fukien. Bruce couldn't bear to be afflicted with an ordinary disease that was killing everyone around him. He always wanted to be rare, exotic, unique. Robert Mapplethorpe had first sent him to me in New York and we'd had sex immediately, standing by the front door, half undressed. That was what people did in the late seventies in New York. I'd been impressed by Bruce's odorless body, constant laughter, and jewel-bright eyes, but we never slept together again. Every time I saw Bruce after that, usually while we were dining in an expensive Paris restaurant, I'd recall us that first time sniffing each other's genitals like dogs—and he'd be regaling the table with his latest anecdote, sounding out and working up a version of the novel he was working on. I saw him several times while he was researching and writing *On the Black Hill* and *The Songlines*, his Australian novel. Interestingly, or tellingly, the real-life stories he told me were much gayer in the original than those ending up in the book.

Bruce was a relentless raconteur; you felt that his audience didn't matter as much to him as his need to polish and reshape the same story at a different table the following evening. He lived in London in a tiny flat on the top floor of an Eaton Square mansion. He was more concerned with the address than with the actual living space.

One evening he had what I took to be a peroxided rent boy with him, but later, I realized was Jasper Conran, the wildly successful clothing designer, son of the famous designer Sir Terence Conran, and favorite of Princess Diana. Bruce and Jasper were lovers, it seemed, for a long time, though ultimately Bruce went back to his wife, who nursed him until he died. Since he was a connoisseur as much as he was a compulsive raconteur and writer, and since he had worked as an auctioneer at Christie's, he had an almost pharaonic urge to pile up goods to be used in the afterlife; his wife would have to return the extravagant daily purchases.

John Purcell, when he was still my roommate, couldn't bear Bruce's monologues, which demanded too much respectful silence and close listening. John wanted to drink and be casually merry with an older man who would ask him questions about himself, and he hated Bruce's long involved narratives about Australian aboriginals, which amounted to drafts of his next book. His art seemed to be entirely oral, a form of performance art. I assured John that Bruce kept crowned heads mesmerized with his soliloquies. John's only reply was a spat-out "They can have him."

I loved England, but its upper classes seemed maddeningly light-hearted and privileged to me. I remember one evening walking near Regent's Park by myself and feeling lonely. A troupe of youngsters in evening clothes with posh accents stumbled past drunkenly. I felt so alienated, I who belonged nowhere, who was cursed by AIDS, who was no longer young, who was broke and always would be. I guess in Paris everything was so alien that I never compared myself to anyone;

everyone was incommensurable. But in London, because of the familiar language, I felt close enough to the culture to envy the bright young things. Giving in to self-pity is considered a great sin in England, but it was one I was guilty of committing.

Chapter 16

Susan Train, an American so old she had "no age" (as the French say), had been running the office of French *Vogue* since the 1950s. Susan remembered that when she'd first arrived in Paris, she'd had so little money that she'd bought fabrics and devised shawls for herself. The art of tying the shawl or foulard or scarf is one of the mysterious talents of French women. In the early eighties, the French Minitel, a forerunner to the computer (it was a keyboard and small screen that made use of the phone lines), was employed by people I knew as a place to advertise for hook-ups. Little girls were writing, "I'm ten and live on the boulevard de Courcelles. Meet me on the corner for sex in your car, bring an Hermès scarf."

People would do anything for an Hermès scarf, with its traditional design and loud colors. Girls and teens alike shared this taste with their mothers. Everyone seemed to be the same age in Paris. Rock stars on TV were all old, like Johnny Hallyday, Serge Gainsbourg, or Véronique Sanson, and Juliette Gréco was still giving a concert on her eightieth birthday. Girls didn't want green hair or facial piercings or black leather, but were content to wear pearls, black dresses, and heels, carry handbags, and dress up their good suit with an Hermès scarf for accent. The look that was in was "bcbg" (*bon chic bon genre*), which could be translated as "preppy."

The Minitel was given free to phone subscribers in lieu of fat telephone books. It was a bulky box with an eight-inch screen—a bit like a small television. You could make transportation reservations on it with your credit card and obtain theater tickets. The cruising facility was the *ligne rose* (pink line), where users typed out their preferences for all to see. It took some doing to learn the abbreviations. *JhCh TBM pour plan hard, pour SSR, look Santiag* meant "Young man (*Jeune homme*) looks for (*cherche*) a very handsome guy (*trés beau mec*)—or, alternately, very well-hung (*très bien monté*)—who wants rough sex (*plan hard*) and safe sex (*sexe sans risque*) who wears Western-style cowboy ("Santiago") boots. Users could click into a private dialogue with another subscriber, their comments unavailable to the other onlookers.

I met many men this way and also through more traditional cruising in parks, bars, and back rooms and on the street. One of Mitterrand's first acts when he was elected president was to legalize homosexuality and to abolish the vice squad (*police mondaine*). Napoleon, out of deference to his gay second consul, Cambacérès, had legalized homosexuality, but then the pro-Nazi Vichy government had recriminalized it. There were movie theaters where guys went to meet Arabs. I heard that there was even a ring of firemen available for a fee, but I never obtained this precious number. On July 14, Bastille Day, the firehouses were open to the public for all-night dancing and I'd often go to stare at the *pompiers* in their stylish silver helmets.

Due to the new freedom, gay men would jump over the fence at night on a warm evening and have sex in the Tuileries Gardens as they had been doing for centuries anyway according to a book called *Sodome au Bucher* (*Sodomy at the Stake*).

Since I lived on the Île Saint-Louis, I'd go to the gardens at the tip of the island where there were steps leading down to a quay right next to the water. On the stone walls were giant metal hoops used to tie up boats in the past, I supposed. It was so beautiful to see the lights of passing barges dancing on the Seine, to feel the coolness floating off the water, and to embrace a tall, dark stranger. If I liked someone, I could invite him home, which was only two blocks away. John Purcell was usually out drinking or back in America. Once I crouched in the bushes in the park and attracted the eye of a muscular man twenty years my junior. He came home with me. He had the smallest penis I ever saw and a beautiful body, and insisted on being the active partner despite his little cock. I was happy to play my passive role since he was so ardent, so beautiful, and such a master at kissing and frottage. I doubt that most women can understand how romantic anonymous sex can be, mainly because women are often more vulnerable and female sexuality is slow to ignite, though eventually it burns with such a bright flame and can be doused only slowly. What men like about anonymity is that it allows free rein to any fantasy whatsoever. There are no specifics to contradict the most extravagant scenario.

Of course specifics come with the postcoital chat. When I asked Monsieur Littlecock if I could see him again, he said no, he was kept by an older man, a German millionaire who was very jealous. The rich German had installed him in a town house in the Marais. Yes, he'd been a dancer—he still took classes, that's why he was in such good shape. He'd seen by the way I'd knelt by the bushes that I was submissive; that's what he liked, an older man who was submissive. I thought, He's right to ignore his small endowment and build up an enviable body and impose his will on older men. I thought I would have made a good kept boy, with my geishalike, easygoing nature and my ability to find almost any man sexy.

The French were tyrannical about weight—"the fat police," I called them. Maybe that's why they have such long life expectancy; many, if not most of them, were thin, though reputedly obesity has become a new hazard even in France due to fast food restaurants and fewer bicycles and more cars. Although by American standards I was at the time not grossly overweight, I was turned away at the door of certain gay baths for being fat. This policy infuriated me. At first I thought I was being rejected for being too old, but I saw men older than me being readily admitted. In my mind I formed monologues in which I pointed out to the insolent desk clerk that I was a pioneer of gay liberation, that I had fought for their right to exist, and that it was the worst sort of discrimination to exclude me because of my body size. I was rejected every other time by the IDM baths, which we pretended stood for "Institut Danielle Mitterrand," the name of the president's wife. It was my favorite sauna.

We used not only the Minitel but also certain numbers on the telephone where eight or nine people could talk at once. You'd call out a little advertisement for yourself ("sucker looks for big dick"), and if someone responded you'd shout out your telephone number, hang up, and wait. Using that clamorous and chancy method, I met a guy. He said he was nineteen and would come over after a soccer match, though his time was limited since he also had to babysit his little sister.

He came directly from the game he'd played in, not attended. He had purple lips, pale matte skin, huge eyes, and a freshly scraped knee. He was tall. He was Yugoslavian (the word he used, not Serb or Bosnian or Croatian). He'd been born in France to parents who came from Yugoslavia. Someone told me that Yugoslavs were the best hustlers in Paris but also the most violent. A study had shown they had the biggest dicks.

Etienne was not violent but very pleasant, if somewhat mocking in an adolescent way. He thought of himself as bisexual and for quite a while he had had an African girlfriend. Above all other kinds of women, he prized *une belle black*. That was the word he used, "black," not *noire*. He told me that girls in Paris were aggressive. Later, after we'd had a number of encounters, I saw two girls, total strangers on the métro, slip him their phone numbers. No wonder. He was tall, well dressed in trendy clothes, had straight, dark hair. He worked at the reception desk of a gym in the *banlieu* where he lived and was allowed to exercise on the machines for free. I could just imagine him joking with the girls. Etienne liked to hang out at heterosexual bars on the boulevard du Montparnasse and at the end of the night scrape up another "straight" guy who hadn't yet teamed up with a woman. He preferred meeting men there to going to a gay bar, where the regulars would have descended on him like piranhas on a baby.

I never questioned Etienne and was just grateful that I was sufficiently old and bulky and foreign, sufficiently "other," to fall into his comfort zone. I always gave him a bit of money at the end of the evening. He seemed neither to expect it nor to be shocked by it. I offered no explanations, but I thought surely he'd need it for what the French call *arrondir les fins de mois*, making ends meet at the end of the month—that time between paychecks when most people run short and have bills and rent to pay.

Things changed over the many years I knew him. *La belle black* vanished one day from his life and his conversation—when I asked him about her he just shrugged. He started to shave his body entirely and he told me he now preferred men who were active rather than passive ones. He still thought of gays as a race apart. Once he stayed in my apartment with a girlfriend when I was traveling and he did a funny imitation of a gay waiter who lisped over him with delight and was openly hostile to his girlfriend. When they asked about desserts, the waiter began listing ice cream flavors: "For Monsieur we have chocolate and vanilla and peach and pistachio," in a baby-talk lisp—then he turned to Etienne's girlfriend and shouted harshly, *"Et Madame?"*

Chapter 17

Dominique Nabokov and I went to Marseilles and interviewed and photographed everyone in that city. The centennial of Victor Hugo's death was 1985 and Edmonde Charles-Roux, the talented and impeccable wife of the Socialist mayor, Gaston Defferre, who was also Mitterrand's minister of the interior, organized a museum exhibition of works by Hugo's descendants. Then she invited them all—and many friends and journalists—to a big banquet at a bookstore called Les Arcenaulx on the Old Port; the low-ceilinged store (now a restaurant) had originally been a naval warehouse built under Louis XIV. I was seated next to a ravishing, elegant blonde, the daughter of a senator. She pointed out her lover at the table of honor, a tall young descendant of Victor Hugo. I felt I was in a novel—seated with a duchess, the beautiful, middle-aged mistress of a Hugo boy.

After we had interviewed everyone and seen everything and spent thousands of *Vogue*'s dollars on meals and transportation, I said to Dominique, "There's nothing here. No *Vogue* lady would ever want to come to Marseilles. It's the French equivalent to Akron." She was quick to agree with me. Marseilles, with its souk all up and down its main street, its frozen then nuked bouillabaisse served in cafés where diners were plagued by beggars, its mafia, its riffraff who joined the Foreign Legion (the office was next to our ugly modern hotel on the Old Port) instead of serving jail time, its hill of old neighborhoods so dangerous that the Nazis, *after* conquering the city, bombed it back into the Stone Age (the only example in history where the conquerors gave up on the captive city and reduced it to rubble)—this Marseilles struck us as irredeemable, though its partisans kept claiming there was a wonderful hidden Marseilles we hadn't yet discovered.

Edmonde Charles-Roux was one of those perfect French older women who seem to have everything under control. She had worked for Coco Chanel and later written her biography. She'd directed French *Vogue* but parted ways in the sixties when Condé Nast had not permitted her to put a black model on the cover. She'd written a novel that had won the coveted Prix Goncourt, the equivalent to the American Pulitzer or the English Booker. And now she was married to the mayor of Marseilles. Years later, when I interviewed her about her unlikely friendship with Jean Genet, criminal and prostitute, she showed up on time for the meeting in an impeccable Chanel suit, well coiffed and perfectly manicured, her notes arranged so that she could give me the most information in the shortest possible time. While conducting the scores of interviews for the biography, I'd learned that other writers were the best—they remembered colorful details, used specific, nuanced descriptions, and avoided all the "marvelous" and "fabulous" talk. I couldn't help but admire Madame Charles-Roux for her powers of organization and her resolve to do every job, no matter how minor, properly.

From my roost on the Île Saint-Louis, I'd often see the Rothschilds, in their eighties, tottering forth for yet another dinner party—beautifully dressed, slender, on time, impeccable. No wonder these people lived so long with their drive to perfection in everyday life.

Dominique Nabokov and I went to Lyons to interview Pina Bausch, who was one of the most original choreographers of our day and was about to bring her company to the States for the first time to dance at the 1984 Summer Olympics in Los Angeles. Having appeared in films by Fellini and Almodóvar, she would later be the subject of Wim Wenders's splendid 3-D *Pina*, shot immediately after her death from archival footage and new sessions with her company. But at the time, I'd never heard of her. We attended rehearsals for a week in a dreary, working-class neighborhood of Lyons before she agreed to see us.

Bausch liked to work with dancers of all ages, sizes, and

nationalities. Her home base was the German industrial city of Wuppertal, where she was first hired to do ballets for the local opera company, though soon she'd formed her own troupe and was doing evening-length original dances. One of these we saw her revive was *Café Müller*, a recollection of her days growing up in her parents' provincial hotel and restaurant.

The women were dressed in heels and dresses, their legs bare and muscular. The men were usually in suits and ties, looking like thirties gangsters. The music was often romantic, sentimental, German ballads or South American tangos. If the clothes and music were decorous, the dancing was violent and confrontational. Women slammed into walls self-destructively and men pulled them away and held them repeatedly. People ran and collided. Sounds and words were emitted, a break with the balletic rule of silence. The dancers were Asian or Mediterranean as well as blond and Germanic.

They were also rehearsing a new piece in which a young woman came out center stage, stopped, and said, "*Bonjour, j'habite Paris*," what seemed like a thousand times. Bausch, who was seated in the audience, didn't seem to give her any guidance. She just wanted this moment to be repeated again and again, as though this wearisome repetition itself would eventually wear itself down into the right dimensions. The dancer had a very pugnacious way of saying "*J'habite*," almost as if she were saying, "I beat!"

One of the most interesting things about Bausch's method was the way, one by one, she'd ask her dancers to show her what they did or said when they were anxious, thrilled, or frightened. She'd then take this intimate personal moment and assign it to another performer or to the rest of them, but not to the originator. It was sort of like method acting, in that the director was pulling out of the memory or private repertory of individuals their idiosyncratic expressions of deep feeling, except that the expression was more an action than anything verbal. Certainly repetition seemed to be crucial to her method, too. A man endlessly sets aright chairs that a woman keeps knocking over; a man extends the arms of a second man and drapes a nerveless woman over them, then the arms give way and dump her on the ground. The interactions often seemed nightmarish and transgressive, violations of decorum, and I couldn't help noticing they were almost all heterosexual. Rarely did two members of the same sex touch each other.

She liked to play with the elements of earth and water. In one piece, a woman repeatedly shovels dirt on another woman writing on the ground. In another piece the dancers scoop water into buckets, then drench each other. During rehearsals Pina said little, and then only in intimate hushed conferences with individuals. It was like a combination of exercise class and psychotherapy. Her main advice to her performers was "Dig deeper," as if everything were coming from them, not from her. People compare Pina Bausch to Robert Wilson, but Wilson was never interested in the psychological makeup of his performers, only in stage pictures. They both favored small idiosyncratic hand gestures and beautiful sets, although Wilson's were more beautiful and he designed the lighting as well.

After we waited around for a week in this dreary Lyons neighborhood, we were finally given a time to interview and photograph Pina Bausch: at midnight in a local café filled with noise and smoke. A gay male nanny with a ginger mustache, a German, brought her three-year-old son, Saloman, to her and she nursed him with her flat breast. She said the child's name had come from a gay man who'd designed the sets for *Café Müller*, a man who'd died—while the kid's biological father was just some transitory man she'd slept with. That sounded like the most German thing I'd heard in a while.

Of course, France had its own odd ducks, especially the writers I was meeting—a whole generation of *poètes-maudits*. One was Gabriel Matzneff, an outspoken pedophile who'd written a book called *Less Than Sixteen* (*Les moins de seize ans*) about his attraction to—and adventures with—boys and girls who were under sixteen. He was a bald man who had his gleaming scalp polished at Carita. He was a practicing Russian Orthodox believer. In 1985 I wrote a novel, *Caracole*, and he protested my use of this title in France since he had a 1969 pamphlet called *La Caracole*. My Paris editor immediately backed down, afraid of a lawsuit, and I chose the alternate title *Le héros effarouché* (*The Startled*

Hero), from a Mallarmé poem I used as an epigraph: "Let me introduce myself into your story as the startled hero."

Matzneff came from a White Russian family and started riding horses at age ten. He majored in classics and studied philosophy with Gilles Deleuze and Vladimir Jankélévitch. He became close to President Mitterrand, who wrote an article testifying to their friendship (imagine Bush or even Obama bearing witness to a friendship with an artist, much less a notorious pedophile). He was considered one of the most original writers of his generation, admired by Mauriac, Aragon, and Julian Green (who became a close friend).

As for his pedophilia, he explained that he was less attracted to males or females than he was to those under sixteen, who for him constituted a third sex. When he first presented these ideas, I think for French readers they had a classical, old-fashioned sound about them. After all, for years there had been a homophile publication in France, *Arcadie*, and André Gide, the Nobel Prize–winning author, had said he was not a homosexual but a boy lover. Loving boys sounded Greek, like something Plato or a bucolic poet might do. Matzneff admitted that sixteen was not an absolute cut-off age for women, although he said he would never have a central relationship with a boy over seventeen. He claimed that the two most sensual beings of his life were a girl of fifteen and a boy of twelve.

When I met Matzneff, he had just been accused of having sexual relations with retarded children at a facility called the Corral. The names of other intellectuals, such as Michel Foucault, René Schérer, and Félix Guattari, were wrongly dragged into the affair. All of the accusations against Matzneff were withdrawn—although seven of the educators at Corral eventually served prison sentences. A young man at Corral raped and murdered a patient there after he'd spent time in a psychiatric hospital. As everyone admitted, it was imprudent to have allowed him to stay at Corral.

Guy Hocquenghem was a killingly handsome young novelist who published a book about the Corral scandal defending his friends, called *Les petits garcons* (*The Little Boys*). Guy, whose curly hair and sharp features impressed everyone, usually wore a sardonic smile. He seemed fondly contemptuous of everyone. He and his friends were often stoned, and when I visited Guy in his Montmartre apartment, the air was thick with pot smoke. I'd first met him in New York when he was still in his mid-twenties, soon after he'd published his first book, *Homosexual Desire* (1972), which was surely one of the first works of queer theory, along with Dennis Altman's *Homosexual: Oppression and Liberation* (1971).

Hocquenghem was usually with René Schérer, his high school philosophy teacher whom he'd started having an affair with when he was sixteen and Schérer was in his forties. Twenty years later, they were still close friends and they somewhat programmatically called themselves lovers. Schérer was yet another apologist for pedophilia. He was the younger brother of the filmmaker Éric Rohmer. When I knew Schérer, he'd been inculpated in the Corral affair and his career was destroyed. To be sure, in his writing, he'd advocated pedophilia as the point at which the loving adult—who was neither a parent nor an instructor—might help to "liberate" the child from the killing strictures of society and parental control. Schérer had been influenced by Félix Guattari, whose *Anti-Oedipus* (coauthored with Gilles Deleuze) marked an entire generation, and by Charles Fourier, the nineteenth-century utopian philosopher. He championed a closer look at Fourier's previously unpublished *Le nouveau monde amoureux* (*The New World of Loving*), a text that advocated the free expression of everyone's desires.

I met most of these people through Doug Ireland, an American leftist gay journalist I'd known for years. Altogether Doug lived in France a decade, but before that he'd managed Bella Abzug's campaign, making her the first truly radical politician in Washington in years. Doug was a columnist for the *Village Voice* and later wrote in French for *Libération*. Doug was a big, smiley guy who'd contracted polio as a youngster because his parents were Christian Scientists and wouldn't allow him to receive the Salk vaccine. When I knew him, he was still in pain and drank a lot. I'd first met him when I ran the New York Institute for the Humanities, a think tank at New York University that counted among its members Susan Sontag, Joseph Brodsky, and Derek Walcott. Doug raised quite a few eyebrows by living in his institute office and washing out his clothes in the bathroom. I think he also cooked on a hot plate. As a leftist critic of the Democratic Party during the Clinton years, he also wrote the widely syndicated "Clinton Watch" column, having been a member of the Dump Johnson movement in the sixties. Later, he began writing a blog called *DIRELAND*.

Doug, René Schérer, and Guy Hocquenghem were the core group of these evenings, though Matzneff was sometimes on hand. I think the Corral scandal spelled the end to a lot of the rhetoric of the seventies which had advocated liberation of all sorts and had conceptualized individuals as "desiring machines." I didn't realize it at the time, but I was witnessing a crisis not only in the careers of these men, once so influential, but also an end to a whole anti-psychiatry movement advocated by Guattari. Guy had also made a rather amateur movie called *Race d'Ep*, with his ex, the charming Lionel Soukaz, who is still alive. The title of their film could be translated as *The Race of Faggots*, since *d'Ep* was a sort of anagram of *pédé*, a pejorative for homosexual. (This kind of colloquial word reversal, trendy with young people, is called *verlan*, which itself is itself a near anagram of the word *l'envers*, or "inverse." *Verlan* still constitutes a youth argot of amusing code words. For instance, women, *femmes*, are called *meufs*.)

The greatest pedophile writer was Tony Duvert, who lived a tormented country life in his mother's house in Loir-et-Cher and was constantly in a struggle with poverty and the scorn of his neighbors. He wrote many books, notably in the seventies *Journal of an Innocent*, *When Jonathan Died*, and *Atlantic Island*. Duvert was published by Beckett's publisher, Éditions de Minuit, often in very limited editions; his advocacy of pedophilia and his hostility to families made Jérome Lindon, the publisher, nervous. He was such a hermit that no one noticed when he died; his decomposed body was found in his house many days after his death in 2008. A biography of sorts, *Tony Duvert: the Silent Child*, came out two years later, written by Gilles Sebhan. I say "of sorts" since there were so many factual gaps in the story, often filled by sentimentalizing and generalizing.

The strangest writer I knew was Pierre Guyotat. He was a heavy, bald man who looked like the great god Baal. For a while Guyotat wrote in a language of his own invention that seemed to be composed mainly of consonants. Later, he returned to regular French, what he called "the normative language." He wrote about such violent aspects of rape, torture, slavery, prostitution and homosexuality that for a long time his works were banned. When Mitterrand was elected in 1981, one of his first acts in office was to lift the ban on Guyotat's *Eden, Eden, Eden* and to encourage Antoine Vitez's staging at the magnificent Théâtre National de Chaillot of Guyotat's *Tomb for 500,000 Soldiers*—a book about the Algerian war, in which Guyotat had participated as a soldier. When he deserted he was arrested by the French authorities. (The Chaillot would be the equivalent of the National Theater in London or the Kennedy Center in Washington.)

I first met Pierre Guyotat at the apartment of Gilles Barbedette. He was a heavy, sepulchral man with some but not much conversation whenever the subject strayed from him and his work. He had undergone an injury as obscure as Henry James's; apparently he'd had a psychotic episode and lived in a trailer and failed to eat and had fallen into a coma. He'd written a book about it, *Coma*, and other books about other moments in his life, such as an adolescent visit to relatives in Scotland.

These more autobiographical books were beautiful and accessible, and again like the late-period James, Guyotat dictated them. From time to time he spoke ad lib. I once saw him onstage, seated, talking, while dancers whirled about him. He appeared for several days at the Centre Georges Pompidou. A hundred people attended every night. He sat enthroned on a stage with a microphone, his presence impressively basaltlike. He intoned phrases sometimes in French and sometimes in his made-up language. Often it sounded as if he were saying the French word for testicles (*testicules*). There was no clear idea how long this would go on, and I, who hate attending readings, was itchy but then settled into the experience, nearly mesmerized. Clearly he had been deeply traumatized by his own experience of the Algerian war—his visual memories of severed limbs, rape, violence of all sorts—to which, phantasmagorically, he'd added slavery. I'd known a few English-language writers in America (like William Burroughs, Kathy

Acker, Dennis Cooper, Samuel Delaney) who loved portraying violence and sexual cruelty for its own sake. But in France, land of Sade and Bataille, such extremes are more common.

Guyotat sometimes referred to himself in the third person and once sent me a postcard saying, "No one has done more for Guyotat this year than you." Stephen Barber, the man who wrote my biography, *Edmund White: The Burning World,* and is interested in Antonin Artaud's drawings, took care of Guyotat in England for a while until Stephen's patience wore thin. Whatever other vices he may have, Guyotat is at least not a pedophile. In fact, someone in the know once told me, "Guyotat's sexuality does not involve other people."

The French still believe in the avant-garde and imagine that someone extreme must necessarily be the next good thing. By that way of thinking, Guyotat is the main literary embodiment of the avant-garde in France, though he seems to be haunted by his childhood, by his coma, and by the atrocities of war, and has sought only the most vivid, not the most experimental, way to explore these subjects.

Sometimes he is seen as an heir to Jean Genet, and once, during a staging of Genet's *The Balcony* at the Odéon theater, we invited Guyotat to do one of his monologues before the play to a smaller audience. The stagehands said he had to end his "act" at least a half an hour before the play was due to start so they would have time to dress the stage. We told Guyotat this, but he replied, "Time is inscribed within the work—it is not exterior to it." We prayed that time would be inscribed in time, and it was; just at the last moment, Guyotat left the stage, applauded mainly by his biographer, a charming, young woman.

Recently in New York, I hosted Guyotat for the Department of French at New York University. Guyotat, who is very shy but warm, said, "Please don't ask me to read"; someone from the French embassy whispered to me, "Monsieur Guyotat doesn't want to read"; then the first thing he did was to stand and read aloud in a completely incomprehensible English. Absurd as he can be, there is no doubt Guyotat is a genius, one of the truly remarkable people I've known in my life.

All of these French writers had the courage of their eccentricities: Marguerite Duras announced in *Libération* that she knew who'd killed "le petit Gregory"—a small-town boy who was the victim of a notoriously grisly unsolved murder. Duras had visited the house and intuited it was the mother, though no evidence to incriminate her was ever turned up and she was cleared in 1993. Duras was certain the woman had murdered her child because the garden was neglected.

We were far from America with its tenured creative writing profs, each blessed with a loving wife, many children, and a local church—men who spoke gravely about the Third World and once served in the Peace Corps. I remember a novella that Henry Miller once wrote called *A Devil in Paradise,* about his married happiness and his life in the Big Sur. All is disturbed when a prewar Parisian friend from his sexual heyday—a friend who is sickly and unhealthy in his values and attitudes and covered with sores—invites himself to stay with Miller and his family. Eventually, Miller has to ask the broken-down syphilitic, dirty and all dressed in black, to leave. Although the decision to oust the creep is a painful one, Miller realizes that his bohemian, transgressive days are over. So many of the pages of *Big Sur and the Oranges of Hieronymous Bosch* symbolized for me the clash between healthy but bland America and the diseased but deep France.

Alain Robbe-Grillet was a friend of mine and I spoke at his memorial ceremony, along with Bernard-Henri Lévy and a dozen other people. With Nathalie Sarraute, Robbe-Grillet was one of the first proponents and practitioners of the New Novel. He'd written the most influential critical book of the era, *For a New Novel,* in which he'd commanded novelists to banish psychology and anthropomorphic metaphors—"The sea struggled with the sky"—in favor of very precise, almost scientific descriptions (he'd trained as an agronomist). Robbe-Grillet had written influential novels such as *The Erasers* and *Jealousy* (or maybe the French title, *Jalousie,* is better, since it also refers to the tropical louvered window, which is the same word in French). In *Jealousy* there is a famous "scientific" description of a banana stand, how many centimeters apart was each tree, etc. There was a major dispute at the time between those who said that the book was "objective," as Robbe-Grillet himself claimed, or "subjective," written from the jealous husband's point of view. Today most of the people who still read the book take the subjective, psychological point of view.

I first met Robbe-Grillet in the early seventies at a cocktail party hosted by Tom Bishop, head of the French department at NYU and a great defender of the New Novelists. I went with Richard Howard, Robbe-Grillet's translator, a close friend of mine at the time and of Susan Sontag, who dedicated her *Against Interpretation* to him. As Alice Kaplan has said in *Dreaming in French*, her book about the role Paris played in the lives of Jacqueline Kennedy, Sontag, and Angela Davis, during the sixties Susan and Richard were allies introducing French artists and intellectuals to America, she through her essays and he through his translations. At the party for Robbe-Grillet, Richard translated for me; in those days I couldn't say a complete sentence in French and Robbe-Grillet, though he'd taught for years in the States, at least pretended he couldn't speak English. Working at a cultural magazine then, I took it on myself to commission an article from him on Forty-second Street—a seedy strip in Manhattan of porn stores, hookers, and dirty movies and a place that excited his imagination.

Ten years before that I'd seen the film *Last Year at Marienbad*, which Robbe-Grillet had written for director Alain Resnais. I'd gone with my favorite English professor at the University of Michigan, Caesar Blake, a gay black man. I'd loved its stylish *anomie*, as formal as French topiary. Caesar said that he hadn't quite been able to "isolate" its themes.

When I first met Robbe-Grillet I was surprised that he was always smiling and seemed to be taking a rueful pleasure in all the absurdities of American life. It was the same sort of smile I later recognized in Philippe Sollers, the editor of the influential journal *Tel Quel*, a smile that embraced everything ridiculous or aggressive and that seemed to be saying, "Bring it on!"

Years later, in the late nineties, after I'd returned from France to

America, I was asked to dine with Robbe-Grillet and his wife after a *colloque* on Roland Barthes, who was discussed as if he were passé (news to me). Robbe-Grillet and his diminutive wife, Catherine, were invited with some of the NYU faculty to a local eatery where men played bocce ball in the back. It was an unusually warm spring night and the waiter had propped open the door. Suffering from the usual French fear of drafts, the fierce Catherine, who was reputed to be Jean de Berg, the sadomasochistic novelist, said to the waiter in French, "Close the door."

"Oh, no, madame, it's too warm—"

"Close the door, I said," she repeated with a tone that could not be contradicted.

And he did.

I heard rumors that Catherine liked to torture fashionable couples from Paris in their Norman château-fort, complete with a dungeon. I asked my informant what role Robbe-Grillet played. "Well, he is the author of *Le Voyeur.*" Reputedly Catherine kept track in a diary of which tortures were administered to which victims, just as old-fashioned hostesses used to paste wine labels and inscribe the menu in a *livre d'or* beside her guests' names so they wouldn't be subjected to the same dishes twice.

After the disaster of 9/11, Catherine appeared in New York with the young humorous novelist Frédéric Beigbeder (he and several other alert French authors churned out their World Trade Center books before any Americans managed to). Catherine was complaining that all the S&M places in New York had been shut down by Mayor Giuliani and that tonight she would suffer the indignity of beating *lesbians,* of all things. Frédéric, who'd awarded me a literary prize at the film festival at Deauville, tried to console her. I said that on Twenty-third Street near Sixth there was a restaurant where slaves lapped water on all fours out of dog bowls.

"Gone," she said mournfully. "Closed."

I saw Robbe-Grillet at the medieval nunnery that the Institute Mémoires de l'Édition Contemporaine (IMEC) was redoing as a study center outside Caen. I'd heard that IMEC, though an archive dedicated to modern writers and editors, was building a greenhouse for Robbe-Grillet's precious collection of cacti. He told me that the plural in French should be *cactées* and explained the etymology. For the privilege of taking care of the *cactées*, IMEC received all of Robbe-Grillet's papers and the many, many films he shot.

Chapter 18

Marie-Claude invited me to stay for two weeks in her summerhouse. It was a fisherman's cottage on the Île de Ré, in a small village that smelled of the brackish sea. Her house was at the end of a tiny street just wide enough for one car, a street called the ruelle des Musiciens. A high wall around her house was pierced by a green-painted wood gate, inside which was not only the cottage but also, somewhat unusually, a garden (another house had been torn down to make room for the garden). The cottage had a large eat-in kitchen, quite modern, with big windows and French doors letting on to the garden. The kitchen flowed into the sitting room, where there were twin couches and a rattan chair, its back swelling like a cobra's hood, drawn up beside the blackened fireplace. On every wall were curious pictures, suitable, I suppose, for the tastes of the whimsical artist of *Babar*. Upstairs there were three bedrooms, one of which had a double bed for the lady of the house, the other two tiny.

Everything smelled of the sea, and every morning Marie-Claude would dash off on her bicycle to do her *courses*, her shopping in the town market, which was covered and the size of a New York block. There, she would buy us the fish we would eat every night, broiled, the vegetables she'd make into a sumptuous ratatouille, and the tiny sardines that she'd decapitate, gut, and marinate and that we'd eat raw in olive oil and green peppercorns. Unpeeled potatoes she'd cook on top of the fire in a closed clay pot called a *diable*, which she'd rest on top of an asbestos pad over a low flame. That was a strange dish for the French, who normally are incapable of eating an unpeeled potato. They

would dry up and shrink and become deliciously charred in the *diable*—
we'd eat them with salt and pepper and lavish lashings of butter.

It was a house consecrated to peace, beauty, and reading. MC
always brought home fresh flowers, especially sunflowers and the
hollyhocks that grew wild outside the gate and on abandoned plots
on the island. She would arrange her vased flowers in a still life
composed of that day's eggplant, tomatoes, purple-edged lettuce, and
feathery fennel.

MC's daughter, Anne, was in her element, too. She worked day and
night in the garden. She was an accomplished photographer who had
published a book of pictures of ornate tombstones in Italy. She had also
taken the definitive photo of Georges Perec, with his wild, Einstein
hair, from which the French government had made an honorary stamp.
(Imagine if the States made a stamp with John Ashbery's portrait, or if
the UK made one of Ronald Firbank.)

Ré was the Hamptons of France. Because of high-speed trains, it was
only three hours away from Paris. In my first days there, you had to
take a ferryboat over to the island, but in the late eighties they built a
bridge, which many people opposed because it made the island too
accessible to hordes of day trippers. Luckily, MC's village of Ars-en-Ré
was farther out on the island than the larger, more popular scenic port
of Saint-Martin-de-Ré. Ars had been a fishing village for the working
poor, but now politicians (including a prime minister, Alain Juppé)
mingled there with writers, film directors, and actresses.

In the center of the village stood a church that had a bumpy, tapering
steeple, half black and half white for maximum contrast and visibility
to those at sea. Around the church were the post office, a newsstand, a
café, and a snack bar. Down by the harbor were a couple of good restaurants and a shop selling expensive nautical wear and equipment (such
as a brass circular compass and cut-glass liqueur bottles set in a mahog-
any caddy that would always right itself even when the boat was
severely listing to one side). And there were all the moored boats, of all
sizes and kinds, and the dry docks, and beyond, an antiques shop.
Marie-Claude and I would often go walking out on the long, earth-
filled breakwaters.

By some magical fetishism, I sometimes think that if I dialed old phone numbers of friends, long since dead, they'd answer even if, in those days, there was one less digit in the number than now. By the same token, I think that if I flew to Paris and took the TGV to La Rochelle and a hundred-dollar taxi to Marie-Claude's green door in its whitewashed wall, she'd be there, sitting in the garden, smoking, drinking good Lapsang souchong tea from a bumpy black metal teapot and a small glazed cup. She'd be in her rattan chaise longue, which she folded up at night and stored in the garden shed. There would be the pierced round metal picnic table painted a dull green and the matching hard-metal chairs under the fig tree (I understand why nudes are outfitted with fig leaves, which are enormous).

There was another building alongside the garden, a stone garage, with a bathroom attached to its side. The bathroom had the only shower, a toilet, and a large sink and vanity, as well as the washer-dryer. The whole setup reminded me of Junichiro Tanizaki's essay "In Praise of Shadows," which begins with a description of a Japanese bathroom (all shadows and dim shoji screens and pine branches and wooden fixtures) and compares it favorably to Western bathrooms with their surgically bright surfaces, all antiseptic metal and porcelain. This bathroom definitely seemed on the Japanese end of the spectrum. Even its smells were those of fresh herbs, Proust's iris root, lavender soaps, Roger & Gallet Extra Vieille toilet water, and the ocean.

Upstairs, above the garage, was a large guest bedroom under the exposed beams with an unframed double bed on the floor covered with a nubby white fabric. A staircase dropped down and pulled up by rope-pulley. Double windows looked down on a small garden where every flowering plant was white. The room was full of lazy buzzing wasps and dead spiders immobilized in the center of sticky webs, white pebbles and gaudy shells brought back from the beach.

Late in the afternoon, in the summer, the sun didn't go down till ten o'clock. MC and I would bike to the beach, walk through a pine forest, and cross the dunes onto what the French called *une plage sauvage,* to distinguish it from a manicured beach with cabanas, like those along the Riviera. The beaches of Ré are dotted every half mile or so with a massive series of concrete pillboxes built by the Nazis as a defense against a coastal Allied invasion. It would have taken a lot of dynamite to dislodge them from the dunes. The elements had tilted and shifted them and they'd become the make-out sites for teens, who'd left their empty booze bottles and used condoms on the uneven sandy floors; the walls inside and out were covered in graffiti.

The Atlantic coast, unlike the Mediterranean, is subject to major tides. The Atlantic-side beaches of Ré swoop gently toward the ocean floor and when the tide is out, miles of extra sand and rock are exposed, leaving pond-sized tidal pools and providing a happy hunting ground for gatherers of mussels and clams. At low tide, morning or evening, you can see bathers, bucket in hand, inspecting every uneven and algae-strewn stretch of wet sand for their supper.

Sometimes we'd go to a closer beach where there was a bar shack, and we'd have a drink before riding our bikes along the path on the top of a retaining wall. To get there, we'd have to bike through what the French call *un camping*, a vacation trailer camp that functions only in the warm weather. I suppose these camps, scattered throughout Ré, make it more democratic, as if the Hamptons on Long Island were host to many campgrounds; the poor in their trailers (what the French call caravans) were always present.

I've always suspected these French campings were witness to the hottest teenage sex in the country. While the parents from France and Germany and Holland reclined in plastic and aluminum chairs or cooked wieners on the portable grill, the adolescent girls and boys ran off together, excited by a sudden lack of supervision and the randy exoticism of all this freedom and all these nationalities. In fact, the now middle-aged French novelist Michel Houellebecq, author most famously of *The Elementary Particles* (*Les particules élémentaires*), and the great white hope of the French novel, has explored in the bitterest terms the laxity of his parents' generation—the *soixante-huitards* (sixty-eighters), with their sun-battered faces, receding hairlines, and gray ponytails (whose tents and trailers you still see in *campings* all over France)—and he blames them for the moral fecklessness of his own generation. As Houellebecq recounts it, the *campings* were notorious wife-swapping (*échangiste*) venues—and at least as he'd like to tell it, the reason for so many divorces and fractured families and fucked-up offspring in France.

Many of MC's Paris friends had substantial summer houses on the rue du Palais in Ars, and we'd sometimes drop in on them for a drink. Her best friend was also named Marie-Claude, and is now buried next to MC on the Île de Ré under white rosebushes, rather than in MC's ghastly family crypt in the Montparnasse cemetery. Marie-Claude Dumoulin was an editor at *Elle,* her husband one at *Lui,* and their son one at *L'Express.* They were the most *knowing* family I'd ever met. There wasn't a single vacation hotspot in Cambodia they hadn't visited, a single new Romanian novelist they hadn't read, a single nautical race anywhere in the world they hadn't competed in, a single bid for power in the mayoral race of Clermont-Ferrand they hadn't already investigated and profiled. Marie-Claude Dumoulin knew everything about clothes and home furnishings, her husband was a tireless sailor, and their son was a crack political reporter. Conversations seldom got off the ground before taking a nosedive, because the Moulins weren't interested in ideas and were impatient with gossip. What they prized above all else was usable information, grist; but they all three already knew all about whatever subject you might mention.

Harry Mathews, who's lived in France since the fifties, told me that in his opinion every nation shares the faults of all others, but each nation has developed one fault to an extravagant degree. The French fault, he said, was always wanting to be right. A French person will deny the proof of his senses and all the savants of the world and cling to the notion that the world is flat, if he or she started out with that view. Concomitant to that fault is a simultaneous impatience with—and hunger for—the new. Impatience because admitting that something is new to you is humbling, information that has not already been absorbed. Hunger because the only way to one-up friends and relatives is to know the new before they do. The easiest tactic is to dismiss a new bit of information from the outset as not worth knowing. I remember traveling to Istanbul with MC and a stylish young Parisian, Guillaume Bouvier. As we entered the Grand Bazaar, the vast covered market, with its hundreds of stalls, Guillaume said, "There's nothing here. Let's go," and MC quickly concurred.

I exploded, "You've already dismissed the biggest bazaar in the world?"

I thought they might be right, as stand after stand sold the same aubergine-colored car coats and the same rubber tires, boxes of Tide and industrial dish towels. But then at the very center, within a locked cage, was an old mosque and the small jewelry district, with its antique brooches and rings and sand-blasted tea glasses from the 1940s—all the things we loved and would buy. Of course the French, like the Japanese, want their *luxe* to come from half a dozen brand names, such as Gucci or Hermès or Christofle, and it's no wonder that ripped-off products, such as Chinese copies of Izod shirts, are confiscated by French customs officers and the offenders are arrested and fined.

The French will not admit not knowing something. The most that they'll concede of their own ignorance is that they "no longer know it": "*Je ne sais plus.*" At any museum exhibit in Paris, the biggest crowds aren't looking at the paintings but standing in front of the explanatory plaque telling the history and provenance of the whole concept of the show. Here is where the know-it-all culture vultures are feeding themselves so they can overwhelm their friends who've not yet seen the exhibit. The United States is a fractured culture in which every subgroup has its own website and fanzine, and no two *chapelles* (as the French call small in-groups) can or want to communicate with each other. The gun hobbyists don't want to know the antique doll collectors, who scorn collectors of black mammy cookie jars. But in France, there is still some sense of the collective, which is reinforced by this uniform "knowingness."

Once the Dumoulins had heard about something or professed to know about it already, they immediately lost interest in hearing any more. Suddenly the subject had lost all of its savor.

On the Île de Ré, MC had her athletic side. She could swim vigorously for half an hour in the freezing Atlantic. She loved to bicycle long distances, through the fields beyond which the black and white church tower of Ars floated and shifted, like the twin Combray steeples in

Proust endlessly playing with each other. Ré was famous for its salt farmers (usually old women), who would fill ditches with seawater, let it burn off in the sun, then rake the salt into piles; this is the salt that sells for twenty dollars a bottle at Zabar's in New York or Hédiard in Paris. The utterly flat land, the huge, blue skies animated by soft white clouds lined in gray, the steeple dancing over the green fields, the Wordsworthian solitude of the lady salt farmer bent over in the drained ditch, the sun's warmth on the back of one's neck—these were some of the exhilarating elements of a bike ride to the next village. It might be Saint-Clément-des-Baleines (St. Clement of the Whales), the snobby Les Portes-en-Ré, or the "big-city" commune of Saint-Martin, with its handsome prison, which always makes me think of Manon's deportation to Louisiana.

In the winter Ré was deserted. The summer population of two hundred thousand would dwindle to twenty thousand. It rarely snowed, but the air was briny and chilly. Thick fogs often descended over the garden. The shopkeepers seemed friendlier and less harried. MC bought me a *cire*, a green, knee-length, impermeable raincoat that had a hood. Since it didn't breathe, I could work up a considerable sweat under it just by walking around. She and I would make a fire in the fireplace and settle in on our matching couches, sometimes with a matching book. I remember one year we were both reading Ishiguro's nightmarish *The Unconsoled*. We'd look up every few pages and say, "The poor man is about to play a concert but he doesn't know where he is or who all these people are." Maybe we both loved the book because we were so happy being together, with no distractions beyond MC's long international phone calls. She might talk to her daughter Anne back in Paris, who wanted to know details about fertilizers in the garden, and the window repair in the dining room. Or book talk with Ben Moser in Holland, living with an older gay literary couple. Ben— tall, intelligent as only a Texan can be, enthusiastic, young—was one of MC's most devoted fans. He found everything about MC glamorous, fascinating, *attachante*.

May 1968, the moment when the students in Paris took to the streets and revolted against the stiff class consciousness of traditional, Gaullist

France, still fired MC's imagination. She often referred to the rapture of the whole city of young comrades ("Under the paving-stones, the beach!" had been a popular slogan). Despite or because of her age, she seemed to represent that romantic long-ago time. She had watched the skirmishes in the streets from the window of her elegant Boulevard-St-Germain apartment.

The intellectual Julia Kristeva and her husband, the novelist Philippe Sollers, spent the summers on the Île de Ré in a remote house on a peninsula that overlooked a huge empty bay. Julia and Philippe were a fascinating couple who had no equivalent in America. She wore big barbaric jewelry and designer clothes and was a feminist only in America, at Columbia, where she often taught. In France, she was way beyond anything so primitive as feminism (too seventies!). She was, among other things, a psychoanalyst—a job title that in France requires no special training or accreditation, nothing beyond hanging out a shingle and opening an office for business. She and Philippe were always up to date. If there was an exhibit dedicated to Vivant Denon, the artist whom Napoleon appointed the first director of the Louvre Museum, Philippe had already written a book about the subject. He'd also written about Watteau, Nietzsche, James Joyce (whose *Finnegans Wake* he had translated in part into French), Mozart, Casanova, De Kooning, Sade, Francis Ponge, and countless other writers and painters and thinkers. Italy and the eighteenth century were two topics he kept returning to. All the arts, including music, obsessed him. MC said that every September he went to Venice with a Belgian woman novelist, Dominique Rolin, his lover, twenty-three years older than he. MC found his constancy to her admirable. In fact, Rolin published an account of their love story, *Thirty Years of Crazy Love* (*Trente ans d'amour fou*), and in 2000, Philippe wrote *Passion Fixe*. Although he was always welcoming with me, I found his know-it-all attitude annoying. When Genet's *The Balcony* was presented at the Odéon, he participated in a *colloque*. Sollers's stance was that he alone had actually read Genet and that everyone else was talking through his or her hat (I'd heard him adopt a similar strategy about Céline and Sade). If anyone dared to challenge him, he drew on his cigarette and exhaled a cloud of smoke,

smiling all the while a big, mocking smile. His smoke was the equivalent of a skunk's odor. There he was on stage with Albert Dichy, the
world's most erudite Genet scholar, Sollers all knowing and all the
while puffing. (To be fair, Sollers wrote a laudatory review of my Genet
biography in *Le Monde des Livres*, for which I was entirely grateful.)

As it happened, Sollers and Kristeva were the most famous people
MC knew. Around Sollers she was very quiet, as if afraid to say something foolish, though she was more expansive when we were alone
with Kristeva. Sollers was mercurial. In the past, among other things,
he had been a semiologist and a friend of Roland Barthes. In the seventies he became a Maoist. When I knew him I think he was in his
Catholic stage. Sollers often railed against people he regarded as fools.
He thought his hit novel *Femmes* should have been published in the
States for a lot of money. (Columbia University Press eventually
brought it out, probably without paying him a big New York advance.)
He blamed this "failure" on Tom Bishop, who'd organized at NYU a
French production of Virginia Woolf's play *Freshwater* in 1983 with the
roles played by such luminaries as Ionesco, Robbe-Grillet, Nathalie
Sarraute, and Jean-Paul Aron—"the flowers of French literature,"
Sollers grumbled. "All making fools of themselves. Their foolishness
cost me two hundred thousand dollars at Random House or Doubleday.
If only these writers had not disgraced themselves! We were all
tarnished by their absurdity."

Kristeva had written a roman à clef about French literary types
called *Les Samuraïs*—which was supposed to repeat the success of
Simone de Beauvoir's *Les Mandarins* but failed to do so.

Legends already, oddly both Sollers and Kristeva wanted to sell out.
But they were condemned to remain fixtures of high culture, famous
but never rich.

I once took MC with me to London, where we attended a big party for
lots of literary people. MC wore her long, Japanese-style layered clothes,
mostly beige; her gaudy outsized necklaces she created herself out of
baubles she bought at the market in Ré; and her red shoes and eternal
cigarette holder. This very contrived look won her nothing but mocking

looks and comments from English literary ladies in their tweeds and genuine pearls and hand-me-down cardigans. Suddenly I hated the English all over again for their dowdiness and smugness, their horrible sense of humor, and their common sense. And I thought that it was no wonder England never had a bold avant-garde in painting, no wonder their response to Picasso was so feeble, far less imaginative than that of Czechoslovakia, for Chrissake. In the 1980s the Tate had its first ever show of Cubists—in the 1980s! Walton and Britten were the best they could do in music. Only in fiction, where gentility and the wretched class system are actually viable subjects, did the English excel. The horrible, deflating English sense of humor, the terrible tendency to "take the piss out of" everyone and everything. You'd think, I thought bitterly, that the English would be ashamed of their commonsensical reaction to all the great modernist tendencies. Their failure to have a Giacometti or Stravinsky or Balanchine or Günter Grass, their sickeningly merry way of laughing at whatever is "pretentious" or "takes itself too seriously." And this disgusting piss-taking response only goes on. Only the English have failed to recognize Robert Wilson's genius. They alone rejected Schoenberg in favor of Elgar.

For the French bicentennial celebrations in 1989, I did a commentary for the BBC with Germaine Greer and the Oxford historian J. H. Plumb, who couldn't understand what the astounding costumes by Jean-Paul Goude and Alaïa "symbolized." For my part, I said that they were original and beautiful, which was enough for the Parisians, who, after all, lived in the world capital of fashion. All these black ballerinas in long white skirts; the Russian girl waltzing with a polar bear on a rink borne high by sailors in their midi blouses; thousands of soldiers marching with lit tapers in their hands; those spectacular red and blue fireworks above the Arc de Triomphe; the Marseillaise sung by Jessye Norman in the place de la Concorde. After the splendors of the most expensive spectacle in history—and Goude's masterpiece—the deflating English questions about what it all "symbolized" seemed characteristically stunting.

I guess I'd been the target of English scorn as an out gay writer. I've had Germaine Greer and the anti-Zionist critic and poet Tom Paulin attack my novel *The Farewell Symphony* for being "disgusting" on a late-night chat show, *Late Review*. Paulin took the novel to task for its "sexual boasts," and Greer described a sexual scene I hadn't written. A few years before, A. S. Byatt and Germaine Greer, also on TV, had condemned the erotic pursuits of the narrator of Alan Hollinghurst's novel *The Folding Star*. And now Greer described a moment of "anal jackhammering" on an elevator in *The Farewell Symphony* that I'd never even imagined, much less rendered. More recently, Greer attacked my Rimbaud biography for its supposed advocacy of anal sex, which she for one was categorically opposed to.

Naturally there is an ancient rivalry and even enmity between England and France. For many French people England is still a country of comical snobbishness, outworn traditions, and bowler hats. The French are unaware of lowering English social phenomena. For the French, skinheads have never existed anywhere (except maybe in Germany) and lager louts are some forgettable exception to the cult of the gentleman.

Despite bouts of strangely selective and fleeting Anglophilia, the French have largely resisted England and the English. For a century, a store near the Palais Garnier called Old England has been selling tartan skirts, tweed jackets, and Barbour coats. Upper-class French families send their children to England every summer to acquire the language (those who are really upper class also send them to Vienna).

I attended Culture Club's first Paris concert, in October 1983 at L'Espace Ballard. Here were all these teenage French girls wearing their Hermès scarves and carrying their Gucci bags standing around watching the stoned-seeming English cross-dressing lead singer, Boy George, sing a reggae-style song, "Do You Really Want to Hurt Me?" The evening never really took off. The French girls didn't get this man with the big nose, Kabuki makeup, dreadlocks woven with satin ribbons, and voluminous cloak. Blue-eyed reggae was a bit much for the French, who were so hostile at the time to multiculturalism. It often seemed to me the English Channel was wider and deeper than the Atlantic.

In the pre-Chunnel eighties, we still flew to Heathrow from Charles de Gaulle, on British Airways—with the understanding that English planes alone were equipped to navigate the fog.

The myth was that people ate poorly in London and superbly in Paris, but increasingly exactly the opposite was true, especially for everyday bistros at normal prices. In London one was served large helpings of roast beef and fresh peas with mint and delicious summer pudding for dessert, whereas in Paris at a comparable restaurant one had a greasy *confit de canard*, soggy fries, and a stale crème caramel. The English server might easily be a fresh-faced, superpolite debutante hoping to get a job as a publicist at Faber and Faber, while the waiter in France, as likely as not, was a sullen Moroccan who'd worked twenty years at the same crappy place.

Of course I'm not talking about temples to haute cuisine, where the French win every time hands down. I ate at the Tour d'Argent, with its view of Notre Dame, slow, fussy service, and tagged and numbered roast ducks put in a press to extract the blood for the sauce—the press looked like some medieval torture device. I remember the owner, Monsieur Terrail, swarming about. Once, a very fat, middle-aged American who liked to have his ice cream served on a plate, not in a bowl, was served it the wrong way by an uninitiated waiter. The customer, who always dined alone, snapped his fingers; Monsieur Terrail rushed over and saw the terrible offense just as the chubby customer indicated his disappointment merely by opening his hands reproachfully, as though opening a book to a particularly damning passage.

Monsieur Terrail, as thin and nervous as a Boldini portrait, hissed at the waiter, "Are you trying to ruin me?"

Americans were often angry in the better French restaurants. Their idea of an expensive restaurant was one where the service was rapid, obsequious, and obliging. Yet in the French tradition, the more expensive the restaurant, the slower; the three-hour lunch would leave many American executives apoplectic.

If you could hear only one person in a restaurant, you could be sure it was an American. John Purcell's theory was that Americans thought they were interesting and wanted everyone to hear what they were saying.

In Proust, characters, often aristocrats, don't mind talking to someone dubious, but they don't want to be introduced. What was the big deal? It turned out that in La Belle Époque, you could *call* on someone once you'd been introduced. No longer were you dealing with chance encounters; now you were obliged to *receive* someone or pay calls on him or her. Today the phone and Internet have made visits like that obsolete, but still the French feel no obligation to someone they haven't formally met. Whereas Americans are helpful to total strangers who ask directions, the French breeze right past foreigners asking where the Louvre is, or even deliberately point them in the wrong direction. Meanwhile, there is a law in France punishing those who do not help a person in danger—a woman fighting off a rapist, say. In America, no such law would be necessary (although there is one in Massachusetts). In France an article of the penal code states that whoever could prevent a criminal act against a stranger and does not intervene (when by doing so he would run no risk to himself) can be sentenced to five years in prison and a fine of one hundred thousand euros. Of course, in America, even good Samaritans are wary of being sued. In America, St. Martin himself, when he gave half of his cloak to the beggar, might have been sued for infecting the beggar with bedbugs.

Why this difference? Since the United States was, for so long, a pioneer culture, helping was a survival skill. In France, people only move once, from the provinces to Paris, and in your new city you're stuck for the rest of your life with everyone you regularly meet. No wonder the French are so cautious about rushing into intimacies.

Americans weren't the only eccentrics in restaurants. Once I was at Le Grand Véfour, my favorite restaurant and one of the oldest in Paris, situated in the beautiful neoclassical peristyle of the Palais-Royal. The arcades of the Palais-Royal used to teem with prostitutes and cutthroats. Now the gorgeous complex is an island of tranquility, with its shaggy gardens designed by Marc Rudkin, the Pepperidge Farm heir.

Le Grand Véfour had velvet chairs topped with the names of great French writers. On the walls were Pompeiian-style paintings and on two sides were big plate-glass windows. One afternoon, a much older man at the next table was presented with a dessert intricately decorated with nets of spun sugar that formed an abstract sculpture in miniature. I couldn't resist asking him what it was. The man—who was French—turned from his wife to me and gaily explained that he'd mounted a campaign to erect a monument to the "noble asses" that had fought in 1916 in the terrible battle of Verdun and this *pièce montée* was in honor of the poor animals.

I couldn't help smiling, and he turned grave and began to expostulate, "But no, Monsieur. Thousands of little donkeys from northern Africa were wounded or gave their lives for France at Verdun!"

Later, when I checked, I figured this man might be Raymond Boissy, the president and founder of a donkey-appreciation society called ADADA (L'Association Nationale des Amis des Ânes) to honor the beasts that brought bread, wine and munitions to French soldiers on the front lines.

Chapter 19

MC stuck with her art, her Cornell-style boxes. These boxes were filled with found objects forming surreal or else drily witty scenes, and were given droll titles that helped explain the connections to their origins in, say, literary-salon gossip from Proust's day, classical myths, operas, or the lives of writers, composers, or visual artists. Over the years her craftsmanship had become more honed and sophisticated, her handling of the tools she used to fashion her fantasies in her studio more dexterous. Two floors up from her apartment, her atelier had been a maid's room. It was small and crammed with a large work table, several smaller work surfaces, and shelves that hung from every wall and held everything from pliers and hammers to strings of tiny white Christmas lights, dolls, vacation souvenirs, and rolls of colored cellophane and gaudy wallpaper. As her craft improved, MC began to light the scenes in dramatic and clever ways (a bracelet of fake diamonds became a chandelier illuminated by a hidden bulb); she hired assistants to help her miter-saw the frames a gallery director had advised her to add and to wire each box so that it came to life like a stage set. This was still before her work began selling—she blamed the owner of the first gallery to show her for somehow undermining her career and ruining her chances for sales—and we worried that she would go broke on her quest for recognition. Contrary to what some might have thought, Marie-Claude had profited little from Babar's international fame, and she worked believing that an imaginary clock was running out on her and that she needed to prove herself to Laurent and to La Dame and her allies.

The whole place smelled of formaldehyde, and I was surprised that in the close, stuffy, and poorly ventilated little room she could even breathe this air, so reminiscent of a taxidermist's shop, for the hours and hours she applied herself. In spite of a lot of bluffing to the contrary, she wasn't at all sure of her ideas, and this uncertainty was a constant source of anguish. Should the pyramid be painted gold? Should the whale fly on invisible strings above the landscape? Should the geisha be standing or kneeling behind her lute?

The boxes brought together her interests in literature and history and the struggles of her own life. I own a large box depicting sea lions playing a duet on a piano filled with colorful beads. They are in a mirror-lined room lit by a chandelier. In the doorway stands a man made of feathers. The room beyond is a library. The man is framed by gilt Art Nouveau screens. The sea lions are Marcel Proust and his boyfriend Reynaldo Hahn in the act of being surprised by Charlus. Of course, no one could guess who was depicted from studying the box. In other boxes Phaedra and Alice in Wonderland floated about, as did a Scottish reverend on ice skates. MC had certain talismanic book titles and paintings that often recurred in her boxes. It was all very "cultured" in the familiar European fashion, this curatorial appreciation of traditional artistic references (the German term is *Bildunsburgertum*). After her death, one collector swooped in and bought them all, and they vanished into his château.

I sometimes mildly enthused over her boxes, especially when she started illuminating them and when they became smaller and smaller. I disliked the kitsch objects, highfalutin' cultural references, and Surrealist collision of pearls and sharks—it all seemed so old-fashioned to me. I wanted her to paint or sculpt new things and ditch all the references to literature. I'd have preferred that she create purely imaginative and speculative works, as if she were giving us a glimpse of some new mental drama. But she didn't have the confidence to invent wholesale, nor did she trust her skills as a painter or sculptor.

She was very much a victim of the way women were brought up in her era. She'd had a poor education, and I don't know if she ever received her baccalaureat. And after all, she'd been brought up in a

French (mainly Jewish) colony of refugees in Mexico City. After her breakdown when her husband left her, her sister told me that when MC was a teen in Mexico their father had submitted her to electroshock treatments because she had started sleeping with a black American soldier. MC never talked to me about the soldier or the shock treatments. She did like to allude to her racy sex life in the distant past, but only in the vaguest possible way.

Certainly her family had been very strict. Her mother and grandmother had forbidden her ever to mention money, and my frank American way of talking about the prices of things shocked her mildly. Sometimes I wondered if her horror of talk about money was an aversion to behavior and talk that might be considered "too Jewish."

She was worried about being unmasked as a fraud. When she failed to pick up on how blasphemous *The Satanic Verses* would be considered, she tormented herself endlessly about this lapse in judgment, and yet I doubt if many or even any literary scouts like her around the globe had foreseen this horrible development. Certainly Salman himself hadn't, but MC took the fatwa as a very public exposure of her incompetence. I assured her that no one could blame her for not anticipating the evil whims of some flea-bitten cleric in Iran, but at the same I wondered whether or not she might have been more sensitive to cultural clashes if she'd come from a religious melting pot like America instead of the completely secularized France.

She loved the opera, and in 1985, the year after she got out of the madhouse, I convinced *Vogue* to buy me a subscription for two. The opera was still being held in the old Palais Garnier, which was far more elegant than the new house at the place de la Bastille. The Palais Garnier, with its gilt and red velvet, its rows of balconies, its Chagall ceiling and marble staircases and uniformed ushers unlocking the doors to the box seats—well, it was something out of Proust, and one could easily picture his liquid black eyes and little mustache and pale face above the crisp evening clothes, a white shirt and white bow tie as he lurked in the corridors on the lookout for a duchess or a young man . . .

MC loved the luxury of our orchestra seats. She was still slightly batty and felt that the plot devised by Calvino for Luciano Berio's new opera *La Vera Storia* contained coded secrets intended for her decrypting and eventual instruction. She would nod with familiarity at the subscribers in adjoining seats, elderly couples from Lyons or Lille, I imagined. That same season we saw Gluck's *Iphigenie en Tauride*, staged by the Italian film director Liliana Cavani, with sets by the brilliant Ezio Frigerio and sung by Shirley Verrett. I remember the opening storm scene with huge black banners rippling across the stage to dramatize the high winds and the ship blown off course. The next year we saw Cherubini's *Medea*, in which the singers precariously explored a giant silver cracked skull that filled the stage. Over at the Opéra-Comique we heard Ravel's *L'heure espagnole* and Puccini's farcical *Gianni Schicchi*.

Chapter 20

My sex life had come down from the paradise of promiscuity it had been in the 1970s. When I'd first arrived in France, I was thin and still presentable in my early forties—and soon I'd get rid of the mustache. Nevertheless, I was a middle-aged man and not exactly a head turner in a city that, like so many others, idolized youth. Older people in Paris, a remarkably high percentage of them, keep on having sex, but they have to bring something valuable to the bed, failing the self-evident glamour of youth.

When I arrived in Paris, a few bars in the Marais had back rooms. It seemed as if in the dim light I was often surrounded by short, hairy, perfumed men with unworked-out bodies. One such guy I met I ended up inviting to dinner at the eighteenth-century restaurant Lapérouse, on the quai des Grands Augustins. He trembled throughout the meal, I suppose because the atmosphere was so *guindé* ("uptight") and the food was so expensive. In those days, when the dollar was at its strongest, I thought nothing of going to all the most famous eateries, although as a freelancer I sometimes scrambled to pay my American Express bill at the end of the month.

I could barely speak French at that point, and I put phrases together in my head before I pronounced them. They were utterances of such a startling, sometimes nonsensical banality they sounded straight out of some manual of conversational English for geishas: "I have often heard the camel is called the Ship of the Desert" was an actual phrase recommended to geishas entertaining American sailors.

I met one big-dicked, heavy-smoking guy in the bushes of the park at the end of Île Saint-Louis. He was a twenty-something waiter with a diamond ear stud who was constantly hanging out with a hairdresser his age. They would discuss (I think) the latest gossip about French pop stars I'd never heard of. Gérard's only pillow talk was a frantic hectoring to hurry up and come, as if his only concern were to terminate this hateful but necessary activity with an aging American john. I paid for meals, of course, but nothing else until he decided his fondest wish was that I buy him a twenty-karat gold ID bracelet called a *gourmette*. I went to a jeweler on the rue de Rivoli and plunked down a couple hundred dollars for this vulgar chain; he was genuinely happy that night and even slowed the orgasm talk down to a more reasonable pace. When I broke up with him (I found the rancid smell of menthol cigarettes daunting), all he did was warn me that I was getting old and should settle down before it was too late. "*Tu viellies, Edmond,*" he hissed. If only he'd known how many more decades of gallantry lay before me. Which didn't stop a reporter from the London *Times* from calling me and asking me politely, with a nice Oxford stutter, what I thought of "intergenerational sex." I answered him sincerely and described my relationship with Michael, who's twenty-five years younger than me. A few days later, as we were about to board a plane to London, Michael opened a newspaper and found an article about ourselves headlined "The Frisky Old Goat Is Still At It."

I'd been living for years in France without a visa. My frequent trips to London and Zurich meant I left the country every three months, as required by law. Since I never earned a single franc, I wasn't taking money away from a French journalist. If by chance I wrote something for *Le Monde* or *L'Express*, I was careful to tear up the check they paid me. I wasn't going to risk attracting the attention of the "fisc" for a few hundred bucks. In my mind, I was doing nothing unethical, since I was spending all my American dollars in France and not taking advantage of any of the more costly French services. I had no children enrolled in state-run schools and I always paid my doctor out of my pocket (no more than thirty dollars, anyway, for an office call). I thought the French had invented a neat system, one that stopped foreigners from earning francs but invited them to spend all their dollars. I was careful to avoid altercations, anything that might draw attention to myself. I was a faceless member of the bourgeoisie. Even my apartment I rented "under the table," or, as the French say, "under the overcoat" (*sous le manteau*).

I had a regular hustler who was a small, hairless guy, pneumatic with youth. He called himself Boble, which he thought was an English-language name, though I'd never encountered it before. He couldn't speak a word of English and he claimed my French was too good and perfect, that I didn't speak like "real people," by which he meant in argot. In this complex sublanguage of French, which is old and somehow rarely changes, *bagnolle* is a more common usage than *voiture* for "car"; *fric* is in higher circulation than *argent* for "money"; a cop is a *flic*, not a *gendarme*. (This is to say nothing of the playful youth argot *verlans,* which reverses syllables to turn a word like "bizarre" into *zarbi*.) I learned a lot of argot reading about underworld figures for my Genet biography, although Genet didn't use anything but the purest French except in his dialogue. He used prison argot as well: *dorer une biche* (literally, to gild a doe), for instance, means "to take the virginity of a young boy."

Even though Boble was a little guy, he usually was the active partner. Once we got stoned and I topped him. He was angry and accused me of raping him. I thought of how often straight guys must be accused of rape—when you're drunk or stoned, you don't even notice whether the other person is consenting, and you assume that the other person wants the same thing you want.

Boble sent me a beautiful guy from the Pyrenees. This guy was in Paris on some sort of marijuana delivery deal and he spent the night with me. He was an educated young man, unlike Boble, and very hand-some, with his olive skin and Mediterranean features.

Boble was a character right out of Genet, whom he'd never heard of. He had met a girl he was in love with, but she was bullied by a man she hated. They were working in one of those little amusement parks that spring up on an empty lot or on the meridian of a boulevard in Paris, a collection of five or six rides where local mothers take their kids. Boble had bought a pistol to threaten the carnival worker with, and when he showed it to me I was shocked by his anger and begged him not to go out and use it.

He thought of me as English, like the putative father he'd never known. I tried to point out to him that Americans weren't like the English, but for him this was a distinction without a difference. Perversely, I thought, he needed to think I had something in common with his father.

Chapter 21

MC liked to think of us as the scandalous couple in *Les Liaisons Dangereuses*, calling herself Madame de Merteuil and me Valmont. Once we went to hear Hubert Selby Jr. read at the Village Voice bookshop. The punked-out audience was disappointed that Selby was no longer transgressive; in recent years he had joined AA and found his higher power.

MC nudged me in the ribs and indicated an extremely handsome redhead wearing designer clothes: "There's one for you!"

We chatted him up after the reading. His name was David and he was from Dublin, Georgia, and a grad student at the Sorbonne. He made his living as the *physiognomiste* at a chic disco, Les Bains (where Margaux Hemingway was always passing out). His job was to recognize VIPs on sight and hasten them in.

I asked David what their door policy was.

"First, we let in all the blacks. Then all the gays. Then the celebrities. One night I recognized Allen Ginsberg and William Burroughs. The French girl I worked with thought that they were just a couple of old stumblebums."

David was a favorite student of Mireille Huchon, the Sorbonne professor who wrote an influential study speculating that the great Renaissance poet Louise Labé didn't actually write the works attributed to her, but was merely a front for several male poets. David was an expert in rhetoric and saw all of literature, I think, as mere combinations of rhetorical devices. He said that he loved my novel *The Beautiful Room Is Empty* and Harry Mathews's *Cigarettes* for their "deployment of rhetorical figures"—a way of discussing literature that absolutely mystified me.

Though he was noble and handsome, with big muscles, he was a major masochist. He claimed proudly that no one had ever touched his penis. He liked to be severely lashed and fucked by his French lover, who was courtly and handsome, "a big nobody." After his lover beat him, he would draw David a hot bath to ease the welts. I took David on a road trip through Morocco. At Taroudant, he pulled me into his bed and socked me in the stomach.

When David became ill with AIDS, his lover threw him out and he went home to Georgia. There his parents, who were poor Scottish immigrants, put him in a state hospital, which would never release him. Though there was nothing to be done for him and he wanted to die peacefully in his mother's garden, the hospital was afraid of a lawsuit.

After he died I met some of his friends: the daughter of a deputy from the Franche-Comté who'd shot up heroin with him and an old college pal who'd attended college with him at the University of Georgia in Athens. From these friends I found out that in Paris "Davey" would get drunk and beat up fags under the highway in front of the Gare d'Austerlitz beside the Seine. He'd gloried in his steroid-hefty muscles, in how tough he was—and how much abuse he could take and hand out. And yet he'd had a refined way of talking, sipping air before every sentence as he was discussing the poetry of Ronsard.

I ended up going with another language scholar, Gilles, who wrote his prizewinning dissertation on the seventeenth-century writer Claude Favre de Vaugelas, a savant who was so poor that he sold off organs of his body to anatomists for collection after his death. MC and I, she outfitted in her shawls and dark glasses, attended Gilles's brilliant defense of his thesis. His professorial parents from Marseilles were also there—and stared daggers through Valmont and Madame de Merteuil. Gilles was a *mélomane* who could listen to one symphony on the radio while humming another.

MC had laughingly given up on love, claiming she was too old for it. But several men floated mysteriously through her life. There was "the

Chinese," who wasn't Chinese at all but a Peking correspondent of *Le Monde*. There was an Italian prince I'd found for her. MC was always banging on about how she longed to have an affair with an Italian prince, but when I located one, she decided he was underbathed and wouldn't do at all. Then there was a man I'd never met, whom she called her *transi*, which means "bashful lover." They would have private dinners together.

Once, when we traveled to Bruges to see a Memling show, the hotel had misunderstood and put us in a double bed. It was embarrassing to both of us, but we pretended the situation was *normale*, as the French say. Romantically, the French pride themselves on being "realistic," and Marie-Claude never once got drunk and became amorous. If she had, it would have been torture to turn her down. Once, when she was serving dinner in Ré to her daughter and Michael and me, we were all looking at her silently with big eyes as she spooned out those great blistered potatoes. She became angry and said, "Stop looking at me as though I'm your mother."

Chapter 22

I always write a book in longhand and then dictate to someone who types it. Of course I change lots of things as I go along and try to eliminate repetitions, unsnarl grammatical constructions, and correct mistakes. It usually takes a week or two. The whole process of dictating is tedious, since in order to get a clean manuscript you have to pronounce every comma and accent mark and spell out foreign words.

When I finished *The Beautiful Room Is Empty* in 1985 I dictated it to Rachel Stella, who became a close friend. Her father was the famous painter Frank Stella and her mother was Barbara Rose, the art critic, who had divorced Stella and married Jerry Leiber, half of the songwriting duo who'd written "Hound Dog." Rachel's mother loved to speculate in Paris real estate. Rachel and I started out working in a ground-floor studio on the Île Saint-Louis, and then we had to move to a grim studio a block away from MC. Rachel's old, arthritic chow dog, with his blue tongue and sweet smile, kept us company. Rachel seemed like a tough chick because she spoke out of the side of her mouth in a hard-bitten way, but she was as sweet as her chow. Many things struck her as funny that left me cold; she had a very satirical eye. Even though her artist father was rich, he was married to a woman not Rachel's mother, kept expensive polo ponies, and had grown up rich (self-made men, in my experience, can be more generous). He wasn't very liberal in helping Rachel—in fact, very little if at all. French bourgeois parents would have been shocked; they usually buy their newly adult children their first apartment or house at least. The American sink-or-swim attitude strikes the French as cruel, and the idea of kids working horrible summer jobs to learn the value of a euro seems to them unreasonable. That so many Americans put their aging parents in old-age homes seems to the French harsh and unfeeling. If French people inherit wealth or property, they think of it as the patrimony of which they are only the custodians before it's handed on to the next generation.

Eventually I introduced Rachel to the man she would marry, Pierre Aubry, a filmmaker with a permanently startled expression and the French equivalent of an Oxford stutter. For once I hadn't planned on playing the matchmaker. Pierre came to dinner with a Chinese girlfriend he'd been with for ages. The Chinese woman offered to translate and get my work published in China, which seemed like a very remote possibility. Unbeknownst to me, that evening Pierre had a *coup de foudre* for Rachel, a life-changing event that had occurred to her as well. The very next day they were a couple. The Chinese woman left a tearful message on my machine saying that she couldn't translate my work after all. Soon enough Rachel and Pierre were married; their daughter Rebekah Edmonde became my goddaughter.

Rachel had a gallery in the sixteenth where she sold works on paper. She was kind to my lover Hubert. When he was ill with AIDS she helped him turn from architecture to cartooning by publishing his first book of *bandes dessinées*. We met many people at her parties, some of whom Hubert caricatured, including the Albanian author Ismail Kadare. Hubert pictured himself with me and MC fawning over Kadare, and then in the next frame admitting none of us had ever read a word he'd written.

One couple I liked immensely was the illustrator Pierre Le-Tan, who'd illustrated many covers for the *New Yorker*, and his spunky English wife, Plum. He was always driving them into debt buying at auction beautiful hand-painted furniture that had belonged to the Duke and Duchess of Windsor. We liked to clown together. We would dine at Davé, a Chinese restaurant frequented by models and owned by the flamboyant Davé himself. Once we were discussing as we walked to the restaurant how we could avoid being kissed on the lips by our host. Neither Plum nor I could think of anything and got roundly bussed, but then clever Pierre went down on one knee at just the right moment and kissed Davé's hand. Then we got Davé to show us photos of himself in drag. He had endless scrapbooks, which may have seemed less boring to Pierre than it was to me.

Pierre had grown up in Paris. He was Vietnamese and had known the last Vietnamese emperor in exile. He'd known everyone from Jean Marais (the actor and Cocteau's lover) to the charming Baron de Rédé, who lived in the Hôtel Lambert on the Île Saint-Louis with Guy and Marie-Hélène de Rothschild and who invited me to lunch once with the photographer Ariane Lopez-Huici and her sculptor husband, Alain Kirili. Rédé and I had drinks in the Lambert's perfect reception room, with its wood carvings of the labors of Hercules. Then we ate truffles and scrambled eggs in a small dining room painted by Mignard with murals showing this very room. From the windows we looked down on the garden designed by Le Nôtre. I'd always see Rédé at the Voltaire with Juliette Gréco's sister; they were like little lovebirds, though in their eighties. I remember once introducing him to Leo Castelli, the art dealer, in the lobby of the Crillon. I thought the most famous man-about-town in Paris should meet his New York counterpart; they couldn't have been less mutually interested. Leo was too obsessed with his new Italian wife, a twenty-something art historian.

I got to meet many American or Canadian writers in Paris I'd never encountered in New York. Foremost among them was Raymond Carver, whose granitic integrity as a man inflected the way I read his work—which had seemed mannered and faux naïve until I knew him. Because there were so few American writers living in Paris in those years, Odile Hélier at the Village Voice bookstore used to call on me to introduce visitors. The high point for me was publicly presenting Peter Taylor, who'd just won the lucrative Ritz-Hemingway award, to Carver, two of our greatest practitioners of the short story. Later Carver invited me to join him and Richard Ford and my old schoolmate Thomas McGuane on a salmon-fishing expedition in Oregon; I was flattered but said I didn't know what to wear. Another memorable moment was meeting the mysterious Mavis Gallant, one of the few English-language writers who dared to write about French people interacting with other French people; everyone else, including Edith Wharton and James and Hemingway, wrote about Americans abroad. Gallant told me that she'd learned French as a girl in Montreal, though her parents were Anglophone and she always wrote in English. She'd lived in France so long that many of the men she'd known had died and their widows were helpless, like so many women of that generation, and she had to help them pay bills and handle their affairs. She was deep into the research for a book about Dreyfus, but she has never written it. I told her that my favorite book of hers was *The Pegnitz Junction,* about postwar Germans, and she told me, perhaps out of politeness, that it was her favorite, too. The last time I saw her she was completely bent over like a hairpin, but she straightened herself out and had lunch with several of us at the Select. We often saw each other at parties given by my friend and Princeton colleague, the poet C. K. ("Charlie") Williams, and his effervescent French wife Catherine, a jewelry maker.

Charlie Williams introduced me to Ted Solataroff, the former editor of the *New American Review*, where I'd first read a chapter from *Portnoy's Complaint.* Years later I met Philip Roth through his fellow New Jerseyite Charlie, though I doubt if Roth remembers me. It was an honor to meet authors whose work brought me so much pleasure, though I remembered James Merrill once saying to me about some young fan, "Why does he want to meet us in the flesh? Doesn't he realize the best part of us is on the page and all he'll be meeting is an empty hive?"

Chapter 23

A year after Hubert died I received a long letter from a thirty-year-old writer named Michael Carroll, who was living in Pilsen, in the Czech Republic. He was teaching English in the university there for the Peace Corps. My then agent sent the letter along (hers was the only address he had for me) and scrawled in the margin, "Sounds like a live one." Now we've been together eighteen years.

I'd been terribly lonely and thought I'd never meet someone else. He'd given me an address, so I wrote him a postcard and told him if he was ever in Paris to come by for lunch. I jotted down my phone number.

On Easter weekend he called me from a nice youth hostel near the rue Saint-Martin. I invited him right over. He thought Hubert was still alive and had no idea I was prospecting for someone. He was handsome, sweet, but not demonstrative; though he was thirty he looked twenty. Later I found out his whole family is genetically favored toward youthful looks. We shared a southern background of sorts. My parents were from Texas. I'd lived in Texas. He'd been born in Memphis. My paternal grandfather had been a college teacher because he said he wanted a job "out of the sun." Michael's father (a year younger than I) had been the first person in his family to go to college; he manufactured wallboard. Michael had grown up in northern Florida, which is very redneck. And yet he'd had a very good education in public schools, in "gifted" classes where they'd read Greek plays, Shakespeare, the Victorians. He'd gone to grad school for English and then creative writing, but he wasn't very confident about his own stories—though he was very sure, even adamant, about his taste.

He had such a cozy, unemphatic way of becoming intimate. I read him out loud a story I'd just written and he said sensible things about it. He sat on the floor and I on the bed. We went to bed and that, too, seemed very intimate. I was fifty-five but still randy; I hadn't yet learned to wait for encouraging signs from the other person. I was far too old to be everyone's cup of tea, but I hadn't learned that yet.

I realized it had cost Michael a month's salary and sixteen hours to come on a bus to Paris from Pilsen. I insisted he move out of his hostel and stay with me. On subsequent trips I paid his airfare to Paris and back to Prague. And I flew to Prague twice to court him. I was in love with him almost instantly, but he was much cooler, which slightly miffed me. He told me that in August his term of duty in the Peace Corps would be up; I wanted him to move to Paris.

Michael and I were lying in bed at the end of August 1997 when Jonathan Burnham phoned and said, "Isn't it terrible what happened in your city?"

I'd sung a few scales before lifting the receiver and now I tried to drive the sleep out of my voice. "What happened?"

"Princess Di died in a car crash there in Paris last night," he said.

Only a year before Jonathan had had dinner with Diana and said what a hysteric she was, gabbling and fiddling with her hands nonstop—and I'd always wanted to believe this version.

And yet I knew how compassionate she was as well. I had done a profile of Marguerite Littman, a southerner who'd joined her AIDS charity to those of Princess Diana and Elton John. Lucretia Stewart's husband's brother had died of AIDS. The princess was one of the first people who'd visited him in the hospital and had not been afraid to touch him. Somehow she knew the disease wasn't catching. Everyone who'd worked with her on her AIDS charity was awe-struck by her warmth and courage (she'd lost many friends to the disease) and her unfailing dedication.

In the next few days we were scheduled to fly to the States for the American book tour of my novel *The Farewell Symphony*, and the following winter I was planning to begin teaching on a trial basis at

Princeton. Suddenly Princess Di's death consumed the media, and gone were most of my choicest interview and coverage prospects, including an appearance on Charlie Rose. *The Farewell Symphony* took in the whole period of New York gay life leading up to the AIDS crisis, sweeping in the euphoria of gay liberation as its cruel prelude, and one by one killed off most of its characters—and it was the capstone of my autobiographical trilogy.

So much for my triumphant return to native soil.

I'd emphasized the phrase "trial basis" when relaying the news of my upcoming teaching gig, but MC, perhaps sensing my deeper hopes, wasn't buying it. Her work had advanced, and more and more I admired some new effect she'd managed to achieve in her boxes, but she had yet to find a new gallery to show her latest efforts. Though her energy never flagged, she was the same old little girl in search of approval to shore up her confidence. She turned to Michael and asked him if we weren't in fact planning a permanent move.

Then, one evening as I was saying good night to her after one of our small quiet dinners together, just the two of us, she confronted me with a mixture of command and frail emotion and pleaded, "Just give me one more year!"

I was relieved finally to have a job. I was sick of scrambling at the end of every month to pay my rent. And Michael had never taken root in Paris. His whole life he'd dreamed of living in New York, and as an aspiring young writer it seemed the perfect place for him to be. The first year we had to live in Princeton till I officially got tenure, but then we moved to New York into an apartment I bought—or rather the bank did. My hand shook as I signed the mortgage agreement, the first one I'd ever signed. Before I got tenure and we began the apartment hunt, however, we rented professors' houses in Princeton the first two semesters, and I whimpered every evening as the dog next door howled.

There we were in a subdivision. The doors to the neighbors' houses were all shut, the lights in most of the windows extinguished, and I complained to Michael, "Why don't people ever come outside?"

"What are they supposed to do when they come outside, get in their cars? It's winter."

"But it's like they're hiding. It all seems so sordid. What are they doing in there?"

"What everybody anywhere else does. Eating, watching TV, reading, and going to bed."

Michael had grown up in a suburb, and though it had never been his dream to stay in one, it didn't bother him as much as it did me. He enjoyed being able to drive to a grocery store that stayed open late into the evening instead of having to hurry out to the markets before dark.

At the first hint of spring, MC came for her first drily amused visit, and on our tours of the New Jersey countryside rode in the front seat next to Michael (terrified of cars and accidents, I prefer to ride in the back). She looked out at the profusion of shocking-magenta redbud bushes in bloom on the lawns and croaked, *"Mais c'est vulgaire."*

For months she'd been ramping up her satirical and alarmist colorings of small-town life in America, which—remember—she'd had a taste of back during the Babar tours in the old days. Suburbia was where the true horrors were perpetrated, bastions of puritanical pettiness and hypocrisy, with all that wasted space and all those locked doors to help hide it.

And the food could be good or it could merely be amusing and "typical." *Typique* was one of her favorite words to launch a zinger against the country that had bewitched and abducted us. Once she called from Paris and Michael answered. She asked him what we were having for dinner and he began to describe the main course.

"And three vegetables," she said haughtily, "the Americans and their three vegetables!"

And of course at first I was gloomy and discontented to be back in America. My greatest accomplishment, speaking French, was useless here. I'd hear French spoken at the next table or on the street by tourists and joyfully assault perfect strangers who, as often as not, reacted coldly to this old man's effusions. And yet their very coldness seemed heartwarmingly French to me.

After sixteen years of living in Paris I was out of step with Americans. The same day a friend of mine named Hal Rubenstein wrote in his column that you must never arrive at a dinner empty-handed and must always bring flowers or wine, I'd said to him, purely by coincidence, "I wish people would never bring flowers—the host has enough to do without finding a vase and pricking his fingers on thorns. And never wine—he's already carefully selected them. All right, some chocolates, maybe . . ."

I went on to explain that I'd interviewed the Duchess of Beaufort, who owns Badminton House, one of the great English country houses, and she had thought all house gifts were a preposterous, newfangled custom. "Curious, that," she'd said.

This snobbish effusion didn't make me popular with my friend.

I was much older now, in my sixties, an age when it's difficult to make new friends. The people who were willing to befriend me, young gay writers, would eventually ask for a blurb or a Guggenheim recommendation and then vanish as soon as I delivered them. Other people would call me their "new best friend" and then stop returning my calls—not from any hostility but from negligence. Americans were so enthusiastic on first meeting; I'd forgotten that enthusiasm didn't mean anything. The cliché among Europeans was that friendships with Americans didn't go anywhere.

And I now had a fatal Old World sense of conversation—that it should be exciting and frivolous and provocative and preferably scandalous. I'd mentally prepare two or three hot topics before every evening. But my style was withering to Americans, who like to graze peacefully in conversation, and my "sparkling" style inhibited general conversation—which would revive, I would notice, whenever I went into the kitchen for the next course.

Four old friends—Marilyn Schaefer, Sigrid MacRae, Stan Redfern, and Keith McDermott—were welcoming. At Princeton, Joyce Carol Oates did everything to make me feel welcome, gradually introducing me to many people of interest at the university. A couple of times I lost old friends because I gossiped about them. I'd forgotten that Americans had the bad habit of running back and tattling to the injured party: "I think you should know there's something Edmund is saying about you . . ." (Usually something sexual.) I'd forgotten, too, that Americans can be puritanical and self-righteous snitches. In France most people enjoyed sex scandals, which shocked no one but titillated everyone. Moreover, everyone knew that the *milieu* was more important than any one member of it, and no one would rock the boat to save one passenger. Or rather, no one saw any harm in a bit of spicy gossip, certainly no reason to set off feuds and cause ruptures in the group cohesion. Boris Kochno, who'd been Diaghilev's last assistant, friend to Stravinsky and Picasso, and the lover of Christian Bérard, said to me in his nineties that he could see that the most important thing was to preserve the *milieu*. Though he was Russian, he'd lived his whole life in France, and his wisdom seemed typically French. Americans, I remembered, to my chagrin, didn't esteem the group but only conceded value to the individual friendship (unless the American was old, worldly, and female, and could recognize the sanctity of the group).

I'd acquired a lot of odd habits in France. Michael and I rented a car and went on an extended tour of Charleston, Savannah, and New Orleans, then flew home. My American friends were puzzled—were you on a book tour, they'd ask, giving a lecture? No, I'd say, we were on a pleasure trip. Pleasure? Were you visiting relatives?

Then I had too much social energy. I'd ask people to dinner and they'd say, "Dinner? Next Tuesday? At eight? Well, usually I work till seven and then work out for two hours. And remember I'm a gluten-free vegan. But yeah, I guess I could come. What's the occasion—is it your birthday?"

I ended up at first socializing with foreigners, other writers such as Salman Rushdie and Peter Carey and Francine du Plessix Gray, or Europeanized Americans like Ned Rorem. I didn't want to fall back into an all-gay ghetto, as I'd done in New York before going to Paris, but it was tempting, given the way people socialized. Many gay guys were as awkward around women as prep school boys, and straights were overeager to establish their tolerance of gays.

I was used to devoting a large part of my budget to inviting people to dinner or to the theater, but the gesture took most Americans by surprise and often confused them. In Princeton everyone went Dutch, carefully dividing the bill down to the last cent, which shocked me.

People dressed up less often, yet even Paris now was much more casual. I remember Sydney Picasso, Claude's American ex-wife, once saying to me, "Remember how we used to dress in the eighties? All those crazy outfits? Now we wouldn't dare."

In America I became obese, I suppose because the portions were bigger in restaurants and sugar was added to so many foods. It seemed to me that the secret of French cuisine was smaller portions, multiple appetite-quenching courses starting off with a big salad, and unexpectedly rich small indulgences—a sinfully gooey cheese or dessert. But no one in Paris took seconds, at the risk of being labeled *gourmand* (greedy). Only after I had become uncomfortably fat did I go on a diet and lose eighty pounds, though most people would say I was still heavy.

Until I became old and fat I was still going to saunas, but soon I discovered the whole paradise of cruising gerontophile chubby chasers on the Web.

People in the general public (on planes or even at dinner) had never heard of me. People said, "Should I have heard of you?" And I was so embarrassed by the whole subject that I said, "No. No one's ever heard of me."

Cheekier writers I know answer that question by saying, "Only if you're cultured."

If someone knew my name he was usually a middle-aged gay. I got used to supposedly educated men saying brightly, "I don't read. But my wife does." And she was brought up to meet the writer, but she would turn out to be clueless, a reader of foil-covered airport paperbacks.

In America I had to confront the writer's loss of prestige and the public's neglect. In France and England I'd been on endless radio and TV chat shows. In London, Jeremy Isaacs had interviewed me for an hour on *Face to Face* when everyone assumed I'd soon be dead from AIDS. In America literary writers didn't have the same access to the media. We had reality show stars for that.

My old friends in New York had been decimated by AIDS. I passed so many apartment buildings in the Village or Chelsea where a lover or trick or friend had once lived. There's where I once went to dinner with that cute airline steward. I'd shown up with three bottles of wine for two people—that's when I admitted to myself I was an alcoholic. Also it was the third time in a month I'd lost my contact lenses. Where was that guy now? I'd sat by several deathbeds at St. Vincent's, but not all the people who'd disappeared were accounted for. Gay life was organized in such a way that one day you realized you hadn't seen an acquaintance for months, years.

My old comfortable, dowdy New York was gone. St. Vincent's had closed. Whereas everyone used to rent and move every few years as they could afford a bigger place, now everyone bought and gentrified their property. The cobblers and that strange little shop in Noho that sold pink sugar were gone, and the very New York institution of the "coffee shop" that sold cheap, delicious food had been replaced by an influx of nail shops and branch banks. There were no more bookstores. Someone said there were more bookshops in Paris than all of America— could that be true?

Luckily I came back to America with Michael. He might rant against the empty decorousness of our old life in Paris, but he had lived in Europe for four years and at least knew what I missed. He made the new New York bearable by introducing me to a whole gang of gay writers in their thirties and forties. And of course I gradually made new friends of my own, my age and younger (everyone was younger).

And we went back to France, but to Provence rather than Paris. We'd rented an old peasant house just outside Saint-Rémy-de-Provence, where we spent many summers. Michael found the local accent more understandable than Parisian French, which was spoken too quickly for him. The house, called the Mas de Fé (the "mas of faith"—a mas being a Provençal farmhouse), had acres of grounds and a spring-fed swimming pool (*un basin*), pines at the top of the hill and olive groves at the bottom. We were in the Alpilles, across the street from the same convent, now a retirement home, where Van Gogh had been confined after he cut his ear off.

The owner of the house was Madame Daudet, the very old widow of Léon Daudet's son, a doctor. Léon and Charles Maurras had founded Action Française, a far-right party that was protofascist. *His* father, Alphonse Daudet, was a famous novelist of the late nineteenth century who financed the publication of *La France juive*, the central text of modern French anti-Semitism. He also wrote one of my favorite novels,

Sapho, which is about a penniless young man from the provinces who falls in love with a beautiful woman. At first he assumes she is a *grisette*, one of those poor girls who make artificial flowers, like Mimi in *La Bohème*, but who he eventually discovers is much older, close to forty, and a famous courtesan. As a child he played around his father's desk and would look with awe at a miniature version of a statue of her—a voluptuous Sappho. I've always thought that would make a good situation for a gay story set now, the forty-year-old New York model who hooks up with a twenty-year-old Iowan who thinks they're the same age but doesn't realize the New Yorker is the same man whose nude photos he used to jerk off to. Now please, no one steal that idea.

Alphonse Daudet, a native of Provence, also wrote *Letters from My Windmill*. Though Daudet never lived inside one, *Windmill* became perhaps the most famous book about Provence—the real windmill he had in mind was just a few miles away. Then he wrote a diary about his case of terminal syphilis, *La Doulou*, which is dialect for *la douleur* (pain). Julian Barnes translated it as, "In the Land of Pain." He'd heard that the Daudets had died out, but I arranged for him to have tea with our Madame Daudet. Julian found her to be a tough, royalist, formidable woman. I almost forgot to say Alphonse's other son, Lucien Daudet, was Proust's lover for a while and the author of one of my favorite camp books, *Dans l'ombre de l'impératrice* (*In the Empress's Shadow*), about his years as unofficial gentleman-in-waiting to the widowed Empress Eugénie. Proust was a close family friend of the Daudets'; maybe they chose to ignore that he was Jewish—as he did.

Proust's mother had first suspected that he was gay when she saw a photo of her son and two other young dandies with big eyes, pale faces, black bee-stung lips, and clipped mustaches. These were Lucien Daudet and the young Jewish composer from South America Reynaldo Hahn (another lover). For years Proust was drawn to look-alike aesthetes until, like us all, he went for straight rough trade: a chauffeur and two waiters, one French and one a Swedish giant.

Madame Daudet gave me a new red paperback anthology of her father-in-law's writings. No wonder he'd been such a successful right winger. Unlike our own Republicans, with the exceptions of George

Will and William F. Buckley, Léon could write with spirit and eloquence. Though she must have deplored the fact that I was openly gay, she seemed to like that I was a writer beavering away in her family house every July. In August, when we'd left, she took up residence with her twenty-two children and grandchildren. It was a miracle she could fit them all in, but we kept finding rolled-up blue rubber mats in out-of-the-way places. I would picture children placed head-to-foot (*tête-bêche*) in each of the wide, lumpy double beds with their horsehair mattresses.

One year I tried unsuccessfully to argue the rent down by pointing out to Madame Daudet that the two bathrooms and kitchen hadn't been modernized since the 1950s, that one salon was filled with her junk and sealed off, and that the furniture was all decrepit.

"Decrepit!" she stormed. "That shows how much you know. They're all museum pieces. You can find things just like them in many Provençal museums."

She was referring to a dark wooden cage hung halfway up one wall for storing flour out of reach of the rats. Oh, that and a raised wooden receptacle with a sliding panel for the salt.

In truth, I loved that house and we felt privileged to stay there. One morning a car came rattling up the half-mile-long gravel driveway, trailing dust. Out stepped a bearded man with his wife. He said he was the son of Augustus John, the English painter and famous portraitist of W. B. Yeats and T. E. Lawrence. He and his parents had lived in this very house for twenty-five pounds a year, and were among the last Brits to leave the Continent before the Nazi invasion.

Beside one of the beds upstairs was a painted lifelike Virgin, four feet tall, staring down at the bed with glass eyes. We had to put underwear over her head if we wanted to sleep or have sex. The one window in that room was tiny and the walls were a foot thick, all designed to keep out the cold in the winter and heat in the summer. There were two mammoth armoires richly carved; we could never figure out how anyone had got them in there unless they'd been built in the room.

In another bedroom with one window, there were two double beds and a single bed in an alcove. Next came a smaller room with a single bed and prie-dieu and a crucifix on the wall, again with one small window. It felt very monastic in there.

Finally there was a larger room with a little wrought-iron balcony and French doors beside its own small bathroom. Downstairs there were just the big brick-floored salon, with a huge refectory-size dinner table and ladder-back chairs, and the sorry little kitchen with its primitive equipment from another period. High-flying American friends who rented it from us for a week in July complained of the lack of modern appliances. I forgot to say that through a blocked-off door from the kitchen was the three-room apartment of the guardian (the *gardien et concierge*), his wife, and his six-year-old son, who was lonely and in love with Michael and would ask me plaintively in his heavy Provençal French, "*M'suh, can your son come out to play with me?*"

The guardian kept two large, fierce dogs in a kennel behind the house. We felt safe until the day some tan and rowdy teenage boys from town decided to swim naked in our pool. I didn't know whether to scare them off or befriend them—silly me, I opted for shooing them away.

Though I wrote a lot in that house, with the slat ceilings expertly crafted like the bottom of a boat, my favorite thing was to read in the prie-dieu room all night long with no fear of the hour, the besotted way one reads as a child. I bought the Pléiade editions of Jean Giono's novels. He quickly became one of my favorite writers, with his sexy Stendhalian heroes and lyrical nature descriptions, his notion of Provence closer to Milan than Paris. Years later I found out that some of the first talkies were of Giono's novels. Certainly one of the best recent big-production French films was of his *Horseman on the Roof*. He was my secret fetish author, the one I didn't want to write an essay about because I didn't want to share him with my few readers.

Still, why wasn't he better known? I discovered he'd once been famous but that he'd made two disastrous career moves. On the eve of World War II he'd come out as a pacifist, and then after the war he'd been condemned, incorrectly, as a collaborationist (in fact he'd hdden several Jews on his various farms). For a few years after the war his books couldn't be published in France because of his unpopular political stands. Whenever I tried mentioning him to French friends in the nineties, they'd shrug at me as if for some perverse reason I'd lighted on some insignificant and now justly forgotten French author, impossibly dust covered. The French intellectuals were so conformist that they even had iron-clad trends in their antiquarian enthusiasms. The odd thing is that they revered Céline, who was actively pro-Nazi.

Marie-Claude, Michael, and I made a pilgrimage to Giono's uninteresting hometown of Manosque, which has a museum dedicated to his memory. MC had learned to indulge my strange whims for writers of the past whose reputations had dimmed, such as André Gide, who'd taken one of the first anti-Soviet stances, or Daudet, whose *Numa Roumestan* I was reading, a masterful study of the difference between the Provençal and the Parisian characters; although Daudet was brought up in Provence, he preferred the cool, measured character of Parisians to the flamboyance of the southern blowhards he had known. Or what about Daudet's *Le Petit chose*, a touching story of his difficult youth, his version of *David Copperfield*? Dickens himself was a Daudet admirer.

Living in Provence and cooking Provençal recipes, everything from the labor-intensive soup called *pistou* to saffron-flavored milk in which you soaked fresh pasta overnight, I was haunted by the region's two greatest writers, Giono and Daudet. On the wall next to one toilet in the house was a banner on which was inscribed a poem by Frédéric Mistral, the modern champion of the Provençal dialect and a Nobel Prize winner. One of my translators shyly confessed to me that her left-leaning parents had met in the thirties in one of the summer camps Giono had organized in Provence at Contadour for workers who were having their first paid vacations. She seemed embarrassed by the connection, which she suggested history had eclipsed. Her parents became Communists.

I'm sure Giono would have despised me, an American snob and fag, although he was sufficiently aware of American culture to adapt the story of Johnny Appleseed for the well-paying *Reader's Digest*. He'd posited his Johnny as a Provençal folk hero who'd really existed and had reforested the arid local landscape, but Giono hadn't counted on

American fact checkers, who couldn't turn up any such personage of Provençal myth and eventually canceled the publication. Giono also translated *Moby Dick* and was an avid reader of Faulkner.

Hubert was long since dead and buried in the Père Lachaise cemetery, but his thirty-something brother Julien and his companion, François, who was my age, would come visit for two or three days. They'd drive from Nice, about two and a half hours away. They were nice guys who owned a TV repair shop; with them my greatest anxiety was preparing large lunches and dinners of many courses in the tiny, antiquated kitchen. We'd sit out on the huge terrace and look up at the starry night sky, profiled by pointy cypress trees, which seemed as blazing and animated as in a Van Gogh painting. They brought our basset hound Fred (I'd named him after the young psychiatrist Frédéric Pascal, not knowing there was a comic-book character named Fred the Basset). Fred now belonged to Julien and François. They doted on him and told endless anecdotes about him, as people do about their children.

We had lots of visitors, including the poet Sharon Olds, whom we hurt unintentionally by asking about her ex-lover. The following morning she descended from the room of the Virgin Mary statue with two new poems, each mentioning a different one of us and using some of the offending parts of our conversation the day before as ideas for the opening lines.

One day Jean Stein, who as a teenager had been one of Faulkner's last loves, came by for dinner on the terrace with an actress, Natasha Parry, wife of the stage director Peter Brook, and Kennedy Fraser, the former *New Yorker* fashion writer. More and more Saint-Rémy was becoming a spot for fashionable international people to stop off in. It had a charming maze of streets that wound among the buildings, including the birthplace of Nostradamus. Princess Caroline of Monaco had a house in the area. The English writer Peter Mayle had recently enshrined the region with the series of books that began with *A Year in Provence*.

James Lord came and stayed in a nearby hotel but was always drunk, lunch and dinner, so we got fed up and dropped him. I thought he'd just let our silence pass, but he confronted me and I had to explain. I'd written a flowery dedication to him in one of my books; James cut it out and sent it back to me without comment. Bernard Minoret was vexed with me: "*Ecoute!* Call him. He's an old man." The truth was I could bear a drunk evening with James every once in a while in Paris, but here in Provence we were three hours at table for lunch and three more for dinner, and often, while drunk, he would drive us in his powerful Mercedes a hundred miles per hour back from Aix and scream at a woman we were passing, "Get out of the way, you cunt!" He would become belligerent with strangers at an adjoining table in a three-star restaurant: "What are you staring at, you cow?" Now both James and Bernard Minoret are dead, and I miss the glamor and excitement of their company not to mention their immense erudition. One of my books is called *The Burning Library*, an allusion to the saying that when an old person dies a library burns. Bernard's mental library was the size of the Bibliothèque nationale.

But our most eagerly anticipated guest was MC, who took a strange little sleeper train from the Île de Ré (or rather from nearby La Rochelle, on the mainland), which cut across France and ended up at 6 A.M. in Nîmes. Normally all train traffic in France went through Paris. The usual thing would have been to take a fast train (TGV) from La Rochelle to Paris and another from Paris to Avignon. MC preferred her fourteen-hour sleeper.

She was the perfect guest, ready to pitch in in the kitchen, delighting in the Saturday market with its dozens of cheeses and ripe fruits and vegetables and its cheap saffron threads and its tiny, bitter olives. Brightly colored napkins were also sold there, not far from the roaring crowds at the bullrings. We liked to walk what we called the Ringstrasse, the road that encircled the town where the ancient Roman wall had been. We'd linger at the perfume factory, where we could buy flasks of lavender scent and lavender-scented soap. And there, in a junkyard, MC spotted one of those tin dormer windows called a *chien-assis* ("seated dog"), and for a day could talk about nothing but her idea of using it for what would surely be her masterpiece box, even though it had a huge dent on the side of it that would have to be hammered out.

It was ten times larger than her other boxes, too big to fit in the station wagon, too bulky and unstable to go on top—and anyway, how did she expect to get it to Paris? When we talked her out of it she said, "You have saved me from *une grande bêtise*." (A "huge mistake.")

Just half a mile from our house was an ancient Roman cenotaph (a tomb without a body) and a nearly intact triumphal arch. Across the street was a whole excavated city, Glanum, where Marilyn Schaefer one summer spotted Phoenician shards in the dust and took them to the curator, who offered her a job. Glanum was considered one of the most important sites in France, and the whole area was referred to by the locals as "Les Antiques."

One day we took MC to Avignon, where she'd spent a freezing winter during the war as a child before her family escaped the Nazis for Mexico by boat. It took her a while to find her old apartment in the blazing heat, but eventually we located it on a street behind the papal palace and she paused, staring. She remembered how cold and hungry she'd been.

MC hated garlic and claimed even a taste of it would make her sick for days. She had once entered an apartment in London where the hostess had used garlic liberally, thinking it was a way to please a French person. The dinner was inedible and MC had had to invite everyone to a restaurant. Naturally, her phobia made eating in a Provençal restaurant difficult, but we found an expensive little place on the Ringstrasse that served refined Norman food, which is the cuisine of Paris.

Her alimony sounded quite liberal, allowing her to pay for a maid every day, a physical therapist who came to the house once a week, and her own psychiatrist—a Serbian woman I met once at a memorial ceremony for Danilo Kiš. For some reason I associate this woman with copper—the color of her processed hair, her suit, and even her Manolo Blahnik high heels.

At the service, everyone was mad at me since I'd written Danilo's obituary in the *Independent*. Pressed for time, I'd dictated it over the phone and the transcriber had written the name of his female companion and translator in its male spelling, "Dominic" instead of "Dominique." Given my notoriety as a homosexual, everyone would think Danilo was gay, I was told. Susan Sontag, who'd made championing Eastern Europeans her mission after French "pioneering" had been assimilated by American intellectuals, had first introduced me to his work. She was certain he would win the Nobel Prize, which would have been likely if he hadn't died in his fifties. I used to visit him in his studio near the Goncourt Métro, an ideal space with a desk, a cot, a radio, and a good floor lamp beside an easy chair. All a writer needs, I thought, until I found out that he spent most of his time at his mistress's luxurious apartment. He had many rich women friends.

MC traveled everywhere with piles of books, which I usually dipped into. She read the bestsellers for the French version of *Reader's Digest* and serious literary books for possible translation into English at Knopf. After MC's death I told Sonny Mehta, the head of Knopf, that she'd been so proud of her connection with his house and how the seven-thousand-dollar-a-year retainer fee had meant so much to her, and he said, "Yes, and isn't that sad?" But maybe he didn't understand the prestige that the connection conferred on her in France.

She and I wanted to start a series of books in English of forgotten twentieth-century French classics. Georges Limbour is one name I remember. We also discussed making a cookbook of the recipes we passed back and forth over the phone. She lived, as many people do, in a realm of hopes and wishes, and our cookbook was just one more such imaginary plan.

Now we met twice a year at least. One summer a smart, handsome young man named Augustin Trapenard came to the Île de Ré and did six half-hour radio broadcasts with me in French for a series called *A voix nue*, later published in book form. (I noticed that Angela Davis had done the same series when I consulted the notes of Alice Kaplan's excellent book *Dreaming in French*.)

When MC came to New York she stayed with each of her American friends for three or four nights. Suddenly in our apartment there were cashmere shawls everywhere and the smell of honeysuckle. In Paris sometimes I stayed in the little hotel between her apartment and the Cluny Museum. She had many enthusiasms, most oddly unicorns and vampires. She and her friend Julio Cortázar had made a home movie in which he played Dracula and she played Mina Harker. We were friends with the talented Canadian opera director Robert Carsen, and for a while she tried unsuccessfully to persuade him to let her do the set designs for one of his productions. She was as indirect, however, as Proust's aunts thanking Swann for the wine, and I doubt Carsen ever knew her desires.

Then one year her cancer, which had started in her breasts, came back. She'd had a pain in her leg that for a while was diagnosed as sciatica; when they realized at last it was cancer, it had already spread through her bones. I was with her when she got the diagnosis.

"*C'est bête*," she said, "so stupid," almost as if it was a trick in bad taste that fate had pulled on her—or did she mean it was a *bêtise* that she'd committed?

I visited her later in the hospital. Though her hair had gone, she'd arranged some terrific turbans out of gaudy silks and satins tied with a flourish worthy of a maharani. She was gallant to the end. I had to teach, so I couldn't be beside her when she died, but Richard Ford was there.

The book of photos of her boxes and the accompanying stories that writers like Richard and I had devised was planned. She'd finally secured another gallery show, but that was a ways off still. In recent years she'd gone online with a website displaying her expertly photo-graphed work, but it would be a while before the Spanish collector would come upon them at the show following her death and ship them home where they'd be displayed.

I was dry-eyed. My mother had died; John Purcell had died; my best friend, David Kalstone, had died; perhaps a hundred other friends, French and American, had died. James Lord had died, and even for him I was inconsolable. Numb. I was alive in order to—well, to teach, to trick, to write, to memorialize, to be a faithful scribe, to record the loss of my dead.

Certainly my style became simpler and more direct because of living in two languages. As a reader I became more and more impatient with empty locutions and action-free descriptions, not to mention nuanced interior monologues. French—with the notable exceptions of Proust and Saint-Simon—doesn't tolerate long sentences and sinuous syntax. *Le style blanc* (the white, or transparent, style), which is the French ideal, sounds a bit like translated Hemingway minus the hypnotic repetitions, which Hemingway picked up from Gertrude Stein.

Because I spoke French I was sent by *Talk* magazine on the Concorde to interview Catherine Deneuve.

The French consul in New York asked me to dine with the former minister of culture, Jack Lang. Like all good politicians he "stayed on message" and grilled me throughout the evening on Jean Genet. I was invited to dinner in New York by Alain Wertheimer, the billionaire owner of Chanel, after we discovered at a dinner party we were equally passionate about books.

I maintained my French connections to an ever-diminishing extent. We stopped going to Provence in the summer and started going to Maine. My health faltered and curtailed my travels. In the eighties I'd traveled so much that the American embassy in Paris had had to add pages, accordion-style, to my passport, and even now I still kept my wallet half full of euros, more as a superstitious gesture to fate than out of necessity. I spoke French with three of my beloved New York friends, the photographers Ariane Lopez-Huici and Domonique Nabokov, and Beatrice von Rezzori, the widow of the novelist Gregor von Rezzori. Though Beatrice was Italian and spoke perfect English, she found speaking French more restful. It had been her first language, as it once was for most European aristocrats and educated people—and still was, for those of a certain age.

I missed Marie-Claude, our afternoon teas, our early evening couscous dinners, our dueling books on adjoining couches in the winter on the Île de Ré, the conspiratorial way she'd lure me up the stairs to her *cabinet des merveilles*, the stifling room where she worked so assiduously on her eternal boxes. I missed her kindness, her warmth, her unfailing elegance, her tapenade, her enthusiasm for even the most harebrained expeditions (one night I walked her home at midnight, and in half an hour I caught her at the taxi stand headed for the Casbah, the in club).

She was a very game woman. Her beautiful eyes, as soft as a doe's, would take fire whenever some new book or expedition or exhibition was mentioned. She went with me to Naples. A Neapolitan lesbian in Paris had given us a list of restaurants and must-sees. In one restaurant, across from the opera, the proprietress kept fussing over MC: "*Ma la signora e deliciosa,*" she said, when MC complimented her on her pasta. A handsome Neapolitan named Massimo Semprebene led us all over Capri in March while workmen were repairing villas for the summer. Back in Naples, MC's purse was stolen by a teenager who leapt onto his friend's passing motor scooter. MC: "I didn't think he would be a thief, he was so handsome." We visited the American painter Phillip Taaffe in his rented house, the wonderfully dilapidated Villa Pierce, where Churchill had once stayed.

A few years ago when I wanted to fly down from New York to discover Buenos Aires, no one would go with me. MC would have gone!

She was so faithful about attending the huge receptions following the Prix Goncourt or the Prix Médicis. She'd urge me to go with her, as if by attending them I had a better chance to win one of those coveted prizes.

When I had a sick stomach she'd prepare rice and boiled carrots. She was always thoughtful. I must have been introduced by her to a thousand literary personalities. She'd always say, "Pierre, you know Edmund White," and Pierre would shake my hand. That was her formula: "you know," because in Paris everyone already "knew" everyone. Or least you'd never admit a social lacuna.

Of course many people knew who I must be and didn't approve. Michel Mort, who had a rare blood condition that gave him a blue appearance, and who was a literary advisor for Gallimard, disapproved of me because he was an Americanist who disliked the overrefined American "palefaces," the descendants of Henry James. He liked a real "redskin" American like the great Erskine Caldwell—with whom I was supposed to appear on Bernard Pivot's book chat show, *Apostrophes,* except he died on the eve of our "foreign soirée." I ended up with Han Suyin, Fritz Raddatz, and Wole Soyinka, who'd just won the Nobel Prize.

Again and again I met French critics and serious readers who liked strange American authors—John Fante or Philip K. Dick or the great Charles Bukowski, who'd showed up on Pivot's program drunk and abusive and unable to speak French, though he'd promised he was fluent in it—and who'd sold twenty thousand copies of his poems the next day. An American writer was supposed to be hard-drinking and live in a trailer. Camus had said American writers were the only ones in the world who weren't also intellectuals. After World War II, the French, fed up with their own culture, had discovered Faulkner and obtained the Nobel Prize for him. A Princeton French professor, Maurice Coindreau, had translated him and Sartre had written an early influential essay on him.

I was too prissy, too refined, too abstemious, too French to be a good American writer. One blurb called me "the best French writer in English." Every country has a fantasy about every other. I didn't conform to anyone's fantasy of a Hemingway. Curiously enough, MC and I met Ed Hemingway, the writer's grandson, who resembled the grand old man except that he was without a beard and was twenty-one. In Paris he was arrested for drunk and disorderly behavior but was let off when the gendarmes looked at his passport and saw his historic last name. They saluted him and let him go. Only in France . . . just as Cocteau had argued at Genet's trial for theft that Genet was a modern-day Rimbaud, and you didn't put Rimbaud in jail.

It was strange to come back from a country where even the concierge knew what a writer was to a land where people immediately asked, "Any movie deals? Any bestsellers?" Genet had assumed that as a famous writer whose plays *The Blacks* and *The Balcony* were long-running hits off-Broadway, he'd immediately have access to TV and radio in the States in order to defend the Black Panthers—his great cause. But of course no American novelist is shown on TV, except for a few trivial seconds, since Dick Cavett went off the air and the telegenic generation of Vidal, Capote, and Mailer died off. Cultured English people are often astonished that their American counterparts have never heard of me. I used to say that France had become a country of great readers and few good writers, and America was a country of great writers and no good readers.

Did living in France all those years affect my writing? It gave me a lot to write about.

Once a green-haired presenter on TV in Manchester asked me, "You're known as a writer, a homosexual, and an American. When did you first discover you were an American?"

"When I first moved to Europe."

Acknowledgments

I want to thank my partner of two decades, Michael Carroll, for encouraging me as always. Anton Mueller helped me restructure this book. Leo Racicot typed it and made many suggestions.

A NOTE ON THE AUTHOR

Edmund White is the author of many novels, including the classic *A Boy's Own Story* and most recently *Jack Holmes and His Friend*; two previous memoirs, *My Lives* and *City Boy*; biographies of Jean Genet, Marcel Proust and Arthur Rimbaud; and several other works of non-fiction, including *The Flâneur*. He lives in New York City and teaches writing at Princeton University.